The Orlofsky Edition

The Lieberman Open Orthodox Haggadah

THE ORLOFSKY EDITION

THE LIEBERMAN OPEN ORTHODOX HAGGADAH

RABBI SHMUEL HERZFELD

gefen גפן
publishing house בית הוצאה לאור
JERUSALEM ◆ NEW YORK
Est. 1981

Cover Design: Benjie Herskowitz, Etc. Studios
Typesetting: Raphaël Freeman, Renana Typesetting
Illustrations: Copyright © Caryl Herzfeld

Paperback ISBN: 978-965-229-805-8
Hardcover ISBN: 978-965-229-807-2

1 3 5 7 9 8 6 4 2

Gefen Publishing House Ltd.
6 Hatzvi Street
Jerusalem 94386, Israel
972-2-538-0247
orders@gefenpublishing.com

Gefen Books
11 Edison Place
Springfield, NJ 07081
516-593-1234
orders@gefenpublishing.com

www.gefenpublishing.com

Printed in Israel

Send for our free catalog

Library of Congress Control Number: 2015930387

There can be no communal redemption
without it also being an individual redemption.

We will never be redeemed as a community as long as there is even one agunah.

This Haggadah is dedicated to the agunot.
Even one is too many. May they be free!

In honor of the seventieth birthday of our mother and Bubbe, Joan Orlofsky, we dedicate this Haggadah.

As we say to you every Friday night:

> Many daughters have done worthily but *you* surpass them all. Charm is deceptive, and beauty is naught, a God-fearing woman is the one to be praised. Give her praise for her accomplishments, and let her deeds laud her at the gates. (Mishlei 30:30–31)

Anything we do of significance in this world is due to you.

Love,

Aaron, Ahuva, Avigail, Elana, and Izzy Orlofsky

As we remember the Seder tables of our parents,

PHYLLIS PENNER SILVERMAN and **RUBEN SILVERMAN,**

CARYL MEYER LIEBERMAN and **HERBERT LIEBERMAN,** *z"l,*

and of our grandparents

dor l'dor

we embrace the traditions and tastes of Seders past

as we retell the Passover story together with our family.

We dedicate this Haggadah with love to our children

RACHEL, JESSICA, and BENJAMIN.

SHARON & STEVE LIEBERMAN

CONTENTS

ACKNOWLEDGMENTS

The publication of this Haggadah would not be possible without the very generous assistance of two families: Aaron and Ahuva Orlofsky and Steve and Sharon Lieberman.

Aaron and Ahuva's encouragement and support of my work is inspiring for me to see and humbling for me to realize since I know that I am not deserving of such support. Of course, I know that I am but one of the beneficiaries of their largesse. Their acts of kindness to those in need are legendary. In particular, Aaron and Ahuva's support of Sulam allows children with special educational needs to receive a first-class Jewish education.

Steve and Sharon have been a source of strength, counsel, and guidance to me in both a personal and professional capacity for over fifteen years. I cannot even imagine where I would be without their help, but I know I am just one of many people who are supported by their incredible generosity. Steve and Sharon have dedicated their lives to supporting Jewish institutions. It is not surprising to me that Steve and Sharon have been honored for their support of Yeshivat Chovevei Torah Rabbinical School, an institution that enables more rabbis to serve communities that desperately need their help.

It is a tremendous honor for me to have my name associated with these two families.

This project started with the hard work of my dear friend, Baruch Roth. Baruch spent many hours going through all my divrei Torah and collecting the ones that related to the holiday of Pesach. He then edited them slightly and passed them along to me. His creativity and dedication to this effort was essential to this Haggadah. Without him this would never have happened.

I am deeply grateful that my amazing mother was kind enough to provide the illustrations for the Haggadah. Along with my incredible father, they worked on the educational content of the illustrations and the questions relating to the illustrations.

As an Open Orthodox Haggadah it was important to me that my voice not be the only voice reflected in these pages. I felt that it was necessary to include the voices of others to help us better understand the powerful implications of the Pesach story. I am very appreciative of the following people who were kind enough to share their writings for this Haggadah: Maharat Ruth Balinsky

Friedman, Rabbi Jeffrey Fox, Rachel Lieberman, Rabbi Asher Lopatin, Michel Martin, and Rabbi Avi Weiss.

What kind of family encourages their father to wear a matzah suit (i.e., a suit that looks like a matzah) for the entire holiday of Pesach? My family does! Thank you to my children Lea, Roey, Elai, Max, Shia, Kolbi, and Bear, and to my wife, Dr. Rhanni Herzfeld, for everything. Their support and love is what gives me the energy and encouragement necessary to celebrate Pesach properly.

INTRODUCTION

Our synagogue does two things relating to the holiday of Pesach about which I am especially proud.

First, we are one of the few synagogues in America that bake our own *shmurah matzah*. In order to do this project we had to invest an enormous amount of preparation time. We had to install a brick oven and design some special metal tools. We had to study the laws of matzah baking very carefully. It also took us some time to perfect our baking technique. The actual matzot we make are beautiful, but the making of the matzot is even more beautiful. There is a tremendous excitement in the air as we race against the clock to make this sacred food to eat at our Seder. (The process of preparing the matzah for baking cannot take more than eighteen minutes.) That excitement is palpable and it carries over into the holiday itself.

When we bake our matzah the whole room is alive. We are alive. Our faith is alive. Our Judaism is alive. That is exactly the way it is supposed to be.

That is what I want this Haggadah to be for you. I want it to help your Seder be alive, exciting, and relevant. For this reason I have especially included other voices in the Haggadah, provocative voices that will encourage you to discuss cutting-edge ideas at the Seder and will help your Seder be filled with the same level of excitement that I feel when we bake our matzah on the eve of Pesach.

But if a Seder is just about feeling the excitement of the holiday of redemption it falls short of what a Seder should truly be about.

Every year we have a free communal Seder on Pesach night for hundreds of people. Many people from a cross-spectrum of the community participate in our synagogue's community Seder, but it is especially attractive to people who need help making the Seder for a variety of reasons. This free communal Seder of our synagogue is thus both inclusive and heterogeneous.

This Seder is so important to what our synagogue is about because it reminds us that a Seder above all needs to be a gathering that is sensitive to those who need help. A redemption story that is based solely on our own excitement and good fortune is a defective story. In order for our story to be whole we need to be sensitive to the needs of those around us.

This is another major theme of the Open Orthodox Haggadah. I have included voices in this Haggadah to help sensitize us to the needs of our entire community. I hope that you will use this Haggadah to help make your Seder both a place of great excitement and one that inspires us to act with sensitivity toward the needs of others.

A word about the term Open Orthodoxy: As a young rabbi at the Hebrew Institute of Riverdale, I remember when Rabbi Weiss first introduced me to the term Open Orthodoxy. He didn't have to define it for me because I knew who he was. He was both open and Orthodox and so it was natural for him to refer to himself as Open Orthodox.

Knowing Rabbi Weiss as I know him, I can tell you what the term meant to me then and what it still means to me now. Open Orthodoxy means a commitment to the tenets of traditional Judaism that matches that of Orthodox Jews around the world. For example, our requirements for the observance of Shabbat, kashrut, and laws of family purity are no less strict than what one would find in the "most frum" Orthodox community. What separates the Open Orthodox from the Centrist Orthodox and the Orthodox Right is a willingness to approach some of the most critical issues that face our community today in a manner that is neither reactionary nor fundamentalist, but rather in a way that is guided by a combination of deep sensitivity and total commitment to halakhah.

I have asked my teacher and mentor, Rabbi Avi Weiss, to share his thoughts about Open Orthodoxy, which you can read below.

ON OPEN ORTHODOXY

by Rabbi Avi Weiss

What is Open Orthodoxy? It is a movement within Orthodox Judaism that is completely committed to *Torah min hashamayim*, to belief that God wrote the Torah, and to the meticulous observance of *halakhah* (Jewish Law). At the same time, it is open – inclusive, pluralistic, and nonjudgmental.

This balance is at first blush self-contradictory. When one thinks "Orthodox," the last thing one thinks about is open. And when one thinks "open" the last thing one thinks about is Orthodox. And yet, these two dimensions interface.

As I wrote years ago when introducing the term "Open Orthodoxy":

> The key to strengthening Open Orthodoxy is the reconciling of more rigid halakhic practices, which I believe are positive, with our open ideological agenda. It is this tension that is difficult to live with. But it is the dialectic between different ideas that ultimately sets Open Orthodoxy apart from

> the Orthodox Right. The Orthodox Right deals in absolutes – their closed ideological agenda is a natural offshoot of their halakhic fervor. Open Orthodoxy does not see this offshoot as necessary. For the Open Orthodox Jew, true and profound religio-legal creativity and spiritual striving emerges from the tension between the poles of strict halakhic adherence and open ideological pursuits. They appear to be opposites when in fact they are one. ("Open Orthodoxy! A Modern Orthodox Rabbi's Creed," *Judaism* [September 1997])

This dialectic manifests itself in a whole variety of areas. For example, as it relates to women's issues, Open Orthodoxy parts with the heterodox community, as it does not subscribe to egalitarianism. It is rather an approach where women and men share a commonality of roles in more than 90 percent of areas, but there are still clear distinctions. There are certain parts of Jewish law, custom, and ritual that are meant for women and not men, and vice versa. In the same breath, Open Orthodoxy parts with the Orthodox Right in encouraging, supporting, and applauding women's involvement not only in learning Torah on the same quantitative and qualitative level as men, but in leadership roles (including spiritual ones), so that, for example, women can be ordained and receive *semikhah*.

Our attitude towards the gay community is yet another example of an area where Open Orthodoxy carves out a distinct path. While we are well aware of the Torah's prohibition, Open Orthodoxy sensitively welcomes and fully integrates all people regardless of sexual orientation or level of religious observance into our communities – our schools, synagogues, and homes.

Open Orthodoxy also has a distinct approach to "outreach." While the term "outreach" is generally understood to mean that only the person reaching out has something to offer, Open Orthodoxy suggests that both parties can grow. Those being reached are not viewed as having little to contribute to the Jewish community either spiritually or religiously; rather, outreach becomes an experience that offers a great deal to everyone involved. Everyone, regardless of their level of commitment or knowledge, has something to offer. For this reason, a more appropriate term than "outreach" would be "encounter," which describes a mutual interaction in which all parties benefit and acquire deep respect for one another.

Separate from these kinds of cutting-edge issues, Open Orthodoxy carves a unique sense of involvement in spiritual striving, in a constant search to feel God's presence. In this sense, Open Orthodoxy is mission driven. Its synagogues are not only functional, providing services of *tefillah* and learning, but immersed in mission, of inspiring its constituents to follow in God's paths by seeking out ways to love Am Yisrael and the world.

More generally, Open Orthodoxy is distinct in three areas.

It understands *mesorah* not only as a commitment to the past, in the spirit of "ask your elders and they will tell you," but as an understanding that Jewish Law carefully evolves. That is, *mesorah* is also the dictum that in every generation one seeks out halakhic judgment related to new situations and conditions.

Open Orthodoxy also sees great danger in the centralization of rabbinic authority. Concerned that power concentrated in the hands of the few can be corrupting, it believes in the authenticity, learning, and ability of local rabbis. In this sense, Open Orthodoxy is fighting against a trend in Orthodox movements to the right that gives more and more power to fewer and fewer people.

Finally, Open Orthodoxy sees halakhah as a system of *kedushah* – of holiness – leaving it to the decisor of Jewish law and its adherents to discern the *kedushah* inherent within the halakhic system. For the Open Orthodox Jew, the question is not only "what is the halakhah," but "what is the *kedushah*."

In my experience as a rabbi, I have found that people are eager to connect with a Judaism that is deeply rooted in the halakhic tradition as long as it is not frozen in time. At the same time, they yearn for a halakhah that is open to evolving as long as it is still clearly rooted in our tradition.

This in short is the message of Open Orthodoxy, which in the last twenty years has had a tremendous impact. It represents today a growing movement of tens of thousands of supporters.

In addition to its many supporters, Open Orthodoxy has also pushed other movements within the Jewish spectrum to be better. For example, Open Orthodoxy has pushed Centrist Orthodoxy to revamp and retool.

Terms are important. I'm not a fan of the term "Centrist Orthodoxy" as it implies being in the center. It follows then, that when its flanks on the right or left move, it moves. It then becomes reactive instead of proactive. Nor am I a fan of the term Modern Orthodoxy. In the postmodern era, the term "Modern Orthodoxy" is old; it is passé. Furthermore, it does not reflect who we are, as there are many in the Orthodox Right community who today live in the modern world in their businesses and in their social contexts and do so with great success. Open Orthodoxy, on the other hand, is descriptive of a unique approach to Judaism. It is a distinct movement within Orthodoxy.

Movements are not announced; rather, they evolve. Whether one thinks Open Orthodoxy is a movement or not, one point is clear: twenty years ago,

Centrist Orthodoxy was a dying breed. It had moved precipitously to the right and was losing the values that had made it unique. Something new is happening today. With the advent of Yeshivat Chovevei Torah and Yeshivat Maharat, the International Rabbinic Fellowship, the Jewish Orthodox Feminist Alliance, the Institute for Jewish Ideas and Ideals, Uri L'Tzedek, and in Israel Beit Morasha and Beit Hillel, and synagogues like Ohev Sholom – The National Synagogue, there is a new spirit. These entities were not created in a vacuum. No, they were introduced in response to a crying need, a need for an Orthodoxy that not only speaks to its natural followers, but to the more than 85 percent of American Jewry for whom Orthodoxy has been irrelevant.

With Centrist Orthodoxy moving right and Conservative Judaism moving left (even as Reform Judaism is ritually moving right, inching Conservative and Reform closer to merger) the seas are parting. In between is Open Orthodoxy, which must continue to carve out its own agenda.

What's needed now as Open Orthodoxy moves beyond its founding stages is a leadership that is committed, unafraid to advance its own proactive agenda of interfacing Orthodoxy with an openness, thereby impacting Am Yisrael and doing its share to improve the world.

THE HAGADDAH

REMOVING THE LEAVEN

On the night before Passover Eve, immediately after the Maariv evening service, all the leaven in the home is searched out and collected. To make sure that the blessing is not said in vain, a few pieces, usually ten, are placed in various parts of the house and searched out. Before the search, light a candle and say the following blessing:

Be blessed, God, our God, King of the universe, Who has sanctified us by His commandments and commanded us concerning the removal of leaven.

After the search say:

Let any leaven within the precinct of my home, even if I may not have seen and removed it, be considered null and void and as public property, like the dust of the earth.

---

of New York, and his neighbors, despite the tensions that sometimes erupted. He liked people, he respected them, and he was not afraid of difference.

He was, for example, the first person to tell me about Sukkot, the Jewish Festival of Booths; the families eating together on their porches and patios seemed so festive, even in the drizzly fall weather, I wondered why we couldn't do it too.

That might be one reason why, when Rabbi Shmuel Herzfeld asked my husband Billy and me to start buying the community members' chametz under arrangements made through the synagogue he leads, Ohev Sholom – the National Synagogue in Washington, D.C., it was not a difficult decision at all. In fact we are honored to do so.

Rabbi explained that the contract, while of great symbolic importance, is in fact a valid contract; since my husband is a lawyer he knew this is not to be taken lightly. But it is also a gesture of neighborliness, and this too is not to be taken lightly. Neighborliness means we are linked, and we are linked by much more than the random fact of shared space.

We were originally meant to move into our home on September 14, 2001. This proved impossible because I was stuck in New York, reporting on what we now refer to as 9/11. That was not the original reason why I was in New York – ironically I started the week working on a broadcast being filmed at what was called the Angel Orensanz Center, which began its life as the oldest surviving

בְּדִיקַת חָמֵץ

On the night before Passover Eve, immediately after the Maariv evening service, all the leaven in the home is searched out and collected. To make sure that the blessing is not said in vain, a few pieces, usually ten, are placed in various parts of the house and searched out. Before the search, light a candle and say the following blessing:

בָּרוּךְ אַתָּה יְיָ, אֱלֹהֵינוּ מֶלֶךְ הָעוֹלָם, אֲשֶׁר קִדְּשָׁנוּ בְּמִצְוֹתָיו, וְצִוָּנוּ עַל בִּעוּר חָמֵץ.

After the search say:

כָּל חֲמִירָא וַחֲמִיעָא דְּאִכָּא בִרְשׁוּתִי דְּלָא חֲמִתֵּהּ וּדְלָא בִעַרְתֵּהּ וּדְלָא יְדַעְנָא לֵיהּ לִבָּטֵל וְלֶהֱוֵי הֶפְקֵר כְּעַפְרָא דְאַרְעָא.

GUEST VOICE: MICHEL MARTIN

Our synagogue is located in a diverse neighborhood with a variety of races and religions all calling our community home. We consider this a blessing. Our synagogue has the privilege of selling our chametz every year to our neighbors Billy and Michel Martin. Michel is a veteran broadcast journalist and host at NPR; the following is her perspective on this transaction.

ON BUYING CHAMETZ

When I was growing up in Brooklyn, New York, in the 1960s and 70s, my late father was a New York City firefighter; for much of my childhood he was assigned to a firehouse in Williamsburg, Brooklyn, and he made a point of learning about and telling us about the traditions of the people he went to work every day to protect, most especially his neighbors at the firehouse. A lot of it was about the food, because what firefighter does not love to eat? Also, his firehouse neighbors always seemed to be bringing something by, and he would bring some home to share with us. Polish sausage, Italian cold cuts, Russian black bread, knishes and bagels, the rice and peas and plantains of the Caribbean – my father had a taste for it all.

I don't want to make it sound like one big picnic. These were tense times in New York and the country; there were times, battling both regular fires and the aftermath of civil unrest, that he didn't come home for days and when he did he was sweaty, exhausted, and tense. Still, he seemed to enjoy the moveable feast

ERADICATING THE LEAVEN

On the following morning burn the leaven and say:

Let any leaven within the precincts of my home, whether I have seen it or not, whether I have removed it or not, be considered null and void as public property, like the dust of the earth.

ERUV TAVSHILIN

When Pesach starts on a Thursday, one is permitted to cook on Friday for Shabbat provided the head of the household has performed the ceremony of eruv tavshilin *on the Wednesday afternoon before the festival.*

Place a piece of matzah and an item of cooked food, such as fish or meat, on a plate, raise it, and then recite the following blessing and passage:

Be blessed, Hashem, our God, King of the universe, Who has sanctified us with His commandments and commanded us concerning the mitzvah of *eruv.*

With this *eruv* it shall be permissible for us to bake, cook, and keep food warm, to light candles, and to prepare all necessary items on the festival for the Sabbath. This will be permitted to us and to all Jews who live in the city.

---

the invisible. Introductions were made; (kosher) lunches were shared. Slowly a community of care has developed that goes in both directions. When our twins were born, members of the synagogue were among the first to welcome them home; when a power outage made it hard for me to get into the house, one of my children was frightened and started honking the horn, and half a dozen men from the congregation came running to my aid. There are many more examples that I cherish, many too personal to share here.

But it is interesting to me how a fact that some may consider a negative – living near an institution that is in constant use – has become a positive to our family because it is not a building but a collection of friends.

Of course, as in my father's era, it is not always a picnic. There have been

/cont. p. 9

בְּעוּר חָמֵץ

On the following morning burn the leaven and say:

כָּל חֲמִירָא וַחֲמִיעָא דְּאִכָּא בִרְשׁוּתִי דַּחֲזִתֵּהּ וּדְלָא חֲזִתֵּהּ, דַּחֲמִתֵּהּ וּדְלָא חֲמִתֵּהּ, דְּבִעַרְתֵּהּ וּדְלָא בִעַרְתֵּהּ, לִבָּטֵל וְלֶהֱוֵי הֶפְקֵר כְּעַפְרָא דְאַרְעָא.

עֵרוּב תַּבְשִׁילִין

When Pesach starts on a Thursday, one is permitted to cook on Friday for Shabbat provided the head of the household has performed the ceremony of eruv tavshilin *on the Wednesday afternoon before the festival.*

Place a piece of matzah and an item of cooked food, such as fish or meat, on a plate, raise it, and then recite the following blessing and passage:

בָּרוּךְ אַתָּה יְיָ, אֱלֹהֵינוּ מֶלֶךְ הָעוֹלָם, אֲשֶׁר קִדְּשָׁנוּ בְּמִצְוֹתָיו, וְצִוָּנוּ עַל מִצְוַת עֵרוּב.

בַּהֲדֵין עֵרוּבָא יְהֵא שָׁרֵא לָנָא לַאֲפוּיֵי וּלְבַשּׁוּלֵי וּלְאַטְמוּנֵי וּלְאַדְלוּקֵי שְׁרָגָא וּלְתַקָּנָא וּלְמֶעְבַּד כָּל צָרְכָּנָא, מִיּוֹמָא טָבָא לְשַׁבְּתָא לָנוּ וּלְכָל יִשְׂרָאֵל הַדָּרִים בָּעִיר הַזֹּאת.

Reform synagogue in New York, became an arts center, and is now known as the Shul of New York. Needless to say, once we knew what had happened the attention of my entire team of journalists turned to covering the story of the attacks. My husband understood – he could see the smoke from the Pentagon from his office window. But after three weeks in New York the people waiting to move into our old home couldn't wait any longer and we needed to make arrangements to move. So I came home.

We found concrete barriers blocking our access to what was to be our new driveway. But after everything I had just seen and smelled and felt reporting on 9/11, I understood the desire to use barriers to be safe. It was my hope, though, that true safety would come in moving barriers...both the visible and

QUESTIONS ON THE SEDER

The word *seder* means order. This reminds us that the Passover Seder follows a specific order as the story of our past is retold and sometimes reenacted. A rhyming Hebrew mnemonic, with the names of the fourteen special events that take place during the Seder, is used to help us remember that order. It is sung at the beginning of the Seder.

Four of the fourteen events that will take place in the Seder can be found in the illustration on the opposite page. What are the names of the four events? What is happening in the four events? *Hint*: The answer is in the Haggadah on the page where the Seder actually begins.

Each section of the Haggadah will be introduced with an illustration and corresponding questions. The answers to the questions can be found at the back of the Haggadah, beginning on page 175.

THE SEDER TRAY

Three matzot are placed between three separate folds of a cloth in a way that no two matzot are touching.

A little basin of vinegar or salt water is prepared.

The Seder tray is prepared as follows:

KARPAS – greens: parsley, chervil, celery, and the like.

MAROR – bitter herbs: horseradish, endive lettuce, and the like.

CHAZERET – some have the custom of adding a second bitter vegetable: celery or lettuce

CHAROSET – apples, almonds, and nuts, minced together and made into a paste with wine.

ZEROAH – a shank bone of a lamb.

BEITZAH – a roasted egg.

There are many traditions regarding the arrangement of items on the Seder tray. Here is a common one:

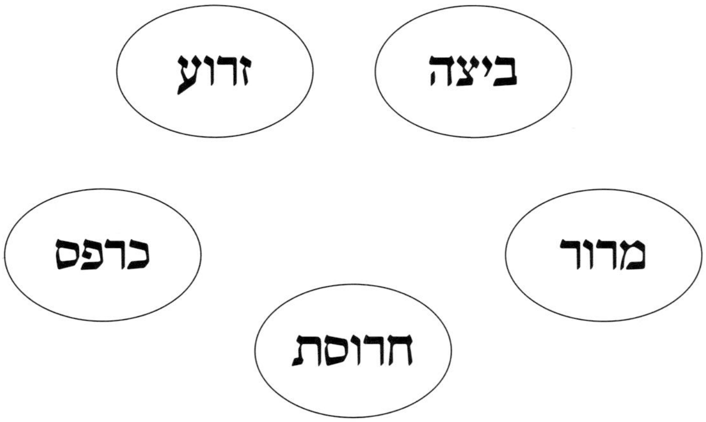

A neighbor is more than a word and that extra dimension only occurs with effort on both sides. We hope that buying the chametz is just one gesture of neighborliness that brings down barriers, the seen and the unseen.

THE SEDER

The person conducting the Seder opens with the following explanation of the order – which is what the Hebrew word "seder" means – of the Pesach night service.

קַדֵּשׁ	KADESH	Inaugurate the festival over wine
וּרְחַץ	U'RECHATZ	Rinse the hands without saying the blessing
כַּרְפַּס	KARPAS	Eat vegetables dipped in saltwater or vinegar
יַחַץ	YACHATZ	Split the middle matzah
מַגִּיד	MAGGID	Recite the Haggadah
רָחְצָה	RACHTZAH	Rinse the hands and say the blessing
מוֹצִיא	MOTZI	Say the bread blessing
מַצָּה	MATZAH	Say the matzah blessing
מָרוֹר	MAROR	Eat the bitter herbs
כּוֹרֵךְ	KOREKH	Eat the bitter-herb sandwich
שֻׁלְחָן עוֹרֵךְ	SHULCHAN OREKH	Eat the festival meal
צָפוּן	TZAFUN	Eat the *afikoman*
בָּרֵךְ	BAREKH	Say the Grace after Meals
הַלֵּל	HALLEL	Chant the Hallel praise and thanksgiving psalms
נִרְצָה	NIRTZAH	Pray that God accept our service and prayer

---

visitors who sometimes treat my family as if we are invisible or treat us as if, for some reason, we don't belong there. Parking is sometimes an issue, as are political opinions shared at inopportune times, as well as noise and ball playing and skate boarding by certain young people who may or may not be related to me.

Buying the chametz is sometimes inconvenient and even a little daunting: as the shul has grown the contract has as well; the figure can be a little intimidating. But neighborliness demands accommodation even when inconvenient.

QUESTIONS FOR KADESH

1. Why does everyone in the picture have his or her own cup of wine?
2. Why do we lean on a pillow when we drink the wine?
3. To what side do we lean?
4. The people at the top of this picture are singing the Kiddush and are standing. At the bottom of this picture the people are sitting. When do we sit? When do we stand?

קדש ורחץ
כרפס יחץ

KADESH

Pour the first cup, everybody stands, recite the Kiddush holding the cup in the upraised palm of the right hand.

Behold, I am prepared and ready to recite Kiddush over wine, and to fulfill the commandment of the first of the four cups, for the sake of the unity of the Holy One, blessed is He, and His Presence, through Him Who is hidden and inscrutable, in the name of all Israel. May the pleasantness of my Lord, our G-d, be upon us – may He establish our work, the works of our hands may He establish.

On Friday night begin here.

And there was evening and there was morning,

THE SIXTH DAY. (Bereishit 1:31) Heaven and earth were completed, and their entire host. On the seventh day God completed all the work He had been doing, and God blessed the seventh day and declared it holy, because on it He desisted from all the work of creation He had done. (Bereishit 2:1–3)

On weekday nights begin here.

By your leave, masters, teachers and gentlemen:

BE BLESSED, GOD, OUR GOD, KING OF THE UNIVERSE, CREATOR OF THE FRUIT OF THE VINE.

The passages in parentheses are said only on Friday night.

Be blessed, God, our God, King of the universe, Who chose us out of all the peoples, exalted us above all tongues, and sanctified us by His commandments. And lovingly You gave us, God, our God, (Sabbaths for rest and) set times for celebration, festivals and occasions for rejoicing, this (Sabbath day and this) Matzot Festival, and this holiday, this holy convocation, the occasion of our liberation (with love): a holy convocation in remembrance of the Exodus from Egypt. Indeed, You chose us and sanctified us from among all the peoples, (and Sabbaths) and Your holy set-times (lovingly and gladly,) happily and joyously did You bequeath to us. Be blessed, God, Who sanctifies (the Sabbath and) Israel and the festivals.

קַדֵּשׁ

Pour the first cup, everybody stands, recite the Kiddush holding the cup in the upraised palm of the right hand.

הִנְנִי מוּכָן וּמְזוּמָּן לְקַיֵּם מִצְוַת כּוֹס רִאשׁוֹנָה מֵאַרְבַּע כּוֹסוֹת לְשֵׁם יִחוּד קוּדְשָׁא בְּרִיךְ הוּא וּשְׁכִינְתֵּיהּ עַל יְדֵי הַהוּא טָמִיר וְנֶעְלָם בְּשֵׁם כָּל־יִשְׂרָאֵל. וִיהִי נֹעַם אֲדֹנָי אֱלֹהֵינוּ עָלֵינוּ, וּמַעֲשֵׂה יָדֵינוּ כּוֹנְנָה עָלֵינוּ, וּמַעֲשֵׂה יָדֵינוּ כּוֹנְנֵהוּ.

On Friday night begin here.

וַיְהִי עֶרֶב וַיְהִי בֹקֶר

יוֹם הַשִּׁשִּׁי, וַיְכֻלּוּ הַשָּׁמַיִם וְהָאָרֶץ וְכָל־צְבָאָם. וַיְכַל אֱלֹהִים בַּיּוֹם הַשְּׁבִיעִי, מְלַאכְתּוֹ אֲשֶׁר עָשָׂה, וַיִּשְׁבֹּת בַּיּוֹם הַשְּׁבִיעִי, מִכָּל־מְלַאכְתּוֹ אֲשֶׁר עָשָׂה. וַיְבָרֶךְ אֱלֹהִים אֶת־יוֹם הַשְּׁבִיעִי, וַיְקַדֵּשׁ אֹתוֹ, כִּי בוֹ שָׁבַת מִכָּל־מְלַאכְתּוֹ, אֲשֶׁר־בָּרָא אֱלֹהִים לַעֲשׂוֹת.

On weekday nights begin here.

סַבְרִי מָרָנָן וְרַבָּנָן וְרַבּוֹתַי:

בָּרוּךְ אַתָּה יְיָ, אֱלֹהֵינוּ מֶלֶךְ הָעוֹלָם, בּוֹרֵא פְּרִי הַגָּפֶן.

The passages in parentheses are said only on Friday night.

בָּרוּךְ אַתָּה יְיָ, אֱלֹהֵינוּ מֶלֶךְ הָעוֹלָם, אֲשֶׁר בָּחַר בָּנוּ מִכָּל־עָם, וְרוֹמְמָנוּ מִכָּל־לָשׁוֹן, וְקִדְּשָׁנוּ בְּמִצְוֹתָיו, וַתִּתֶּן־לָנוּ יְיָ אֱלֹהֵינוּ בְּאַהֲבָה (שַׁבָּתוֹת לִמְנוּחָה וּ) מוֹעֲדִים לְשִׂמְחָה, חַגִּים וּזְמַנִּים לְשָׂשׂוֹן אֶת־יוֹם (הַשַּׁבָּת הַזֶּה וְאֶת־יוֹם) חַג הַמַּצּוֹת הַזֶּה, זְמַן חֵרוּתֵנוּ, (בְּאַהֲבָה,) מִקְרָא קֹדֶשׁ, זֵכֶר לִיצִיאַת מִצְרָיִם. כִּי בָנוּ בָחַרְתָּ וְאוֹתָנוּ קִדַּשְׁתָּ מִכָּל־הָעַמִּים. (וְשַׁבָּת) וּמוֹעֲדֵי קָדְשֶׁךָ (בְּאַהֲבָה וּבְרָצוֹן) בְּשִׂמְחָה וּבְשָׂשׂוֹן הִנְחַלְתָּנוּ. בָּרוּךְ אַתָּה יְיָ, מְקַדֵּשׁ (הַשַּׁבָּת וְ) יִשְׂרָאֵל וְהַזְּמַנִּים.

If the Seder takes placed on Saturday night, add the following two blessings:

Be blessed, God, our God, King of the universe, Creator of the firelights.

Be blessed, God, our God, King of the universe, Who distinguishes between the holy and the commonplace, between light and darkness, between Israel and the other peoples, between the seventh day and the six workdays. You have distinguished between the sanctity of the Sabbath and holiday sanctity, and the seventh day You declared holy above the six workdays. You set apart and hallowed Your people, Israel, with Your holiness. Be blessed, God, Who distinguishes between one sanctity and another sanctity.

The following blessing is always said:

Be blessed, God, our God, King of the universe, for keeping us alive, and sustaining us, and enabling us to reach this occasion.

Drink the first cup, reclining.

If the Seder takes placed on Saturday night, add the following two blessings:

בָּרוּךְ אַתָּה יְיָ, אֱלֹהֵינוּ מֶלֶךְ הָעוֹלָם, בּוֹרֵא מְאוֹרֵי הָאֵשׁ.

בָּרוּךְ אַתָּה יְיָ, אֱלֹהֵינוּ מֶלֶךְ הָעוֹלָם, הַמַּבְדִּיל בֵּין קֹדֶשׁ לְחוֹל בֵּין אוֹר לְחֹשֶׁךְ, בֵּין יִשְׂרָאֵל לָעַמִּים, בֵּין יוֹם הַשְּׁבִיעִי לְשֵׁשֶׁת יְמֵי הַמַּעֲשֶׂה. בֵּין קְדֻשַּׁת שַׁבָּת לִקְדֻשַּׁת יוֹם טוֹב הִבְדַּלְתָּ, וְאֶת־יוֹם הַשְּׁבִיעִי מִשֵּׁשֶׁת יְמֵי הַמַּעֲשֶׂה קִדַּשְׁתָּ. הִבְדַּלְתָּ וְקִדַּשְׁתָּ אֶת־עַמְּךָ יִשְׂרָאֵל בִּקְדֻשָּׁתֶךָ. בָּרוּךְ אַתָּה יְיָ, הַמַּבְדִּיל בֵּין קֹדֶשׁ לְקֹדֶשׁ.

The following blessing is always said:

בָּרוּךְ אַתָּה יְיָ, אֱלֹהֵינוּ מֶלֶךְ הָעוֹלָם,
שֶׁהֶחֱיָנוּ וְקִיְּמָנוּ וְהִגִּיעָנוּ לַזְּמַן הַזֶּה.

Drink the first cup, reclining.

QUESTIONS FOR U'RECHATZ

1. Why are the children holding a pitcher under tap water, a cup with handles, a pail, and towels?
2. Why are the children helping the adults wash and dry their hands?
3. Usually blessings are said after washing the hands and before eating. Will a blessing be said here before the *karpas* is eaten?
4. Why are the hands of everyone at the table washed in this manner?

U'RECHATZ

Rinse the hands without saying the blessing.

וּרְחַץ

Rinse the hands without saying the blessing.

QUESTIONS FOR KARPAS

1. What are the children doing?
2. What is *karpas*?
3. Why do people dip the *karpas* into saltwater or vinegar?
4. What blessing is recited over *karpas*?

KARPAS

Dip vegetable in saltwater or vinegar and say the following blessing before eating:

Be blessed, God, our God, King of the universe, creator of the fruit of the soil.

כַּרְפַּס

Dip vegetable in saltwater or vinegar and say the following blessing before eating:

בָּרוּךְ אַתָּה יְיָ, אֱלֹהֵינוּ מֶלֶךְ הָעוֹלָם, בּוֹרֵא פְּרִי הָאֲדָמָה.

QUESTIONS FOR YACHATZ

1. What is the round thing shown open and closed at the top of the illustration?
2. Why is the matzah round?
3. What is happening to the middle matzah in the second row?
4. What is happening in the third and fourth rows?

YACHATZ

Split the middle matzah; leave the smaller piece in its place between two whole matzot and wrap the larger piece in a napkin for the afikoman.

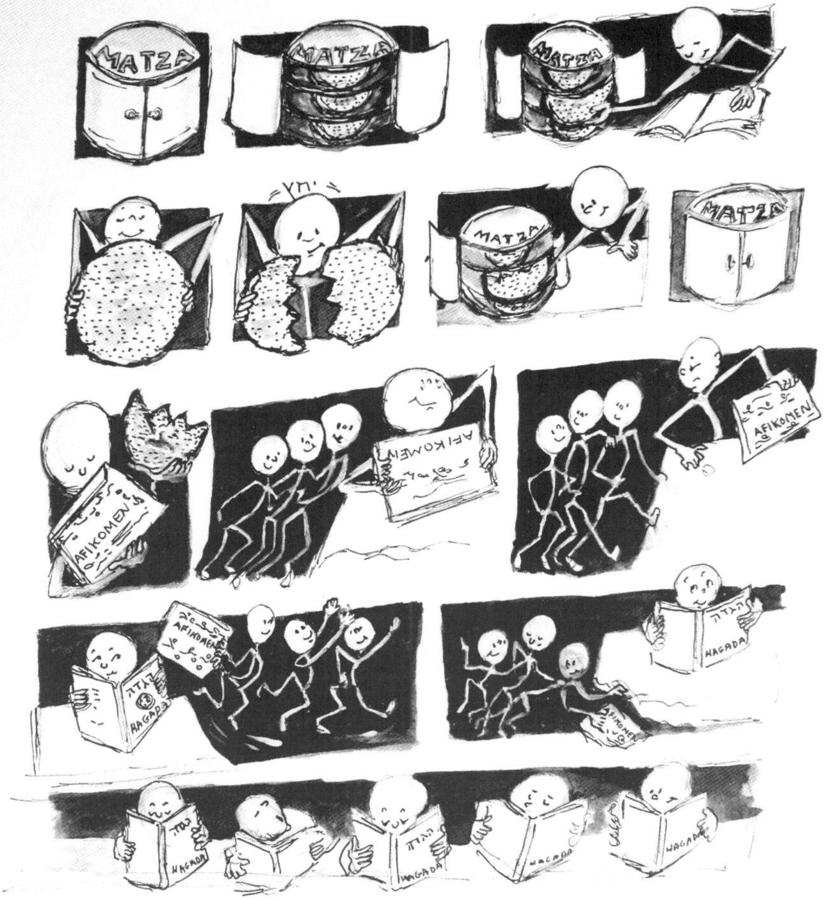

יַחַץ

Split the middle matzah; leave the smaller piece in its place between two whole matzot and wrap the larger piece in a napkin for the afikoman.

QUESTIONS FOR MAGGID

1. Why are the children at the head of the table standing on chairs and singing?
2. What do you see on the Seder plate?
3. Why is the wine off the table right now?
4. Why is everyone so happy to hear the children say the Mah Nishtanah?

Extra credit: What language can you use to say the Mah Nishtanah?

MAGGID

Lift the Seder tray and say:

THIS IS THE POVERTY BREAD that our ancestors ate in Egypt. Let anyone who is hungry enter and eat; let anyone who is needy enter and join us in our Passover feast. This year we are here; next year may we be in the Land of Israel. This year we are slaves; next year may we be free people.

But that is exactly the point of matzah. Matzah is a mitzvah that lives on the edge. By definition, the only grains that can be used for the baking of matzah are grains that can also become chametz. If the grain can't become chametz, then it can't be used for matzah. This shows us that the matzah itself is double edged. It will either be holy matzah or it will be unholy chametz, but it won't be something neutral like, for example, a piece of fruit.

The Talmud (*Pesachim* 40a) records that Rava went a step further. He would actually soak his wheat in water in order to bring it closer to fermenting, but then pull out the wheat from the water just before the matzah fermented. This was done in order to increase the intensity of the mitzvah by watching or guarding the matzah with greater fervor.

What value is there in increasing the possibility that the mitzvah could fail? What is the message here? The essence of baking matzah is to remind us to push ourselves and to challenge ourselves spiritually. This is why we are asked to bake matzah at the most intense and difficult time.

There is a great feeling of excitement in baking matzah on erev Pesach. That excitement comes from the great risk involved in the baking – we might fail. Nevertheless the rabbis teach that erev Pesach is the ideal time to bake the matzah. We are pushing ourselves to succeed. Some rabbis are even afraid to bake matzah on the eve of Pesach out of concern that we might fail. But the overwhelming position is that that is the right time to do it. Sure we might fail, but we are nonetheless challenging ourselves to succeed.

And that is what is needed in order to achieve spiritual greatness. We need to push ourselves at all times. Sure we can fail when we take on a great challenge. But if we don't even try for greatness then we have truly failed.

This same idea is found on the seventh day of Pesach – the day when the Israelites faced the Egyptians at the sea and the Egyptian army drowned. Why did our ancestors have to battle the Egyptians face-to-face? Why did they have

מַגִּיד

Lift the Seder tray and say:

הָא לַחְמָא עַנְיָא דִּי אֲכָלוּ אַבְהָתָנָא בְּאַרְעָא דְמִצְרָיִם. כָּל דִּכְפִין יֵיתֵי וְיֵכוֹל, כָּל דִּצְרִיךְ יֵיתֵי וְיִפְסַח. הָשַּׁתָּא הָכָא, לְשָׁנָה הַבָּאָה בְּאַרְעָא דְיִשְׂרָאֵל. הָשַּׁתָּא עַבְדֵי, לְשָׁנָה הַבָּאָה בְּנֵי חוֹרִין.

RUNNING OUT OF TIME

The *Shulchan Arukh* (458) records the custom of baking matzah specifically on the afternoon of the eve of Pesach. The reason is because that is the time when the Paschal Lamb was offered. Fascinated by this custom, our synagogue decided to bake matzot on Pesach eve.

Baking matzah presents many practical and technical challenges. One needs a brick oven, well water that was left to cool overnight, flour that was watched from the time of the harvest, a special tool to perforate the matzot, a *finner* to crush the dough, and a large group of people to bake the matzah.

Those normal challenges are compounded on the eve of Pesach. Not only is that a time when many people are busy preparing for the Seder, but it is also a time when the laws of chametz are even more stringent. Prior to the afternoon of Pesach, a drop of chametz can be nullified if there is the correct ratio of greater than sixty times the amount of matzah to the chametz. Prior to the afternoon of Pesach it is permitted to own chametz, so it is permitted to own any dough made in the baking process that does not become matzah. But on the eve of Passover it is prohibited to own any chametz and even one drop of chametz can make the entire batch of matzot invalid.

There is thus a special urgency to the making of matzah on erev Pesach. During the eighteen minutes of the matzah baking we had to stop and clean up the dough and burn any remaining pieces. The entire time that the matzah was being made we chanted, "*Kol perurin yiheyu mevutalin*" (May all crumbs be nullified). And if any part of the matzah looked questionable we had to discard the entire piece.

Baking matzah on erev Pesach is so risky – we might wonder why we have such a custom. After all, in the process of making matzah we could inadvertently be making chametz!

Replace the tray on the table, pour the second cup of wine, and the youngest participant asks:

WHY IS THIS NIGHT DIFFERENT from all nights?

Why, on all other nights, do we eat either unleavened bread or matzah,
but tonight we eat only matzah?

Why, on all other nights, do we eat all kinds of vegetables,
but tonight we make a special point of eating bitter herbs?

Why, on all other nights, do we not make a point of dipping at all,
but tonight we make a point of dipping twice?

Why, on all other nights, do we eat either sitting up or reclining,
but tonight we all make a point of reclining?

---

they are all living lives that are short on time and they therefore act quickly and decisively. Here is a quote from the book:

> When an Israeli man wants to date a woman, he asks her out that night. When an Israeli entrepreneur has a business idea, he will start it that week. The notion that one should accumulate credentials before launching a venture simply does not exist. This is actually good in business. Too much time can only teach you what can go wrong, not what can be transformative. (*Start-Up Nation*, 74)

The entire matzah-baking process takes a total of eighteen minutes. From when the flour hits the water, through the kneading, pressing, and rolling, and until the matzah is placed in the oven, we have eighteen minutes. Not a second more.

We experienced this when we baked the matzah for the first time, a few days before Pesach. As we stood there, we gave the children in the room a stopwatch with clear instructions: when we get to one minute start counting out the seconds – 60, 59… And so we began to bake the matzah. As we got closer the energy became greater and greater. And as we entered the final ten seconds there was a mad rush to get as much matzah as possible into the oven. The spiritual energy in the air was palpable.

The countdown represents a broader spiritual idea. It is a reminder that our time on this earth is fleeting; our time is limited. The countdown is at the

Replace the tray on the table, pour the second cup of wine, and the youngest participant asks:

מַה נִּשְׁתַּנָּה הַלַּיְלָה הַזֶּה מִכָּל הַלֵּילוֹת?

שֶׁבְּכָל הַלֵּילוֹת אָנוּ אוֹכְלִין חָמֵץ וּמַצָּה,
הַלַּיְלָה הַזֶּה כֻּלּוֹ מַצָּה.

שֶׁבְּכָל הַלֵּילוֹת אָנוּ אוֹכְלִין שְׁאָר יְרָקוֹת,
הַלַּיְלָה הַזֶּה מָרוֹר.

שֶׁבְּכָל הַלֵּילוֹת אֵין אָנוּ מַטְבִּילִין אֲפִילוּ פַּעַם אֶחָת,
הַלַּיְלָה הַזֶּה שְׁתֵּי פְעָמִים.

שֶׁבְּכָל הַלֵּילוֹת אָנוּ אוֹכְלִין בֵּין יוֹשְׁבִין וּבֵין מְסֻבִּין,
הַלַּיְלָה הַזֶּה כֻּלָּנוּ מְסֻבִּין.

---

to walk through a sea that only split at the last second? Couldn't Hashem have manufactured a situation in which we escaped without facing the Egyptians?

Hashem intentionally orchestrated a confrontation with the Egyptian army because the Israelites needed to face off against it. In order to be truly liberated in a spiritual sense they could not run from their enemy; they needed to wrestle with it and defeat it. The intensity of the direct encounter with the Egyptian army showed the people that they could succeed spiritually.

So, too, with the matzah: When we bake matzah we are pushing ourselves and awakening our spiritual adrenaline. We are reminding ourselves not to be afraid to fail and not to settle for mediocrity when it comes to spirituality, but to seek a deep and exciting connection with Hashem. In order to realize that connection we must always be willing to challenge ourselves spiritually.

The mitzvah of matzah contains another component, which has to do with how we value time. In the book *Start-Up Nation: The Story of Israel's Economic Miracle* (Dan Senor and Saul Singer [New York: Twelve, 2009]), the authors wonder why Israel has had such phenomenal success in the world of hi-tech start-ups. After the US, Israel has launched more successful start-ups than any other country in the world. One theory for this is that Israelis recognize that

Uncover the matzot and say:

WE WERE PHARAOH'S SLAVES in Egypt, and God, our God, took us out of there with a strong hand and outstretched arm. If the Blessed Holy One had not taken our ancestors out of Egypt, we, our children and our children's children would still be enslaved to Pharaoh in Egypt. And even if all of us were wise, even if all of us were clever, even if all of us were sages, even if all of us knew the Torah – we would still be in duty bound to talk about the Exodus from Egypt. And the more you elaborate on the story of the Exodus from Egypt, the more praiseworthy you are.

IT IS TOLD about Rabbi Eliezer, Rabbi Yehoshua, Rabbi Elazar son of Azaryah, Rabbi Akiva, and Rabbi Tarfon: One Passover night they were reclining together in Bnei Brak talking about the Exodus from Egypt. This went on all night, till their disciples came and said to them: "Masters, it is time to recite the morning Shema."

RABBI ELAZAR son of Azaryah said: Here I am like seventy years old, yet I never understood why the story about the Exodus from Egypt should be recited at night until Ben Zoma explained it on the basis of the verse (Devarim 16:3), "So that you shall remember the day of your departure from Egypt all the days of your life." If it had been written "the days of your life," it would have meant the days only; but "all the days of your life" means the nights, too. The other sages explain "all" to mean the messianic era, in addition to "the days of the present time."

---

days (Vayikra 23:15) – from the second day of Pesach until the giving of the Torah at Sinai. Immediately upon being liberated on Passover, the holiday of redemption, we must begin to count. We are reminded that that with our liberation comes responsibility, for our time in the world is finite.

This, then, is the dual message of matzah. We should push ourselves to succeed spiritually with great intensity and remember that our time is running out. We simply don't have that much time left to accomplish everything we need to do. "Rabbi Tarfon said: The day is short, the work is great, the laborers are lazy, the reward is abundant, and the Boss is impatient!" (Mishnah Avot 2:15).

Uncover the matzot and say:

עֲבָדִים הָיִינוּ לְפַרְעֹה בְּמִצְרָיִם. וַיּוֹצִיאֵנוּ יְיָ אֱלֹהֵינוּ מִשָּׁם, בְּיָד חֲזָקָה וּבִזְרוֹעַ נְטוּיָה. וְאִלּוּ לֹא הוֹצִיא הַקָּדוֹשׁ בָּרוּךְ הוּא אֶת־אֲבוֹתֵינוּ מִמִּצְרַיִם, הֲרֵי אָנוּ וּבָנֵינוּ וּבְנֵי בָנֵינוּ, מְשֻׁעְבָּדִים הָיִינוּ לְפַרְעֹה בְּמִצְרָיִם. וַאֲפִילוּ כֻּלָּנוּ חֲכָמִים, כֻּלָּנוּ נְבוֹנִים, כֻּלָּנוּ זְקֵנִים, כֻּלָּנוּ יוֹדְעִים אֶת־הַתּוֹרָה, מִצְוָה עָלֵינוּ לְסַפֵּר בִּיצִיאַת מִצְרָיִם. וְכָל הַמַּרְבֶּה לְסַפֵּר בִּיצִיאַת מִצְרַיִם, הֲרֵי זֶה מְשֻׁבָּח.

מַעֲשֶׂה בְּרַבִּי אֱלִיעֶזֶר, וְרַבִּי יְהוֹשֻׁעַ, וְרַבִּי אֶלְעָזָר בֶּן־עֲזַרְיָה, וְרַבִּי עֲקִיבָא, וְרַבִּי טַרְפוֹן, שֶׁהָיוּ מְסֻבִּין בִּבְנֵי־בְרַק, וְהָיוּ מְסַפְּרִים בִּיצִיאַת מִצְרַיִם, כָּל־אוֹתוֹ הַלַּיְלָה, עַד שֶׁבָּאוּ תַלְמִידֵיהֶם וְאָמְרוּ לָהֶם: רַבּוֹתֵינוּ, הִגִּיעַ זְמַן קְרִיאַת שְׁמַע, שֶׁל שַׁחֲרִית.

אָמַר רַבִּי אֶלְעָזָר בֶּן־עֲזַרְיָה. הֲרֵי אֲנִי כְּבֶן שִׁבְעִים שָׁנָה, וְלֹא זָכִיתִי, שֶׁתֵּאָמֵר יְצִיאַת מִצְרַיִם בַּלֵּילוֹת. עַד שֶׁדְּרָשָׁהּ בֶּן זוֹמָא, שֶׁנֶּאֱמַר: לְמַעַן תִּזְכֹּר, אֶת יוֹם צֵאתְךָ מֵאֶרֶץ מִצְרַיִם, כֹּל יְמֵי חַיֶּיךָ. יְמֵי חַיֶּיךָ הַיָּמִים, כֹּל יְמֵי חַיֶּיךָ הַלֵּילוֹת. וַחֲכָמִים אוֹמְרִים: יְמֵי חַיֶּיךָ הָעוֹלָם הַזֶּה, כֹּל יְמֵי חַיֶּיךָ לְהָבִיא לִימוֹת הַמָּשִׁיחַ.

---

core of what the matzah is all about. It is a reminder to perform the mitzvah of matzah with great alacrity lest we miss our opportunity for the mitzvah.

The Torah instructs us "*Ushemartem et hamatzot*" (You must guard the matzot; Shemot 12:17). Rashi (ad loc.) writes: "Do not read this as *matzot* but as *mitzvot*; just like the mitzvah of matzot must be done with great speed and zealousness, so too every mitzvah must be done in the same manner."

The idea of a countdown as we bake the matzah reinforces the notion that our time to serve Hashem in this word is running out. This idea reappears by the counting of the Omer. The Torah tells us to count for ourselves forty-nine

BLESSED IS THE OMNIPRESENT, blessed is He; blessed is the One Who gave the Torah to His people Israel – may He be blessed. The Torah has four sons in mind: the wise son, the wicked son, the simple son, and the son who does not know how to ask.

WHAT DOES THE WISE SON SAY? "What is the meaning of the precepts, statutes and laws that God, our God, has commanded you?" (Devarim 6:20) You are to tell him the rules of Passover: "It is forbidden to conclude the Passover meal by announcing: Now to the *afikoman*!" (Mishnah Pesachim 10:8)

WHAT DOES THE WICKED SON SAY? "What is this service of yours?" (Shemot 12:26) Since he has said "of yours," thus excluding himself from the community of Jews, he has denied God. So you are to take the bite out of him by saying to him: "This commemorates what God did for me when I went out of Egypt!" (Shemot 13:8) – "for me," not for him; had he been there, he would not have been liberated.

WHAT DOES THE SIMPLE SON SAY? "What is this?" (Shemot 13:14) You are to tell him: "It was by might of hand that God took us out of Egypt, out of the land of slavery." (Shemot 13:14)

AS FOR THE SON WHO DOES NOT KNOW HOW TO ASK – you start him off, for it is written (Shemot 13:8): "You shall tell your son that day, saying: 'This commemorates what God did for me when I went out of Egypt.'"

Barukh haMakom; barukh Hu.
Barukh shenatan Torah l'amo Yisrael; barukh Hu.

Blessed be the Omnipresent; blessed be He.
Blessed be He Who gave the Torah to the people of Israel; blessed be He.

Why is specifically this paragraph chosen to introduce the Four Sons? What is the source of this paragraph? It is not a quotation from the Torah or the Midrash. Its source lies in the last Mishnah of tractate *Middot*.

The Mishnah discusses how *kohanim* needed official approval before serving in the Temple. *Kohanim* would come to the Sanhedrin and proclaim that they were of good lineage and worthy to serve as priests. If the Sanhedrin found them unworthy, they would be wrapped in black garments and sent away. If they were found worthy, a great holiday would be declared. Then they would

בָּרוּךְ הַמָּקוֹם. בָּרוּךְ הוּא. בָּרוּךְ שֶׁנָּתַן תּוֹרָה לְעַמּוֹ יִשְׂרָאֵל. בָּרוּךְ הוּא. כְּנֶגֶד אַרְבָּעָה בָנִים דִּבְּרָה תוֹרָה. אֶחָד חָכָם, וְאֶחָד רָשָׁע, וְאֶחָד תָּם, וְאֶחָד שֶׁאֵינוֹ יוֹדֵעַ לִשְׁאוֹל.

חָכָם מַה הוּא אוֹמֵר? מָה הָעֵדֹת וְהַחֻקִּים וְהַמִּשְׁפָּטִים, אֲשֶׁר צִוָּה יְיָ אֱלֹהֵינוּ אֶתְכֶם? וְאַף אַתָּה אֱמָר־לוֹ כְּהִלְכוֹת הַפֶּסַח: אֵין מַפְטִירִין אַחַר הַפֶּסַח אֲפִיקוֹמָן.

רָשָׁע מַה הוּא אוֹמֵר? מָה הָעֲבֹדָה הַזֹּאת לָכֶם? לָכֶם וְלֹא לוֹ. וּלְפִי שֶׁהוֹצִיא אֶת־עַצְמוֹ מִן הַכְּלָל, כָּפַר בְּעִקָּר. וְאַף אַתָּה הַקְהֵה אֶת־שִׁנָּיו, וֶאֱמָר־לוֹ: בַּעֲבוּר זֶה, עָשָׂה יְיָ לִי, בְּצֵאתִי מִמִּצְרָיִם. לִי וְלֹא־לוֹ. אִלּוּ הָיָה שָׁם, לֹא הָיָה נִגְאָל.

תָּם מַה הוּא אוֹמֵר? מַה זֹּאת? וְאָמַרְתָּ אֵלָיו: בְּחֹזֶק יָד הוֹצִיאָנוּ יְיָ מִמִּצְרַיִם מִבֵּית עֲבָדִים.

וְשֶׁאֵינוֹ יוֹדֵעַ לִשְׁאוֹל, אַתְּ פְּתַח לוֹ. שֶׁנֶּאֱמַר: וְהִגַּדְתָּ לְבִנְךָ, בַּיּוֹם הַהוּא לֵאמֹר: בַּעֲבוּר זֶה עָשָׂה יְיָ לִי, בְּצֵאתִי מִמִּצְרָיִם.

BLESSING THE WICKED SON

The Four Sons of the Haggadah are perhaps the most colorful and dynamic element of the Haggadah. Throughout history artists have chosen to depict each of these sons in ways that reflect their views of society. The Wicked Son, in particular, has been portrayed in countless different ways, including a fighter, a gambler, a capitalist, a Sabbath violator, and a robber.

How did the actual editor of the Haggadah view the Wicked Son? The answer to this question can be understood through a close reading of the text and through understanding the context of the Haggadah.

The Four Sons of the Haggadah are introduced through the following paragraph:

In the Haggadah, the rabbis used the same blessing of the Mishnah, but they no longer applied it to the priests. They now directed it to the Four Sons. Indeed, the rabbis applied the blessing to all of the Jewish people. Instead of the *kohanim* serving God on behalf of the people, the people are now reminded that all of them have the ability to serve God. The *kohanim* are no longer essential, says the Haggadah through this blessing, because the Torah was given to everyone. With this reformulation of the blessing the people are reassured that their Seder service has as much validity as the service of the *kohanim* in the Temple.

Why did the rabbis add a fourth blessing to the formulation of the Mishnah? Not content simply to assure people that their service was valid, the rabbis taught that the current rituals of the Seder are actually more expansive and inclusive than in the time of the Temple.

The fourth blessing that the rabbis added symbolizes the expansiveness of the Torah. The Torah has always been interpreted in countless ways by many different types of Jews. The Haggadah reminds us that these interpretations all stem from an encounter with the same Torah. Moreover, the Haggadah teaches that all of these approaches – regardless of their conclusions – are considered a blessing.

The question of the Wicked Son appears in Shemot 12:26 – as the Torah states, "When your sons will say to you, 'What is this service of yours?'" According to the Torah, when the people heard this prophecy, they immediately bowed down. The Mekhilta comments that they bowed down in praise of the good prophecy that they had heard.

If they were told that they would have wicked children, why was it considered a good prophecy? Rav Reuven Katz, former chief rabbi of Petach Tikvah, explains that to have wicked children like this is praiseworthy (*Dudaei Reuven* [Degel Reuven, 1998], 205). A child who engages in Torah study in any capacity is worthy of praise. Whether or not we like his conclusions, the approach of the Wicked Son is considered a blessing. He is wrestling with the Torah, interpreting the Torah, and coming to very different conclusions than the Wise Son. We are to reject his teachings. But the mere fact that he is studying Torah is a blessing.

With the questions of the Four Sons the Haggadah is teaching a powerful lesson about the breadth and vitality of Torah study. Torah study is widely accessible to all and its power is even greater than the rituals of the *kohanim* in the Temple. Since Torah study is so deeply spiritual, the very act of engagement is a mitzvah of the highest level. The conclusions of the Torah study are far less important than the act of study itself. Even conclusions that we find abhorrent and repulsive are to be blessed. The Wicked Son, too, is to be blessed.

be wrapped in white garments and immediately enter to serve in the Temple. On this occasion, the following blessing was recited:

> Blessed be the Omnipresent; blessed be He, for no disqualifying defect was found in the seed of Aharon. Blessed be He Who selected Aharon and his sons to stand and minister before God in the Holy of Holies. (Mishnah *Middot* 5:4)

The blessing is nearly identical to the one that appears in our Haggadah. Both use the phrase *Barukh haMakom; barukh Hu* (Blessed be the Omnipresent; blessed be He). Both repeat the words *barukh Hu* a second time at the close of the blessing. The crucial difference is that the Mishnah uses the word *barukh* three times as an introduction to three blessings, while the Haggadah uses it four times for four blessings.

Historical context helps explain why the Haggadah chose this blessing as an introduction to the Four Sons. Before the destruction of the Temple, the rituals of Judaism were mainly focused on the priests who served in the Temple. Through their religious service in the Temple they had a mandate to represent the people to God. After the destruction of the Temple, the rabbis boldly proposed that all Jews were capable of ritually serving God.

The Haggadah was formulated in the years following the destruction of the Temple. As long as the Temple existed there was little reason for a Haggadah, as Seder night consisted primarily of eating the Paschal Lamb with matzah and maror. After the destruction of the Temple, some rabbis continued to sacrifice a Paschal Lamb even without the Temple. (See for example, Mishnah *Beitzah* 2:7. See the discussion of this topic by Rav Dov Linzer, http://rabbidovlinzer.blogspot.com/2010/03/torah-from-our-beit-midrash.html.)

Other rabbis, like Rabban Gamliel of the Haggadah, argued for a radical transformation of the holiday. The Paschal Lamb would no longer be the focus of the evening. Instead, the discussion of the Exodus story would dominate the evening. As a result, the main ritual of the evening became the Maggid – the discussion of the Exodus. Before the destruction of the Temple, service of God had generally been formulaic and prescribed; now, a new type of ritual developed – a ritual that emphasized wide-ranging discussion.

The rabbis artfully reassured people of the validity of their radical approach by adapting the text of the Mishnah in *Middot*. The Mishnah contained a formulaic blessing that gave praise for the pedigree of the *kohanim*; the blessing gave thanks to God for allowing the *kohanim* to serve in the Temple. But now there was no Temple – who would serve the Jewish people?

WHY SHOULD the telling not begin on the first day of the month of Nissan in which the deliverance took place? Because the verse stresses "on that day," the day on which it began. In that case, should not the telling begin during the day? No, because the text stresses "this commemorates," and you cannot say "this" except when the matzah and bitter herbs are set before you.

---

have nothing to do with the cycle of the moon – the whole calendar revolves around the sun. On the other hand, the Islamic calendar has nothing to do with the sun, and is only dependent upon the moon. That's why any given holiday can appear throughout the year, irrespective of the season.

Why is it that Judaism depends not on the sun or the moon alone, but on *both the sun and the moon*? This question was posed to Rabbi Shimon ben Tzemach Duran, known as the Tashbetz, who lived in North Africa in the fifteenth century. Rabbi Shimon was asked why it is that Judaism must continually insert leap years in order to have its monthly lunar calendar coincide with its yearly solar calendar – why can't Judaism just choose either a lunar system or a solar system?

Rabbi Shimon responded that Judaism's calendar is actually the best type of system because it is able to utilize the advantages of both the solar and lunar calendars. The problem with having *only* a solar calendar is that the months are arbitrarily made up by man. They have nothing to do with the cycle of the moon; man alone decides if the month will be thirty, thirty-one, or twenty-eight days. In a solar calendar, the months are in effect divorced from nature. They are *solely* man made and not rooted in the natural order. (See http://www.thefoundationstone.org/en/beitmidrash/general/3116-tashbetz-ii.html.)

In a lunar calendar, the months are connected to nature. But a system that is entirely dependent upon a lunar calendar is also problematic. In the Islamic calendar, the holiday of Ramadan, for example, does not always come out in the same season, but rather moves throughout the year. It's a calendar that is too transient. There is no permanence and no connection between the holidays and the seasons.

What Judaism does as a result is combine the two calendars. In doing so, we balance the fact that we are always connected to nature through the cycles of the moon, and yet at the same time we are not entirely dependent upon the whims of nature. By anchoring the calendar to the solar system, we have also established some stability to our calendar.

יָכוֹל מֵרֹאשׁ חֹדֶשׁ, תַּלְמוּד לוֹמַר בַּיּוֹם הַהוּא. אִי בַּיּוֹם הַהוּא, יָכוֹל מִבְּעוֹד יוֹם. תַּלְמוּד לוֹמַר, בַּעֲבוּר זֶה. בַּעֲבוּר זֶה לֹא אָמַרְתִּי, אֶלָּא בְּשָׁעָה שֶׁיֵּשׁ מַצָּה וּמָרוֹר מֻנָּחִים לְפָנֶיךָ.

SHABBAT, ROSH CHODESH, AND PESACH: BALANCING DAILY CHALLENGES AND LONG-TERM GOALS

The Haggadah obviously celebrates the holiday of Pesach, but the holiday of Pesach also links to two other special days: Shabbat and Rosh Chodesh.

The Children of Israel were commanded on the holiday of Rosh Chodesh to take a Paschal Lamb on the tenth day of the first month. When the Israelites were slaves in Egypt the first commandment given to them was to observe the mitzvah of Rosh Chodesh (Shemot 12:2–3). The tenth day of that month, the first time the Paschal Lamb was sacrificed, was a Shabbat. It is for this reason that the Shabbat before Pesach is called Shabbat Hagadol (the great Shabbat), as it reminds us of that great Shabbat in Egypt when our ancestors took a Paschal Lamb as the first step in our redemption process (Tosafot to tractate *Shabbat* 87b, s.v. *v'oto*).

As our ancestors gained their freedom the Torah thought it necessary to link this freedom to a new appreciation of time, as represented in the two holy days of Shabbat and Rosh Chodesh.

Shabbat and Rosh Chodesh actually represent two entirely different ways of measuring time in this world. Rosh Chodesh is based upon the lunar calendar. Based upon the cycles of the moon, we declare our monthly calendar. On the other hand, Shabbat is based upon the solar calendar. Shabbat comes every seven days. A day is calculated by the complete cycle of the sun: setting, rising, and setting again. Shabbat occurs on the sun's seventh cycle.

The Jewish calendar is a lunisolar calendar, which means that it is based on both the cycles of the moon and the cycles of the sun. We base our months upon the moon, but we base our holidays upon the sun. The Torah establishes that Pesach must come out in the spring and Sukkot in the fall. This means that these holidays are dependent upon the solar calendar, because seasons are entirely dependent upon the sun.

Why do we need a calendar that is based upon both the sun *and* the moon? After all, the Christian calendar – the Gregorian calendar that is used today throughout the Western world – is entirely a solar one. The Gregorian months

ORIGINALLY, our ancestors were idolators, but now the Omnipresent has drawn us to His service, as it is said (Yehoshua 24:2–4): "Yehoshua then said to the entire people: 'This is the word of God, the God of Israel: Long ago your ancestors lived beyond the river [Euphrates] – Terach,

---

of the greatest frustrations people have in life is that they go through their day-to-day grinding and grueling existence without clearly seeing the benefit of their work. People often ask themselves: What's it all worth? That's why it's important to look at things with a broad-term perspective. Look back after five or six months and see what you accomplished in your job. See what you accomplished in your family or personal growth. With the lunisolar system Judaism is teaching us that when it comes to measuring in life we need to utilize both this short-term dynamic system, and this long term, more static system. If you only focus on the short term, you will lose perspective. But if you only focus on the long term then you forget about the necessity of staying on target every day of your life. The lunisolar system teaches us that both perspectives are important.

What's the highest point of measuring? What's the highlight of the calendar? That is when you fulfill this creed and live a day following both of these calendrical systems. Such a day occurs when Shabbat intersects with Rosh Chodesh. Shabbat–Rosh Chodesh is a day that follows both the solar and lunar calendars. And consequently it's a day that should remind us about the importance of measuring our own growth both in the long term as well as in the short term.

The Talmud (*Sanhedrin* 70) teaches that when they used to eat the special meal for Rosh Chodesh, it would be eaten at a time of day that was neither day nor night. Our commentators explain that the meal would be eaten between dawn and sunrise.

Why was the meal celebrating Rosh Chodesh eaten between night and day? To remind us that we should not focus too heavily on either the lunar or the solar calendar. That is, it reminds us that when we measure ourselves, both our successes and our failures, we should be careful to think both in the long term and in the short term.

As we gained our freedom in Egypt the Torah knew that as a new nation we would have many challenges and frustrations. Whenever we start something new there is a danger that we might lose perspective – by focusing on the present we could forget about our long-term goals, and by only looking

מִתְּחִלָּה עוֹבְדֵי עֲבוֹדָה זָרָה הָיוּ אֲבוֹתֵינוּ, וְעַכְשָׁו קֵרְבָנוּ הַמָּקוֹם לַעֲבֹדָתוֹ. שֶׁנֶּאֱמַר: וַיֹּאמֶר יְהוֹשֻׁעַ אֶל־כָּל־הָעָם: כֹּה אָמַר יְיָ אֱלֹהֵי יִשְׂרָאֵל, בְּעֵבֶר הַנָּהָר יָשְׁבוּ אֲבוֹתֵיכֶם מֵעוֹלָם, תֶּרַח אֲבִי אַבְרָהָם וַאֲבִי

Classically, our commentators see in this lunisolar system the meeting of God and man. God determines the season, yet He allows man – based upon nature – to set the exact dates. In this way the destinies of God and man meet in one calendar.

There is an alternative explanation to the symbolism of having a calendar that is based upon both a lunar and a solar system. Our lunisolar calendar is a system that is set up to ensure that we use time properly and measure ourselves in an effective manner.

How do we measure time? Today we use a watch to measure hours, and a calendar to measure days and months. But in ancient days there were two basic instruments used to measure time: the moon and the sun. It's easy to measure weeks and months with the moon – you can easily see changes in the size of the moon. In a relatively short period of time, the moon goes from being invisible to being full and then back to invisibility again. Therefore, the moon is excellent as a short-term measurement. But using the moon as a long-term measurement is problematic. In order to measure properly in the long term we need to use a more fixed object like the sun. The sun allows four basic measurements throughout the year, dependent upon the four seasons. So the sun is very good as a system of measurement, but only in the long term.

What Judaism teaches us is that we need to use both a lunar and a solar system as a means of measuring time. Both are equally important. The lunar system allows us to measure ourselves on a daily and weekly, short-term basis. It allows us to mark our change daily, based upon the dynamics and hectic changes of a day-to-day existence.

But Judaism teaches us that we need to measure ourselves not just in the short term but also in the long term. This is where the solar system of measurement comes in. The sun, with its dominating pervasiveness, reminds us not to be too caught up in short-term failures or successes, but to measure ourselves over the long term. The solar system teaches us to use the four seasons as four distinct measuring points through the year.

Why is it important to measure ourselves with a long-term system? One

Avraham's father and Nachor's father – and they worshipped other gods. But I took your father Avraham from beyond the river and led him though the whole land of Canaan, and I gave him many descendants: I gave him Yitzchak, and to Yitzchak I gave Yaakov and Esav. Then I gave Esav the hill country of Seir to possess, while Yaakov and his children went down to Egypt.'"

In 2009, at the invitation of President Obama, Rabbi Haskel Lookstein of Congregation Kehilath Jeshurun in New York spoke at the national prayer service that formed part of President Obama's inauguration. This was a courageous position on the part of Rabbi Lookstein, as he was for the most part breaking the precedent of Orthodox rabbis, who had generally refrained from entering churches. Indeed, the Rabbinical Council of America (RCA) immediately criticized Rabbi Lookstein for this.

They issued a statement that read:

> The long-standing policy of the Rabbinical Council of America, in accordance with Jewish law, is that participation in a prayer service held in the sanctuary of a church is prohibited. Any member of the RCA who attends such a service does so in contravention of this policy and should not be perceived as representing the organization in any capacity. (http://www.jta.org/2009/01/22/life-religion/rabbis-participation-in-national-prayer-service-irks-rca)

Rabbi Lookstein responded with his own letter to his fellow members of the RCA in which he justified his actions:

> The *Shulchan Aruch* notes in YD 178:2 that a person who needs to be close to the government may wear even the Torah- prohibited garments of a gentile in order to represent the Jewish community well. [In those days gentiles wore distinct clothing.] The prohibition to enter a church is grounded in the appearance of impropriety, rather than an actual impropriety — indeed, wearing garments of gentiles is a Torah prohibition and this is generally thought to be a rabbinic one. (http://www.jta.org/2009/01/23/news-opinion/the-telegraph/lookstein-why-i-participated-in-national-prayer-service)

Rabbi Lookstein's basic argument is that in general one should not enter a church but in this case he did so for the good of the Jewish community and

נָחוֹר, וַיַּעַבְדוּ אֱלֹהִים אֲחֵרִים. וָאֶקַּח אֶת־אֲבִיכֶם אֶת־אַבְרָהָם מֵעֵבֶר הַנָּהָר, וָאוֹלֵךְ אוֹתוֹ בְּכָל־אֶרֶץ כְּנָעַן. וָאַרְבֶּה אֶת־זַרְעוֹ, וָאֶתֵּן לוֹ אֶת־יִצְחָק, וָאֶתֵּן לְיִצְחָק אֶת־יַעֲקֹב וְאֶת־עֵשָׂו. וָאֶתֵּן לְעֵשָׂו אֶת־הַר שֵׂעִיר, לָרֶשֶׁת אוֹתוֹ, וְיַעֲקֹב וּבָנָיו יָרְדוּ מִצְרָיִם.

---

toward the future we might undervalue the essential need to work hard in the present. The message of measuring ourselves with a lunisolar calendar shows us that when we begin a new project we must focus on the present, but always remember to take stock of our long-term goals. This is the combined message of Pesach, Shabbat, and Rosh Chodesh.

INTERACTING WITH OUR CHRISTIAN NEIGHBORS

The story of Yaakov and his family immigrating to Egypt is in many ways the first story of a diaspora community. For the first time in history, we as a distinct minority interact with the majority population.

Yosef's plan is to manipulate the situation so that his father and brothers can settle in a distinct land within Egypt, the land of Goshen (Bereishit 47:1). Yosef sets up his brothers outside of Goshen, but at the same time he recognizes the need to gain Pharaoh's permission so that his family can continue to live separately in the land of Goshen. In order to achieve this goal Yosef carefully manipulates how his brothers should appear before Pharaoh and exactly what they should say (46:34). He then brings his father before Pharaoh so that Yaakov may bless Pharaoh and thereby further advance good relations with Pharaoh (47:10). Yosef thus carefully orchestrates the entire situation since he knows that the welfare of his family sensitively hinges upon their interactions with Pharaoh.

The question of how we – Jews as a minority community in the diaspora – interact with our neighbors who practice a different faith is an important and sensitive question going back to biblical times. Although this issue is always present in my mind, in 2015 it became particularly relevant.

On January 2, 2015, Muriel Bowser was inaugurated as mayor of Washington, D.C. As part of her inauguration festivities, she invited me to offer words of scripture and prayer at an interfaith prayer service just prior to her inauguration at the United Church of Christ.

I was honored to accept her invitation.

BLESSED BE THE ONE WHO KEEPS His promise to Israel, blessed be He. For the Blessed Holy One predestined the end [of the Egyptian bondage], doing what he told our father Avraham in the Covenant Between the Sections, as it is said (Bereishit 15:13–14): "And He said to Avram: 'Know for certain that your descendants will be strangers in a land not theirs, and they [the host people] will enslave and oppress them [the Jews] for four hundred years. But I will also judge the nation they will serve, and in the end they will leave with great wealth.'"

---

in which a rabbi is being invited into a church in order to offer his own Jewish prayer on behalf of a government leader and not in order to be seduced by the temptations of another religion.

But there is another factor here, which is not discussed openly in these sources: these legal opinions are based upon hundreds and hundreds of years in which the Jews were often brutally and viciously persecuted by medieval and early-modern Christians. Indeed, as part of the persecution there were often explicit attempts to convert Jews and thus these concerns, which might seem distant from us today, were throughout our history very real threats. Now that Christians are often defenders and protectors of the Jewish people, it is fair to question the relevance of these rulings.

I spoke about this issue at length with one of my teachers, Rav Dov Linzer. Rav Linzer suggested that even those who had theological concerns based upon medieval Christianity should draw a distinction in the modern world between different denominations of Christianity. He argued that the theological concerns regarding entering a church really only apply to Catholic churches and are not applicable to Protestant churches which have different theological beliefs. Certainly in my situation in which I was being invited to offer a prayer in a Protestant church, the theological concerns were not comparable to the concerns of rabbis writing in the Middle Ages. (See http://www.yutorah.org/lectures/lecture.cfm/740361/Rabbi_Dov_Linzer/Entering_into_Churches_and_Mosques_12-20-09.)

There is therefore a basis to argue that even though we must be wary of being tempted by Christianity's theology and therefore should avoid entering a church, in this particular case where it was a Protestant rather than a Catholic church I was allowed to enter for the purpose of giving honor to our government and interacting peacefully with our neighbors.

All this being said, I am really uncomfortable with this whole discussion.

בָּרוּךְ שׁוֹמֵר הַבְטָחָתוֹ לְיִשְׂרָאֵל. בָּרוּךְ הוּא. שֶׁהַקָּדוֹשׁ בָּרוּךְ הוּא חִשַּׁב אֶת־הַקֵּץ, לַעֲשׂוֹת כְּמָה שֶׁאָמַר לְאַבְרָהָם אָבִינוּ בִּבְרִית בֵּין הַבְּתָרִים, שֶׁנֶּאֱמַר: וַיֹּאמֶר לְאַבְרָם יָדֹעַ תֵּדַע, כִּי־גֵר יִהְיֶה זַרְעֲךָ, בְּאֶרֶץ לֹא לָהֶם, וַעֲבָדוּם וְעִנּוּ אֹתָם אַרְבַּע מֵאוֹת שָׁנָה. וְגַם אֶת־הַגּוֹי אֲשֶׁר יַעֲבֹדוּ דָּן אָנֹכִי. וְאַחֲרֵי כֵן יֵצְאוּ, בִּרְכֻשׁ גָּדוֹל.

---

that in certain cases one can even violate Jewish law in order to interact with the leaders of the government.

Rabbi Lookstein's opinion is not a radical opinion. In fact, it is based on a responsum of the Rosh (Rabbi Yechiel ben Asher, thirteenth century), who allows one to enter a church in extenuating circumstances (Responsa of the Rosh 19:17). On the other hand, the RCA's approach here was disturbing as it singled out for attack an esteemed rabbi who has dedicated his life to the Jewish community and in this case was doing his best to maintain his loyalty to tradition and also give honor to the newly elected president.

There may be another way to defend Rabbi Lookstein's position without resorting to the argument that extenuating circumstances sometimes allow us to violate Jewish law. The whole argument of the RCA is based upon a premise that Christians are allowed to believe in the trinity as from their perspective it is a form of monotheism, but from the perspective of Jews it is not considered a form of monotheism (see *Darkei Moshe* 156). In addition to this opinion, the RCA must be following the ruling of the *Shulchan Arukh* (YD 150:1) that states, "It is a mitzvah to keep a distance of four cubits" from a dangerous theological belief that can possibly lead us astray. Thus, since in the minds of the RCA a church represents a theological threat to the Jewish people, one cannot enter a church. Furthermore, there is a prohibition of the perception of impropriety (*marit ayin*), as some might think that a Jew entering a church is going there in order to worship.

In contrast, Rabbi Lookstein would argue that *marit ayin* does not apply in this situation since everyone knows that he is going there in a public manner to represent the Jewish community. So, too, the issue of "keeping a distance of four cubits" from a dangerous theological belief would not be relevant in this case as that is based upon the premise that entering a church is a temptation that could sway us to foreign worship. That is clearly not relevant in a situation

Cover the matzot and raise the cup of wine.

AND IT IS THIS WHICH HAS STOOD by our ancestors and us. For not just one has risen up to annihilate us; in every generation they rise up to annihilate us, but the Blessed Holy One saves us from them.

Put down the cup of wine and uncover the matzot.

GO AND LEARN what Lavan the Aramean intended to do to our father Yaakov: Pharaoh decreed death only on the males, whereas Lavan wanted to eradicate all, as it is said (Devarim 26:5): "The Aramean wanted to destroy my father. But HE WENT DOWN TO EGYPT AND SOJOURNED THERE – FEW IN NUMBER. THERE HE BECAME A NATION, GREAT AND POWERFUL, AND POPULOUS."

---

an honor for me to enter the church that day. It is vitally important that we classify our neighbors with tremendous respect and treat them with enormous dignity. This means that we must recognize that our Christian neighbors today are very distant from the ancient and biblical classification of *avodah zarah*. Our neighbors are in most cases righteous and pious people from whom we can learn an immense amount. For us it is a blessing to be their neighbors.

OPEN ORTHODOX DISCUSSION 1

KOL ISHAH: LET US ALL SING TOGETHER TO REACH OUR SPIRITUAL POTENTIAL

After Yaakov received the blessing that had been meant for Esav, he fled to Lavan's home to escape Esav's rage. Years later, when Yaakov finds out that his brother Esav is coming to meet him, Yaakov is unsure of his intentions and prepares for the worst. As part of his preparations, the Torah tells us that Yaakov brings his eleven children across the river to meet Esav (Bereishit 32:23).

Rashi, citing the Midrash, notes that Yaakov has not eleven children, but twelve. Rashi asks: "*V'Dinah heikhan haitah*? (Where was Dinah?). Rashi answers:

> He put her into a box and locked her in, so that Esav would not set eyes on her. Therefore, Yaakov was punished for withholding her from his brother –

Cover the matzot and raise the cup of wine.

וְהִיא שֶׁעָמְדָה לַאֲבוֹתֵינוּ וְלָנוּ. שֶׁלֹּא אֶחָד בִּלְבָד, עָמַד עָלֵינוּ לְכַלּוֹתֵנוּ, אֶלָּא שֶׁבְּכָל דּוֹר וָדוֹר, עוֹמְדִים עָלֵינוּ לְכַלּוֹתֵנוּ. וְהַקָּדוֹשׁ בָּרוּךְ הוּא מַצִּילֵנוּ מִיָּדָם.

Put down the cup of wine and uncover the matzot.

צֵא וּלְמַד, מַה בִּקֵּשׁ לָבָן הָאֲרַמִּי לַעֲשׂוֹת לְיַעֲקֹב אָבִינוּ. שֶׁפַּרְעֹה לֹא גָזַר אֶלָּא עַל הַזְּכָרִים, וְלָבָן בִּקֵּשׁ לַעֲקֹר אֶת־הַכֹּל, שֶׁנֶּאֱמַר: אֲרַמִּי אֹבֵד אָבִי, וַיֵּרֶד מִצְרַיְמָה, וַיָּגָר שָׁם בִּמְתֵי מְעָט. וַיְהִי שָׁם לְגוֹי גָּדוֹל, עָצוּם, וָרָב.

I can't sit comfortably with this classification of any of the Christian people I know (whether Catholics or Protestants) as a seductive theological group who we should avoid interaction with since they are trying to seduce us with their worship. I consider the Christians I know to be holy people who worship a monotheistic God in a way differently than I do. And that's OK for them. They shouldn't worship the way I worship as they are not Jewish. Only Jews need to worship like Jews.

The language we use to discuss other groups of people matters, and the way we interact as a religious community with other communities also matters enormously. We should take great pains to avoid using harmful and alienating language in discussing other religious groups.

Instead of relying upon the highly nuanced legalisms advanced above, I instead relied upon the opinion of the first chief rabbi of the State of Israel, Rabbi Isaac Halevi Herzog. As the State of Israel was being founded a question arose: Should Israel allow churches to exist in Israel? Rabbi Herzog's approach was to recognize that Christianity today is not the same as the Christianity of the Middle Ages. He wrote: "Christianity today, even Catholics, do not worship a foreign god in the original sense of the word, rather their hearts are toward Heaven." He further wrote that if we adopt a harsh attitude towards Christianity it will arouse further "enmity, anger, and hatred throughout all of the Christian lands" (Herzog, "Minority's Rights According to Halakhah" [Hebrew], *Techumin* 2).

Our Christian neighbors are holy, kind, generous, and charitable. It was

"HE WENT DOWN TO EGYPT" – compelled to do so by the word of God.

"AND HE SOJOURNED THERE" – this teaches us that he did not go to settle in Egypt but only to sojourn there, as it is said (Bereishit 47:4): "And they said to Pharaoh: 'We have come to sojourn in the land, as there is no pasture for your servants' sheep, for the famine is severe in the land of Canaan. Pray, then, let your servants stay in the Goshen region.'"

---

box and her being assaulted by Shechem. In the end, her time being locked up in the box did not protect her but actually increased her vulnerability.

I think about this midrashic interpretation of the Dinah story every time I hear of another incident in which a Jewish educational institution prevents girls from singing because of the prohibition of a woman singing, known as *kol ishah*.

What is the prohibition of *kol ishah*? How has it been interpreted by our rabbis?

The Talmud records the following statement: "Shmuel taught: The voice of a woman is a sexual stimulant since it states, 'For your voice is sweet and your face is comely' (Shir Hashirim 2:14)" (*Berakhot* 24a).

This statement is left without further explanation in that Talmudic passage. But another Talmudic text (*Kiddushin* 70a) implies that the concern is not for the singing voice of a woman but for her speaking voice, when a man is conversing inappropriately with a married woman.

In an important article on this topic Rabbi Saul Berman argues that most medieval authorities did not interpret the statement of Shmuel as a blanket prohibition on women singing in the presence of men, but as a prohibition on men reciting Shema while hearing a woman sing, or exchanging warm greetings with married women, or both of those concerns (Rabbi Saul Berman, "Kol 'Isha," in *The Rabbi Joseph H. Lookstein Memorial Volume*, ed. Leo Landman [New York: Ktav, 1980], 45–66).

Nevertheless, many later authorities did consider there to be a blanket prohibition against a man hearing a woman sing. These later authorities form the basis for a *psak* that limits people today from hearing a woman sing, no matter the context.

Yet two rabbis in Israel – Rav David Bigman, rosh yeshiva of Maaleh Gilboa, and Rav Moshe Lichtenstein, rosh yeshiva of Yeshivat Har Etzion – have both

וַיֵּרֶד מִצְרַיְמָה. אָנוּס עַל פִּי הַדִּבּוּר.

וַיָּגָר שָׁם. מְלַמֵּד שֶׁלֹּא יָרַד יַעֲקֹב אָבִינוּ לְהִשְׁתַּקֵּעַ בְּמִצְרַיִם, אֶלָּא לָגוּר שָׁם, שֶׁנֶּאֱמַר: וַיֹּאמְרוּ אֶל־פַּרְעֹה, לָגוּר בָּאָרֶץ בָּאנוּ, כִּי אֵין מִרְעֶה לַצֹּאן אֲשֶׁר לַעֲבָדֶיךָ, כִּי כָבֵד הָרָעָב בְּאֶרֶץ כְּנָעַן. וְעַתָּה, יֵשְׁבוּ־נָא עֲבָדֶיךָ בְּאֶרֶץ גֹּשֶׁן.

> because perhaps she would cause him to improve his ways – and she fell into the hands of Shechem. (Rashi 32:23, from Bereishit Rabbah 75:9)

According to Rashi, Yaakov was punished for locking Dinah in a box. On the one hand, our sympathies are with Yaakov. After all, he was worried that she would fall into the hands and influence of the wicked Esav. But on the other hand, we learn from this incident that by locking Dinah in a box, Yaakov protected her from Esav – but exposed her to the wicked Shechem.

The lesson of Rashi is clear: one cannot protect someone by locking that person in a box. Having been locked in a box, Dinah was totally unprepared to deal with the wicked people of the world.

After the box incident, we next hear about Dinah once Yaakov has returned to Israel:

> Dinah, the daughter of Leah, whom she had borne to Yaakov, went out to look about among the daughters of the land. And Shechem the son of Hamor, the Hivvite, the prince of the land, saw her, and he took her, lay with her, and violated her. (Bereishit 34:1–2)

Although Shechem is the villain of the story, Rashi tells us that Dinah too acted inappropriately:

> The daughter of Leah: And not the daughter of Yaakov? However, because of her going out she was called the daughter of Leah, since she [Leah] too was in the habit of going out. (Ibid. 34:1)

Having been locked in a box, Dinah became a *yatzanit,* a girl who goes out inappropriately. She went out to see the daughters of the land and in the end Shechem sexually assaulted her.

Thus, Rashi draws for us a direct line between the act of placing Dinah in a

"FEW IN NUMBER" – as it is said (Bereishit 47:4): "Just seventy your ancestors numbered when they went down to Egypt; but now God, your God, has made you as numerous as the stars in the sky."

For many girls music and singing is a spiritual outlet. By denying girls the opportunity to perform in school plays and sing in spiritual settings within their communities we are limiting their ability to succeed spiritually and we are potentially turning them away from our Torah.

This was indeed part of the reasoning of Rabbi Yechiel Weinberg (1884–1966), who issued a radical ruling allowing boys and girls to sing Shabbat *zemirot* together:

> In countries like Germany and France, women would feel disgraced and see it as a deprivation of their rights if we prohibited them from joining in the rejoicing over the Sabbath by singing zemirot. This is obvious to anyone familiar with the character of the women in these countries. The prohibition could drive women away from religion, God forbid. (*Seridei Esh*, vol. 2, responsum 8 [Hebrew]; cited by Berman, 64)

Several women have told me that they experience great spiritual difficulties in not being able to sing in the presence of men. So, too, multiple people shared with me that a prohibitive approach to *kol ishah* is a major factor in deciding whether or not to send their children to an Orthodox day school.

If we deny the girls of our community the ability to express themselves through song, we run the very real risk of allowing them to be serenaded by an alternative influence that is truly dangerous. Another midrash cited by *Torah Temimah* says: "Shechem gathered musicians outside Dinah's home and as a consequence Dinah went out of her home" (see *Torah Temimah* 34:1, note 2). Amazingly, the midrash is teaching us that Dinah left her home because she was enticed by the music of Shechem. We should encourage our girls to sing in the context of Torah lest they run to hear the music of Shechem!

A second concern that we should have is not only what drowning out the voices of girls will do to the spiritual advancement of the girls, but also what message it teaches the boys. This point was forcefully made by Rav Lichtenstein. He argues that if we are stringent in the area of *kol ishah* then we are accepting upon ourselves a "stringency that will lead to a leniency."

He argues, based upon the Talmud, that a human being is in part a physical animal and in part a spiritual entity. By teaching boys and men that girls are

בִּמְתֵי מְעָט. כְּמָה שֶׁנֶּאֱמַר: בְּשִׁבְעִים נֶפֶשׁ, יָרְדוּ אֲבֹתֶיךָ מִצְרָיְמָה. וְעַתָּה, שָׂמְךָ יְיָ אֱלֹהֶיךָ, כְּכוֹכְבֵי הַשָּׁמַיִם לָרֹב.

independently written that the prohibition of *kol ishah* should be understood in a much more limited fashion. Their opinions are based upon the writings of great medieval authorities like Raviah, Mordechai, Tosafot Ri, and even in the writings of some modern-day charedi rabbis like the Seridei Esh and Chazon Ish. (Rav Bigman's responsum can be accessed at http://www.jewishideas.org/articles/new-analysis-kol-bisha-erva; Rav Lichtenstein's article was published in *Techumin* 32, 5772.) The relevance of the Chazon Ish for a permissive *psak* can be seen in Rabbi Berman's article, p. 65.)

Rav Bigman writes:

> There is no prohibition whatsoever of innocent singing; rather, only singing intended for sexual stimulation, or flirtatious singing, is forbidden. Although this distinction is not explicit in the early rabbinic sources, it closely fits the character of the prohibition as described in different contexts in the Talmud and the Rishonim, and it is supported by the language of the Rambam, the Tur, and the *Shulchan Arukh*.

After carefully reading the positions of Rav Bigman and Rav Lichtenstein, I feel strongly that their opinion on this matter is one that should be embraced as an ideal approach by modern Orthodox communities.

There are three considerations that should urge us to follow the path advocated by Rabbis Bigman and Lichtenstein. First, we run the very real risk of drowning out a girl's spiritual voice and thereby turning her away from traditional Judaism. We alluded to the fact that Dinah's actions after being locked in a box were seen as rebellious. "*Vatetzei Dinah*" is understood to mean that Dinah went out inappropriately. Ironically, in a commentary to this passage, the *Torah Temimah* draws our attention to another instance in the Torah where the word *vatetzei* appears: "Miriam, the prophetess, Aharon's sister, took a timbrel in her hand, and all the women came out after her with timbrels and with dances" (Shemot 15:20). These women whom Miriam led were on such a great spiritual level that they took their own musical instruments from Egypt in anticipation of being able to praise Hashem properly. Miriam and her followers used music to reach high spiritual levels (Rashi, ibid.). We need to allow our daughters the space and place to attain that level if they so desire.

"THERE HE BECAME A NATION" – this teaches that Israel was distinctive there.

"GREAT AND POWERFUL" – as it is said: "But the Children of Israel were fertile and prolific: they increased and became very numerous and the land was full of them" (Shemot 1:7).

The ideal approach for our community is to allow the voices of women to be heard within the context of halakhic parameters. Such an approach is not merely an ex post facto (*bediavad*) allowance, but an ideal (*lekhatchilah*) approach that is entirely consistent with halakhah and our worldview.

Questions for the Seder Table

1. Is singing an important part of your spirituality?
2. Do you see any female singers today who are spiritual role models for you?
3. How does singing at your Seder table impact your spiritual experience of the Seder?

GUEST VOICE: MAHARAT RUTH BALINSKY FRIEDMAN

In 2013 Ruth Balinsky Friedman joined the staff of Ohev Sholom – The National Synagogue as a Maharat, a full-time member of the clergy. In doing so, she became the first Maharat to lead a synagogue in the United States.

FERTILITY CHALLENGES

At the Seder we celebrate our freedom from slavery and oppression in Egypt and we also remember the harsh suffering in Egypt – the bricks, the bitterness, and the tears. The Egyptians curtailed our physical freedom, but despite those attempts we only got stronger. The Torah tells us that the Israelites were fertile and reproduced, and they grew stronger and populated the land (Shemot 1:17). In his commentary (ad loc.), Rashi teaches that the Israelites accomplished this by giving birth to six children at once, a miraculous occurrence.

These texts can sound sweet to a child studying them in school, but they can also be a source of pain for couples struggling to conceive. One in every six couples encounters fertility challenges. These struggles are both physical and emotional. Proper diagnosis and treatment for fertility-related conditions

וַיְהִי שָׁם לְגוֹי. מְלַמֵּד שֶׁהָיוּ יִשְׂרָאֵל מְצֻיָּנִים שָׁם.

גָּדוֹל, עָצוּם. כְּמָה שֶׁנֶּאֱמַר: וּבְנֵי יִשְׂרָאֵל, פָּרוּ וַיִּשְׁרְצוּ, וַיִּרְבּוּ וַיַּעַצְמוּ, בִּמְאֹד מְאֹד, וַתִּמָּלֵא הָאָרֶץ אֹתָם.

---

such erotic creatures that it is impossible to have an encounter with them that is not erotic (which is actually the simple reading of the one Talmudic text that refers to *kol ishah* in *Kiddushin,* though it is conveniently ignored by most who are stringent about a woman's singing voice), we are in fact reinforcing the notion that our spiritual personality cannot rise above our physical nature. The hypererotic educational message that we are sending is a depressing one, which seems to go against what our tradition teaches us in other places; namely, that the spiritual can overcome the physical.

A lenient ruling in the area of *kol ishah* is thus an important educational tool for all of our children. It is lenient in the area of *kol ishah,* but actually stringent in the area of what we expect spiritually from the people of our community. We are saying that we are ultimately spiritual beings and not purely physical animals.

A third concern is that by focusing on the formal prohibition of *kol ishah* we are acting hypocritically and ignoring the more salient factor of the context in which the singing is taking place. Although this opinion is generally ignored in actual practice, *Sefer Hasidim* (early thirteenth c., Germany) writes that just as a man cannot hear a woman's voice, so too a woman should not hear the voice of a man (*"v'hu hadin l'ishah shelo tishma kol ish,"* p. 614).

The community message should be consistent and emphasize what the Talmud is really concerned about. Our ever-constant focus on the fact that it is a woman singing causes us to ignore the real issue. The underlying issue is not a woman singing or a man singing, but licentiousness and flirtatiousness. These are the activities that our tradition is strongly discouraging.

Licentiousness can be found in women singing and men singing. Instead of teaching the boys and girls that the voice of a girl or woman singing innocuous words is seductive, we should teach them to make the right choices in life about what is appropriate and inappropriate context and behavior. This type of cultural inappropriateness is far too present in all of our lives and we should focus on it. By instead fixating on whether or not a woman is singing we are merely distracting ourselves from the real issue.

"AND POPULOUS" – as it is said (Yechezkel 16:7, 6): "I caused you to increase like wild-flowers, and you throve and grew, and you came to full womanhood, your breasts fully fashioned, your hair grown – but you were still naked and exposed. Then I came by and saw you writhing helplessly in your own blood, and I said to you: In spite of your blood – live! And I said to you: In spite of your blood – live!"

---

experience this, but they don't feel that they can share. It feels too private. But, as I learned from my friend, people cannot and should not face painful challenges alone. Couples struggling with infertility need the support of their community, and their communities must be prepared to provide that support.

Communities can provide support in a number of ways. Firstly, spiritual leaders of congregations should be prepared with texts and rituals to ensure that they are ready to respond to a couple in crisis. Clergy should be prepared to respond to their needs and help provide support for them on their journey.

Secondly, spiritual leaders of all faiths can work to increase public sensitivity to infertility in their communities. At Ohev Sholom we are frequently celebrating births at our shul. As we celebrate with these families, we pause to remember and offer support to the couples in our community who are struggling to have children. In addition to the public acknowledgment of these couples, we have also started a fund to help support couples in our community who are working to pay for fertility treatments. This way we are able to engage our entire community in expressing support for those who are struggling in our midst.

I strongly encourage all spiritual leaders to develop an approach to addressing these concerns in their communities. My friend's experience serves as a powerful lesson to all of us. The cries of the lonely cannot, and should not, be silent. Communities must be present to support couples struggling with infertility, and to provide safe spaces and resources for these couples as they embark on this painful process.

On Pesach we celebrate our freedom from the bondage of slavery. Even though we are no longer slaves to Pharaoh in Egypt, God commands us repeatedly to love the stranger, for we were strangers in the land of Egypt. We must always ask who the strangers are in our own communities, and how we can embrace them and listen to their voices.

וָרָב. כְּמָה שֶׁנֶּאֱמַר: רְבָבָה כְּצֶמַח הַשָּׂדֶה נְתַתִּיךְ, וַתִּרְבִּי, וַתִּגְדְּלִי, וַתָּבֹאִי בַּעֲדִי עֲדָיִים. שָׁדַיִם נָכֹנוּ, וּשְׂעָרֵךְ צִמֵּחַ, וְאַתְּ עֵרֹם וְעֶרְיָה. וָאֶעֱבֹר עָלַיִךְ וָאֶרְאֵךְ מִתְבּוֹסֶסֶת בְּדָמָיִךְ. וָאֹמַר לָךְ, בְּדָמַיִךְ חֲיִי. וָאֹמַר לָךְ, בְּדָמַיִךְ חֲיִי.

---

require many uncomfortable, painful, and potentially embarrassing procedures, which are exacerbated by the feelings of loneliness that often accompany infertility.

Many couples with fertility problems do not discuss their experiences with others. The pain is so deep that it can be difficult to share. As a society, we tend to be private about our reproductive habits, so many couples feel that it would not be appropriate to share their stories with their friends and family. As a result, couples struggling with fertility can feel completely alone in their pain. This pain becomes acute if they are members of faith-based communities that publicly celebrate life-cycle events. Attending services when births are celebrated can be like adding salt to a wound, and the pain can be so great that some couples withdraw from their communities.

A close friend of mine and her husband grappled with this situation. They struggled with infertility for three years, unable to conceive. They were subjected to enormous amounts of both physical and emotional pain as they saw multiple doctors and underwent numerous tests, while watching more and more of their friends have children. And, like many couples dealing with infertility, this struggle was silent. They were surrounded by people they loved, but they were alone.

They stayed silent for three years, until she had her second miscarriage. The pain of losing a second pregnancy was so great that they couldn't bear it alone anymore. They knew that they needed support from their community, and that it was time for them to share their pain with others.

My friend decided to do this through a healing ritual that combined religion and community. She invited her female friends to her home for a healing session. They baked challah together, and shared hopes of recovery for others and for themselves.

In the days following the event, multiple women approached her to tell her about their own struggles with infertility and miscarriage. So many couples

"**AND THE EGYPTIANS ILL-TREATED** US and OPPRESSED US, AND THEY IMPOSED HARD LABOR ON US." (Devarim 26:6)

"AND THE EGYPTIANS ILL-TREATED US" – as it is said (Shemot 1:10): "Let us deal shrewdly with them and prevent them from increasing further, lest – if war breaks out – they join our enemies and fight against us, and take over the country."

"OPPRESSED US" – as it is said (Shemot 1:11): "So they set taskmasters over them in order to oppress them with hard labor. And they built store-cities for Pharaoh: Pitom and Raamses."

"AND THEY IMPOSED HARD LABOR ON US" – as it is said (Shemot 1:13): "And the Egyptians worked the Children of Israel ruthlessly."

---

teaching and tradition is our brightest light through the darkness of life. Yet, if we are too connected to the past we run the very real danger of stultifying our lives and hindering our spirituality. If we are wrapped in the past we run the risk of losing our future.

How do we balance the difficult tension between a slavish commitment to tradition and a need to embrace the present and the future? Rabbi Dr. Norman Lamm, the chancellor of Yeshiva University, offers a beautiful teaching that encapsulates the balance we are striving for.

Rabbi Lamm bases himself on the haftarah for the last day of Pesach, which is taken from the prophecy of Yeshayahu. The prophet states: "And it shall be on that day that Hashem shall again set His hand, for a second time, to recover the remnant of His people" (Yeshayahu 11:11). Yeshayahu is speaking about *she'ar ammo,* literally translated as the "remnants of His people," who will be redeemed by Hashem. But the Zohar adds an additional meaning to this phrase.

According to Rabbi Lamm, the Zohar (Beshalach) says that the phrase refers to *tzaddikim,* the righteous people of the world: "The world exists only by virtue of those who regard themselves as remnants [*shirayim*]." Rabbi Lamm explains that *tzaddikim* are called *shirayim* because they are "creative remnants." The term *shirayim* refers to leftover dough that is used to ferment the next batch of sourdough. Therefore, *tzaddikim* are symbolically referred to as *shirayim* because they are both the link to the past, the yeast from the previous batch of dough, and also the initiators of a new tradition, or a new healthy loaf of

וַיָּרֵעוּ אֹתָנוּ הַמִּצְרִים וַיְעַנּוּנוּ, וַיִּתְּנוּ עָלֵינוּ עֲבֹדָה קָשָׁה.

וַיָּרֵעוּ אֹתָנוּ הַמִּצְרִים. כְּמָה שֶׁנֶּאֱמַר: הָבָה נִתְחַכְּמָה לוֹ, פֶּן־יִרְבֶּה, וְהָיָה כִּי־תִקְרֶאנָה מִלְחָמָה, וְנוֹסַף גַּם הוּא עַל־שֹׂנְאֵינוּ, וְנִלְחַם־בָּנוּ וְעָלָה מִן־הָאָרֶץ.

וַיְעַנּוּנוּ. כְּמָה שֶׁנֶּאֱמַר: וַיָּשִׂימוּ עָלָיו שָׂרֵי מִסִּים, לְמַעַן עַנֹּתוֹ בְּסִבְלֹתָם. וַיִּבֶן עָרֵי מִסְכְּנוֹת לְפַרְעֹה, אֶת־פִּתֹם וְאֶת־רַעַמְסֵס.

וַיִּתְּנוּ עָלֵינוּ עֲבֹדָה קָשָׁה. כְּמָה שֶׁנֶּאֱמַר: וַיַּעֲבִדוּ מִצְרַיִם אֶת־בְּנֵי יִשְׂרָאֵל בְּפָרֶךְ.

OPEN ORTHODOX DISCUSSION 2

WHY MORE SYNAGOGUES NEED A MAHARAT

Many Jews have the custom of placing an orange on the Seder plate. The apocryphal story behind this tradition is that an Orthodox rabbi was once asked if a woman could be a rabbi. He responded, "When there is an orange on the Seder plate, then a woman will be a rabbi."

Well, in our shul we don't have a female rabbi. But since 2013, we do have a maharat. A maharat is a female member of the clergy who functions as a rabbi in many ways. She teaches Torah, officiates at life-cycle events, and offers halakhic guidance.

We were the first Orthodox synagogue in the United States to hire a full-time maharat. It was one of the greatest things our synagogue has ever done and as the rabbi of our shul I encourage every rabbi and congregation to broaden the reach and impact of their congregation's message by also having a maharat as a spiritual leader for their community.

One of the many challenges facing spiritual communities is how to remain connected to the traditions of our ancestors without stunting our own growth. We are an Orthodox community. This means we live for tradition. Our faith is predicated on our link to our ancestors.

How many Orthodox rabbis does it take to change a light bulb? *Change???* We are adverse to change because we know that our tradition is our strongest

"**THEN WE CRIED** OUT TO GOD, THE GOD OF OUR FATHERS, and GOD HEARD OUR VOICE AND HE SAW OUR ILL-TREATMENT, OUR HARDSHIP AND OUR DISTRESS." (Devarim 26:7)

"THEN WE CRIED OUT TO GOD, THE GOD OF OUR FATHERS" – as it is said (Shemot 2:23): "Long after that, the king of Egypt died. But the Children of Israel were still in grinding slavery, and they cried out, and their outcry about their slavery reached God."

This is not an easy tension to navigate, but it is the mandate that we have. *B'khol dor vador chayav adam lir'ot et atzmo ke'ilu hu yatza mi'Mitzrayim.* We say in the Haggadah that people in every generation have to look at themselves as though they left Egypt. This means that every generation must navigate this tension in their own unique way. The challenge confronts every community and every individual.

For many people in my congregation, the challenge to their commitment to Orthodoxy today rests upon the inclusion of women in a traditional, spiritual environment. For some, the texts of our rabbis and our halakhah are overwhelmingly beautiful and meaningful, yet they sometimes fall short in areas that discuss women and rituals.

Let's take an example from a mitzvah that we are all involved in today. In our shul, the women all have the custom of counting the Omer. We teach our boys and our girls to count the date of the Omer before going to sleep. But the great Chafetz Chayim expresses a different perspective in his classic work, the *Mishnah Berurah.* The *Mishnah Berurah* was published in the early twentieth century and is the primary source of halakhah for Orthodox Jews. He states: "Women are exempt from the mitzvah since it is a time-bound positive commandment [Magen Avraham adds: 'and they have accepted it upon themselves as an obligation']. And it seems to me that in our areas the women do not have the practice to count at all. And the work *Shulchan Shlomoh* writes that in any event women should not make a blessing when counting, for they will certainly make a mistake when counting and also most of them do not understand the meaning of the words" (489:3).

Our challenge is to show respect and commitment to the *Mishnah Berurah* but also to make clear that this opinion does not reflect the reality of our own congregation. Many women in our community have a better chance of

וַנִּצְעַק אֶל־יְיָ אֱלֹהֵי אֲבֹתֵינוּ, וַיִּשְׁמַע יְיָ אֶת־קֹלֵנוּ, וַיַּרְא אֶת־עָנְיֵנוּ, וְאֶת־עֲמָלֵנוּ, וְאֶת לַחֲצֵנוּ.

וַנִּצְעַק אֶל־יְיָ אֱלֹהֵי אֲבֹתֵינוּ. כְּמָה שֶׁנֶּאֱמַר: וַיְהִי בַיָּמִים הָרַבִּים הָהֵם, וַיָּמָת מֶלֶךְ מִצְרַיִם, וַיֵּאָנְחוּ בְנֵי־יִשְׂרָאֵל מִן־הָעֲבֹדָה וַיִּזְעָקוּ. וַתַּעַל שַׁוְעָתָם אֶל־הָאֱלֹהִים מִן־הָעֲבֹדָה.

---

bread. "The *tzaddikim* therefore symbolize a past that is great and glorious, but without the self-deprecation suggested by the term 'left-overs,' and without the pessimism implied by the word 'relics.' Rather, they regard themselves as the ferment that will re-create past glory in the present and transmit its creative leavening into the future" (*Festivals of Faith: Reflections on the Jewish Holidays* [Ktav, 2011], 238–240).

Some people consider the past to be best left in the past and visited in museums on occasions. Others yearn to live in the past. They try to wear the same clothing that their ancestors wore and speak the same language, simply because their ancestors spoke it. But Rabbi Lamm argues for a third approach:

> It is we who have the God-given opportunity to become the *shirayim*, the creative remnant that will ferment the batter of the present with the blessings of the past in order to create a better future.

Rabbi Lamm wrote these words in 1966. But this approach of Rabbi Lamm was something that I heard from him in one form or another when I was a student at Yeshiva University three decades later. Without creativity the world cannot continue to exist. Without creativity spirituality cannot exist. Pesach represents the tension between our commitment to tradition and our transforming of that tradition into a new and exciting future.

The holiday of Pesach is all about remembering the Exodus – *zecher li'yetziat Mitzrayim*. But the Exodus story begins with the mitzvah of Rosh Chodesh – the Torah prefaces its commands regarding Pesach with a reference to the new moon: "This month [*chodesh*] shall be for you the beginning of all months" (Shemot 12:1).

Chodesh has the same root as the word *chadash*, "new." In order for our faith to succeed there has to be a freshness connected to an ancient heritage.

"GOD HEARD OUR VOICE" – as it is said (Shemot 2:24): "And God heard their groaning, and God remembered His covenant with Avraham, with Yitzchak, and with Yaakov."

"AND HE SAW OUR ILL-TREATMENT" – this was a forced separation of husbands from their wives, as it is said (Shemot 2:25): "And God saw the Children of Israel, and God knew."

---

model to our girls, and our boys, our women and our men, and shows us that Orthodoxy is about *shirayim*: clinging to the past but forging a new future.

A maharat is on the one hand a role that is forging new ground and on the other hand a position that is entirely consistent with our tradition. In this respect it is rooted in the past but looking toward the future.

The role of maharat breaks new ground. Although there are women scholars serving in other leadership roles within congregations, these roles are either 1) very limited in scope (such as the *yoatzot halakhah*, women who are experts on matters of *niddah*); or 2) very clearly nonrabbinic positions, such as experts on adult education. What the maharat adds is the fact that she has gone through the same institutional training and curriculum that a rabbi goes through. This qualifies her in the same way that a rabbi is qualified to teach, counsel, and provide halakhic rulings.

Yet in many ways, the maharat is continuing a strong tradition of female spiritual leadership in the community. This role was sometimes traditionally filled by a rebbetzin, who in the past was able and willing to transmit the *mesorah* that she received from her parents, themselves often great Torah scholars. Often the traditional rebbetzin was – and in some communities still is – a resource for the community, teaching Torah on a daily basis, even at times in classroom settings.

But in our congregation the maharat's role is very different than a traditional rebbetzin. The maharat is a spiritual leader in her own right and her authority is not derived from her husband's scholarship, but her own skills. Moreover, the maharat is a teacher to both women and men. She is a spiritual leader to the entire community in exactly the same way that a rabbi serves both men and women.

Halakhah is not egalitarian. There are many overlapping roles, but there are also particular areas where there are clear distinctions between men

וַיִּשְׁמַע יְיָ אֶת־קֹלֵנוּ. כְּמָה שֶׁנֶּאֱמַר: וַיִּשְׁמַע אֱלֹהִים אֶת־נַאֲקָתָם, וַיִּזְכֹּר אֱלֹהִים אֶת־בְּרִיתוֹ, אֶת־אַבְרָהָם, אֶת־יִצְחָק, וְאֶת יַעֲקֹב.

וַיַּרְא אֶת־עָנְיֵנוּ. זוֹ פְּרִישׁוּת דֶּרֶךְ אֶרֶץ, כְּמָה שֶׁנֶּאֱמַר: וַיַּרְא אֱלֹהִים אֶת־בְּנֵי יִשְׂרָאֵל, וַיֵּדַע אֱלֹהִים.

---

not making a mistake than certain men, and many women understand the meaning of the blessings more than the men do. It is for this reason that in our congregation we choose to rely on the opinion of others, like the *Arukh Hashulchan* (489:4), who encourage women to count the Omer with a blessing.

The *Mishnah Berurah* is the foremost halakhic source guiding Jewish Orthodoxy today. We need to recognize that every single day of our lives. But we also need to recognize that when the facts on which the Chafetz Chayim based his opinion no longer apply, and when there are other great authorities who argue with his legal ruling, we must make appropriate adjustments for our congregations.

In this context our Orthodox congregation boldly hired a female clergy, Maharat Ruth Balinsky Friedman.

What is a maharat? The following is a description from the website of Yeshivat Maharat:

> Yeshivat Maharat is the first institution to ordain Orthodox women as clergy.... Through a rigorous curriculum of Talmud, halakhic decision-making (*psak*), pastoral counseling, leadership development, and internship experiences, our graduates will be prepared to assume the responsibility and authority to be *poskot* (legal arbiters) for the community. Maharat is a Hebrew acronym for *Manhiga Hilkhatit Ruchanit Toranit,* one who is a teacher of Jewish law and spirituality.

A maharat is not a female rabbi. It is a new concept – a new type of spiritual leader for our time. A maharat recognizes that there is a need for female spiritual leadership in Orthodox synagogues. A maharat undergoes the same training as rabbis do, but she is uniquely situated to help both men and women. In my opinion a maharat can only enhance our community as she serves as a role

"OUR HARDSHIP" – this means the sons, as it is said (Shemot 1:22): "Every newborn boy you shall throw into the Nile, but let every girl live."

"AND OUR DISTRESS" – refers to the brutality, as it is said (Shemot 3:9): "I have also seen the brutality with which the Egyptians are oppressing them."

GUEST VOICE: RABBI AVI WEISS

Rabbi Avi Weiss is the founder of Yeshivat Chovevei Torah and was for many years the rabbi at the Hebrew Institute of Riverdale. Even though this essay about Yitzchak is not directly related to Pesach, it is relevant to discuss at the Seder. When I was an assistant rabbi to Rabbi Weiss and he first published this essay as a dvar torah in the synagogue bulletin it had a big impact upon me and my rabbinate. Every month our synagogue welcomes in residents of the Jewish Foundation for Group Homes for a spiritual service and inclusion program in our congregation.

YITZCHAK: TEACHING US ABOUT DOWN'S SYNDROME

There is something naïve, almost simplistic, about our patriarch Yitzchak, which jumps out of the Bereishit narrative. Indeed, in virtually every chapter that describes his life, reaching a crescendo in parashat Toldot, he is portrayed as being reserved, nonaggressive, and even, dare I say, slow.

The first time we meet Yitzchak in the text, he is described as being mocked (*metzachek*) by his brother Yishmael (Bereishit 21:9). On the surface it seems there was something funny about Yitzchak; when you looked at him, you would laugh.

In the very next chapter, the chapter of the Akeidah (Binding of Isaac; Bereishit 22), Yitzchak is less independent. He goes to Moriah to be slaughtered without persistent argument. He seems to agree with everything he's asked to do, no matter the consequences.

Later, we learn about the burial of Sarah (Bereishit 23). There, Yitzchak is glaringly missing. It's almost as if Avraham wants to spare Yitzchak, Sarah's own son, the grief of burying his mother.

In chapter 24, a wife is chosen for Yitzchak without his input. The text notes that Rivkah, Yitzchak's wife, comforted Yitzchak as she reminded him of his mother Sarah. (Bereishit 24:67). Once again Yitzchak is depicted as one for whom key decisions are made and one who felt especially attached to his mother.

וְאֶת־עֲמָלֵנוּ. אֵלּוּ הַבָּנִים, כְּמָה שֶׁנֶּאֱמַר: כָּל־הַבֵּן הַיִּלּוֹד הַיְאֹרָה תַּשְׁלִיכֻהוּ, וְכָל־הַבַּת תְּחַיּוּן.

וְאֶת לַחֲצֵנוּ. זֶה הַדְּחַק, כְּמָה שֶׁנֶּאֱמַר: וְגַם־רָאִיתִי אֶת־הַלַּחַץ, אֲשֶׁר מִצְרַיִם לֹחֲצִים אֹתָם.

---

and women. Women are unique and have unique spiritual skills. The role of maharat opens a new path for women's spiritual leadership in the Orthodox community. The maharat is limited in some areas; she is not able to fulfill some of the traditional roles of an Orthodox rabbi, such as reciting certain blessings and leading the congregation in prayers that halakhah requires a man to lead. In other areas a maharat has natural advantages – by virtue of her feminine perspective, she brings a unique approach to spiritual leadership. Can you imagine if the *Mishnah Berurah*'s daughter was a maharat? Would he have written that women do not understand the words of the blessings? Can you imagine if the *Mishnah Berurah* itself was written by a maharat? Would it contain the sentence that women cannot be trusted to complete the full forty-nine-day count?

Additionally, there are halakhic barriers that hinder an Orthodox rabbi's ability to connect spiritually with a female congregant. For example, it is not appropriate for a rabbi to embrace a female congregant at a shivah home or dance with her at a wedding or even study Torah together in a *chavruta*. And of course, only a maharat, not a rabbi, can be fully present when a female convert immerses in the mikveh. There is a gap in a spiritual community that is entirely led by male clergy. The maharat's role is not discretionary but absolutely essential.

Questions for the Seder Table

1. Does your community have a maharat? If so, how has that impacted your spirituality?
2. Do women have any leadership roles in your spiritual community?
3. Is there value in the name "maharat" or should the female Orthodox clergy simply be called "rabbi"?

"AND GOD BROUGHT US OUT of Egypt with a strong hand and an outstretched arm and with terrifying deeds, and with signs and with portents." (Devarim 26:8)

> "AND GOD BROUGHT US OUT OF EGYPT" – not through an angel, and not through a seraph, and not through a messenger, but the Blessed Holy One Himself, as it is said (Shemot 12:2): "On that night I will pass through the land of Egypt and I will kill every firstborn in the land of Egypt, human and beast; on all the gods of Egypt I will execute judgment – I, God."

> "On that night I will pass through the land of Egypt" – I, not an angel. "And I will kill every firstborn in the land of Egypt" – I, not a seraph. "On all the gods of Egypt I will execute judgment" – I, not a messenger. I, God – I am the one; nobody else.

OPEN ORTHODOX DISCUSSION 3

HOW TO FORM AN INCLUSIVE SPIRITUAL COMMUNITY

One of my proudest moments in the rabbinate happened in an office with no one else around. When I became the rabbi of Ohev Sholom – the National Synagogue, the congregation was housed in a very old building and had extraordinarily limited access for people with physical challenges.

I explained to the congregation that we needed to work on that right away. And so we set about trying to raise the money for an elevator. As a young rabbi who had not yet turned thirty, I went to see a strong supporter of the shul and asked for a large grant in order to fund the project. This generous individual said to me, "How many people do you have in your congregation who are actually in a wheelchair? Wouldn't you rather use this money for other projects?" I responded, "It doesn't matter. If there is even one person in our community who can't access the building then I believe this affects the holiness of all of our prayers." Looking back at that incident, I am so proud that I had the strength to respond in that way.

On the seventh day of Pesach we read from the Torah about the splitting of the sea. Let us focus today on the people who might have had difficulty walking across the sea. Was the ground smooth or bumpy? Did the legs of the elderly get caught up in the mush of the sea floor? When they looked over and saw

וַיּוֹצִאֵנוּ יְיָ מִמִּצְרַיִם, בְּיָד חֲזָקָה, וּבִזְרֹעַ נְטוּיָה, וּבְמֹרָא גָּדוֹל וּבְאֹתוֹת וּבְמוֹפְתִים.

וַיּוֹצִאֵנוּ יְיָ מִמִּצְרַיִם. לֹא עַל־יְדֵי מַלְאָךְ, וְלֹא עַל־יְדֵי שָׂרָף, וְלֹא עַל־יְדֵי שָׁלִיחַ. אֶלָּא הַקָּדוֹשׁ בָּרוּךְ הוּא בִּכְבוֹדוֹ וּבְעַצְמוֹ. שֶׁנֶּאֱמַר: וְעָבַרְתִּי בְאֶרֶץ מִצְרַיִם בַּלַּיְלָה הַזֶּה, וְהִכֵּיתִי כָל־בְּכוֹר בְּאֶרֶץ מִצְרַיִם, מֵאָדָם וְעַד בְּהֵמָה, וּבְכָל־אֱלֹהֵי מִצְרַיִם אֶעֱשֶׂה שְׁפָטִים, אֲנִי יְיָ.

וְעָבַרְתִּי בְאֶרֶץ־מִצְרַיִם בַּלַּיְלָה הַזֶּה: אֲנִי וְלֹא מַלְאָךְ. וְהִכֵּיתִי כָל בְּכוֹר בְּאֶרֶץ־מִצְרַיִם: אֲנִי וְלֹא שָׂרָף. וּבְכָל־אֱלֹהֵי מִצְרַיִם אֶעֱשֶׂה שְׁפָטִים: אֲנִי וְלֹא הַשָּׁלִיחַ. אֲנִי יְיָ: אֲנִי הוּא וְלֹא אַחֵר.

In chapter 26, Yitzchak digs wells. The Torah notes that they were the ones originally dug by his father (verse 18). Here Yitzchak seems to lack initiative, succeeding in a business his father developed.

Finally, in chapter 27, Yitzchak is deceived. Yaakov fools him as he takes Esav's blessings.

The upshot: Yitzchak is easy to deceive, lacks individuality, does not find a wife on his own, is spared grief, is less independent, and is even laughed at. There is a common thread that weaves itself through each of these characteristics – they are often found in those who have Down's syndrome. It should be pointed out that aged parents are more vulnerable to having a Down's child. Avraham and Sarah were elderly when Yitzchak was born.

There is no evidence whatsoever from the biblical text or from our classical commentators to suggest that Yitzchak had Down's. Still, one wonders why the Torah presents him with some of the characteristics that are often associated with Down's. The fact that his attributes fit into this mold teaches a vital lesson – those with Down's possess the image of God and have the ability to spiritually soar, to spiritually inspire and yes, even to lead.

Far from being limited, those who are physically and mentally challenged are our teachers. For they teach us that everyone has the potential to reach the highest of heights.

"WITH A STRONG HAND" – this is the pestilence, as it is said (Shemot 9:3): "Then God's hand will strike your grazing herds – and the horses, the asses, the camels, the cattle, and the sheep – with a very severe pestilence."

"AND AN OUTSTRETCHED ARM" – this is the sword, as it is said (1 Divrei Hayamim 21:16): "...with his sword drawn in his hand outstretched over Jerusalem."

"AND WITH TERRIFYING DEEDS" – this is the appearance of the Divine Presence, as it is said (Devarim 4:34): "Has a god ever ventured to come and take himself a nation from within another nation by miracles, by signs and portents, and by war, by a mighty hand and an outstretched arm and by great deeds of terror as God, your God, did for you in Egypt before your very eyes?"

"BY SIGNS" – this is the rod, as it is said (Shemot 4:17): "And take along this rod with which you shall perform the signs."

"AND WITH PORTENTS" – this is the blood, as it is said (Yoel 3:3): "I will show portents in the sky and on earth:

---

rest of the community. They cried out to Moshe, "*Lamah nigara?*" (Why should we be diminished?). Moshe goes to Hashem with this query.

And so Hashem teaches Moshe the law of Pesach Sheni: if someone is *tamei* or far away, he can bring the Paschal Lamb exactly one month later, on the fourteenth day of Iyar.

Surprisingly, Pesach does not need to be celebrated on Pesach. Pesach is the only holiday for which the Torah allows a do-over, a chance to make up for missing out on the Passover offering. Why is Pesach unique? Why does Pesach alone offer people a second chance to perform the commandment?

Perhaps it is because Pesach is the first holiday and the Torah wants everyone to have the opportunity to start off right. Perhaps because Pesach celebrates freedom and the Torah allows everyone to internalize the concept of freedom in order to help them properly perform the other commandments. Perhaps because Pesach is the essential holiday that underlies all the other holidays. Or, perhaps it is because no one ever asked about the other holidays.

בְּיָד חֲזָקָה. זוֹ הַדֶּבֶר, כְּמָה שֶׁנֶּאֱמַר: הִנֵּה יַד־יְיָ הוֹיָה, בְּמִקְנְךָ אֲשֶׁר בַּשָּׂדֶה, בַּסּוּסִים בַּחֲמֹרִים בַּגְּמַלִּים, בַּבָּקָר וּבַצֹּאן, דֶּבֶר כָּבֵד מְאֹד.

וּבִזְרֹעַ נְטוּיָה. זוֹ הַחֶרֶב, כְּמָה שֶׁנֶּאֱמַר: וְחַרְבּוֹ שְׁלוּפָה בְּיָדוֹ, נְטוּיָה עַל־יְרוּשָׁלָיִם.

וּבְמוֹרָא גָּדוֹל. זֶה גִּלּוּי שְׁכִינָה, כְּמָה שֶׁנֶּאֱמַר: אוֹ הֲנִסָּה אֱלֹהִים, לָבוֹא לָקַחַת לוֹ גוֹי מִקֶּרֶב גּוֹי, בְּמַסֹּת בְּאֹתֹת וּבְמוֹפְתִים וּבְמִלְחָמָה, וּבְיָד חֲזָקָה וּבִזְרוֹעַ נְטוּיָה, וּבְמוֹרָאִים גְּדֹלִים. כְּכֹל אֲשֶׁר־עָשָׂה לָכֶם יְיָ אֱלֹהֵיכֶם בְּמִצְרַיִם, לְעֵינֶיךָ.

וּבְאֹתוֹת. זֶה הַמַּטֶּה, כְּמָה שֶׁנֶּאֱמַר: וְאֶת הַמַּטֶּה הַזֶּה תִּקַּח בְּיָדֶךָ, אֲשֶׁר תַּעֲשֶׂה־בּוֹ אֶת־הָאֹתֹת.

וּבְמוֹפְתִים. זֶה הַדָּם, כְּמָה שֶׁנֶּאֱמַר: וְנָתַתִּי מוֹפְתִים, בַּשָּׁמַיִם וּבָאָרֶץ...

---

the Egyptians chasing did they quicken their pace? What about the people who couldn't walk any faster – the tired, the elderly, the young, or the sick?

About this one can only conjecture. One assumes from the text that everyone was able to make it without too much difficulty. Perhaps this is a "hidden" miracle of the splitting of the sea – the fact that no one had physical trouble in crossing.

Without explicitly stating so the Torah is teaching us an important lesson: communities must be inclusive. Everyone was able to cross the sea together.

This lesson of inclusiveness is also taught through another biblical teaching about Pesach. Let's say you wanted to celebrate a holiday on a different date. For example, Sukkot in Cheshvan instead of Tishrei. The answer is that you would not be allowed. The holidays need to be celebrated on the dates that the Torah assigned to them.

However, there is one exception to this rule. In the book of Bamidbar (9:6–14) we are told that a group came to Moshe and said that they had been *tamei* (impure) during Pesach and thus had been unable to celebrate with the

Spill a drop of wine out of the cup at the mention of each plague.

"BLOOD AND FIRE AND PILLARS OF SMOKE"

(Yoel 3:3)

Another explanation: "By a might hand" – TWO
"and an outstretched arm" – TWO
"and by great deeds of terror" – TWO
"by signs" – TWO
"and portents" – TWO.

Spill a drop of wine for each of the ten plagues and for each word of the three acrostics.

These are ten plagues which the Blessed Holy One brought on the Egyptians in Egypt:

BLOOD FROGS LICE WILD BEASTS PESTILENCE
BOILS HAIL LOCUSTS DARKNESS
THE SMITING OF THE FIRSTBORN

WHAT WAS THE PLAGUE OF *CHOSHEKH*?

What was the nature of the plague of darkness? The plague itself is described in a mere three verses in the Torah:

> God said to Moshe, "Stretch forth your hand toward the heavens, and there will be darkness over the land of Egypt, and the darkness will become darker [*vayamesh choshekh*]." So Moshe stretched forth his hand toward the heavens, and there was thick darkness over the entire land of Egypt for three days. They did not see each other and no one rose from his place for three days, but for all the Children of Israel there was light in their dwellings. (Shemot 10:21–23)

This is the shortest description of any of the plagues. Even more noteworthy is that this plague seems to be the tamest of all the plagues. After all, the text just tells us that there was a heavy darkness on the land for three days. The meekness of the plague causes us to notice it. Nothing seems to have been destroyed or ruined by the darkness. The other plagues destroyed the economy of the Egyptians, ruining their food and livestock and making their lives

Spill a drop of wine out of the cup at the mention of each plague.

דָּם. וָאֵשׁ. וְתִימְרוֹת עָשָׁן.

דָּבָר אַחֵר: בְּיָד חֲזָקָה שְׁתַּיִם. וּבִזְרֹעַ נְטוּיָה שְׁתַּיִם. וּבְמוֹרָא גָּדוֹל שְׁתַּיִם. וּבְאֹתוֹת שְׁתַּיִם. וּבְמֹפְתִים שְׁתַּיִם.

Spill a drop of wine for each of the ten plagues and for each word of the three acrostics.

אֵלּוּ עֶשֶׂר מַכּוֹת שֶׁהֵבִיא הַקָּדוֹשׁ בָּרוּךְ הוּא עַל־הַמִּצְרִים בְּמִצְרַיִם, וְאֵלּוּ הֵן:

דָּם. צְפַרְדֵּעַ. כִּנִּים. עָרוֹב. דֶּבֶר. שְׁחִין. בָּרָד. אַרְבֶּה. חֹשֶׁךְ. מַכַּת בְּכוֹרוֹת.

Whatever the reason, Hashem responds to the question "*Lamah nigara?*" (Why should we be diminished?): "You should not be diminished!"

An imperative of the Pesach holiday is "Do not diminish others." We who were slaves in Egypt, we who were diminished on a daily basis, cannot diminish others. We certainly cannot diminish others on the holiday of Pesach.

We live in a fast-paced world, where the question commonly asked is "What can you do for me?" But that's a trap. It's not the Torah way. The Torah way is to recognize the glory of others and include as many as possible in our spiritual community. The Torah way is to remember what it felt like to be diminished in Egypt and to ensure that we treat others with the love and respect owed to all human beings.

Questions for the Seder Table

1. Is your spiritual community inclusive of people with physical and mental challenges? What could your community do to improve in this area?
2. Does your spiritual community have families that differ significantly from the biblical paradigm of father/mother/biological child? Are those families an integral part of your community or are they marginalized?
3. How does your spiritual community relate to people of a different faith? Are their views respected?

Rabbi Yehudah made a mnemonic of them:

DETZAKH ADASH BEACHAV

RABBI YOSSÉ THE GALILEAN says: How do you reckon that the Egyptians were smitten with ten plagues in Egypt and with fifty plagues on the sea? Concerning Egypt what does it say? "And the wizards said to Pharaoh: 'This is the finger of God!'" (Shemot 8:15) And concerning the sea what does it say? "And Israel saw the wondrous hand that God had wielded against the Egyptians, and the people feared God, and they put their trust in God and in His servant Moses." (Shemot 14:31) With how many plagues were they smitten with a finger? Ten plagues. Hence, in Egypt they were smitten with ten plagues, and on the sea they were smitten with fifty plagues.

> during the darkness] and saw their [own] belongings. When they were leaving [Egypt] and asked [for some of their things], and [the Egyptians] said, "We have nothing," [the Israelite] would say to him, "I saw it in your house, and it is in such and such a place." (Rashi, 10:22)

The upshot of Rashi's commentary is that the purpose of the plague of darkness was not so much to inflict a heavy blow upon the Egyptians as to provide cover for the Jewish people. Still, according to Rashi, the darkness just seems to be a mildly uncomfortable phenomenon. If we took a vote most people would probably prefer this type of darkness to any of the other plagues, like lice and boils.

A second understanding of *choshekh* can be seen in Ramban. Ramban argues that there was a thick cloud of darkness that came down from heaven. But it was more than just a darkness descending from the sky; there was also an atmospheric change that sucked out the ability for any light to exist:

> There was a great darkness that would descend upon them and extinguish every light, just as in all deep caverns and in all extremely dark places where light cannot exist as it is swallowed up in the density of thick darkness. Similarly, people who pass through the Mountains of Darkness find that no candle or fire can continue to burn at all.

The Mountains of Darkness is a reference to a place described in the Talmud (*Tamid* 32a); the Talmud writes that the Mountains of Darkness are located in Africa and it is impossible to pass through there. Thus, Ramban's interpre-

רַבִּי יְהוּדָה הָיָה נוֹתֵן בָּהֶם סִמָּנִים:

דְּצַ"ךְ עֲדַ"שׁ בְּאַחַ"ב.

רַבִּי יוֹסֵי הַגְּלִילִי אוֹמֵר: מִנַּיִן אַתָּה אוֹמֵר, שֶׁלָּקוּ הַמִּצְרִים בְּמִצְרַיִם עֶשֶׂר מַכּוֹת, וְעַל הַיָּם לָקוּ חֲמִשִּׁים מַכּוֹת? בְּמִצְרַיִם מָה הוּא אוֹמֵר? וַיֹּאמְרוּ הַחַרְטֻמִּם אֶל־פַּרְעֹה, אֶצְבַּע אֱלֹהִים הִוא. וְעַל הַיָּם מָה הוּא אוֹמֵר? וַיַּרְא יִשְׂרָאֵל אֶת־הַיָּד הַגְּדֹלָה, אֲשֶׁר עָשָׂה יְיָ בְּמִצְרַיִם, וַיִּירְאוּ הָעָם אֶת־יְיָ. וַיַּאֲמִינוּ בַּייָ, וּבְמֹשֶׁה עַבְדּוֹ. כַּמָּה לָקוּ בְּאֶצְבַּע? עֶשֶׂר מַכּוֹת. אֱמוֹר מֵעַתָּה: בְּמִצְרַיִם לָקוּ עֶשֶׂר מַכּוֹת, וְעַל־הַיָּם לָקוּ חֲמִשִּׁים מַכּוֹת.

---

miserable. The other plagues inflicted lasting damage, whereas a literal reading of the text indicates that this was just an uncomfortable three days. Our sages are sensitive to this and for this reason understand the plague to be more than simply darkness over the land. We will explore three ways to understand the plague of darkness.

First is the approach of Rashi. Through his commentary Rashi addresses the questions we raised. Rashi says that the *choshekh* was a highly debilitating darkness. Moreover, Rashi suggests that the whole reason for the plague was not to inflict the Egyptians with misery but to either protect the Jewish people from embarrassment or to enable the Jewish people to figure out how to get their parting gifts from the Egyptians when the moment of redemption would arrive. Here are Rashi's words:

> Thick darkness in which they did not see each other for those three days, and another three days of darkness twice as dark as this, so that no one rose from his place. If he was sitting, he was unable to stand, and if he was standing, he was unable to sit.
>
> Now why did He bring darkness upon [the Egyptians]? Because there were among the Israelites in that generation wicked people who did not want to leave [Egypt]. They died during the three days of darkness, so that the Egyptians would not see their downfall and say, "They too are being smitten like us." Also, the Israelites searched [the Egyptians' dwellings

RABBI ELIEZER says: How do we know that each plague that the Blessed Holy One brought on the Egyptians in Egypt consisted of four plagues? For it is said (Tehillim 78:49): "He loosed upon them His burning anger: wrath, and fury, and rage, a legation of evil messengers." "Wrath" – one. "And fury" – one. "And rage" – one. "A legation of evil messengers" – one. Hence, in Egypt they were smitten with forty plagues, and on the sea they were smitten with two hundred plagues.

RABBI AKIVA says: How do we know that each plague that the Blessed Holy One brought on the Egyptians in Egypt consisted of five plagues? For it is said (Tehillim 78:49): "He loosed upon them His burning anger, wrath, and fury, and rage, a legation of evil messengers." "His burning anger" – one. "Wrath" – two. "And fury" – three. "And rage" – four. "A legation of evil messengers" – five. Hence, in Egypt they were smitten with fifty plagues, and on the sea they were smitten with 250 plagues.

---

first three days of shivah and not the rest of the week. The fact that the Torah makes a point of noting that this plague lasted for three days tells us that this reflects a period of depression and overwhelming sadness.

When our world comes crashing down and we realize that our lives are spiritually bankrupt – for this there is often no immediate warning. It is frequently the result of a lifetime of bad mistakes. We can warn someone, "If you drive when you're drunk, you'll crash the car." But it is much harder to say to someone, "If you live a life in this manner, you will eventually enter into a deep depression over the emptiness of your life." And that is exactly what the plague of darkness was. It was symbolic of the Egyptian realization that their whole way of life was tremendously off. The Egyptians had many gods that they worshipped, but the god that was the most widely worshipped was the sun god named Ra. The plague was certainly an attack on the sun god, but even more so it was an attack upon the entire Egyptian society that overvalued the power of light.

We often make the mistake of running after the light. In this sense we are like insects attracted to light. We think that where there is the most light and the most fanfare there is the most strength. The Egyptians were given *choshekh* in order to teach them that all their superficial lights – their strength, their chariots, their Pharaohs, their pyramids – were not illuminating but were really

רַבִּי אֱלִיעֶזֶר אוֹמֵר: מִנַּיִן שֶׁכָּל־מַכָּה וּמַכָּה, שֶׁהֵבִיא הַקָּדוֹשׁ בָּרוּךְ הוּא עַל הַמִּצְרִים בְּמִצְרַיִם, הָיְתָה שֶׁל אַרְבַּע מַכּוֹת? שֶׁנֶּאֱמַר: יְשַׁלַּח־בָּם חֲרוֹן אַפּוֹ, עֶבְרָה וָזַעַם וְצָרָה, מִשְׁלַחַת מַלְאֲכֵי רָעִים. עֶבְרָה אַחַת. וָזַעַם שְׁתַּיִם. וְצָרָה שָׁלֹשׁ. מִשְׁלַחַת מַלְאֲכֵי רָעִים אַרְבַּע. אֱמוֹר מֵעַתָּה: בְּמִצְרַיִם לָקוּ אַרְבָּעִים מַכּוֹת, וְעַל הַיָּם לָקוּ מָאתַיִם מַכּוֹת.

רַבִּי עֲקִיבָא אוֹמֵר: מִנַּיִן שֶׁכָּל־מַכָּה וּמַכָּה, שֶׁהֵבִיא הַקָּדוֹשׁ בָּרוּךְ הוּא עַל הַמִּצְרִים בְּמִצְרַיִם, הָיְתָה שֶׁל חָמֵשׁ מַכּוֹת? שֶׁנֶּאֱמַר: יְשַׁלַּח־בָּם חֲרוֹן אַפּוֹ, עֶבְרָה וָזַעַם וְצָרָה, מִשְׁלַחַת מַלְאֲכֵי רָעִים. חֲרוֹן אַפּוֹ אַחַת. עֶבְרָה שְׁתַּיִם. וָזַעַם שָׁלֹשׁ. וְצָרָה אַרְבַּע. מִשְׁלַחַת מַלְאֲכֵי רָעִים חָמֵשׁ. אֱמוֹר מֵעַתָּה: בְּמִצְרַיִם לָקוּ חֲמִשִּׁים מַכּוֹת, וְעַל הַיָּם לָקוּ חֲמִשִּׁים וּמָאתַיִם מַכּוֹת.

---

tation is that there wasn't mere darkness, but rather a tremendous change in the atmosphere that prevented light from existing.

A third approach suggests that this plague of darkness must also be understood on a symbolic level. *Choshekh* suggests that the Egyptians were in such a place of spiritual darkness that their world was crashing in around them. At the end of the entire series of plagues, as they realized the might of Hashem, they also finally understood that their lives were based on falsehoods and emptiness. The Egyptians now realized with clarity that their lives, their society, their culture, and their values were meaningless and empty; this realization led them to a place of darkness as a deep and immobilizing depression overcame their society. There are strong hints to this symbolic interpretation in the text of the Torah. The Torah tells us, "*Lo kamu ish mitachtav*" (No man rose from his place). This is reminiscent of people suffering from depression – immobilized by their emotional darkness, they lie down and are unable to move.

The Torah states that the plague lasted for three days. Our sages often understand three days as a sign of intense depression and immobilization. For example, the Talmud distinguishes between the first three days of shivah and the rest of shivah. As it states in the Talmud, "Three days for weeping and seven for lamenting" (*Moed Katan* 27b). There are laws that apply only to the

SO MANY ARE THE FAVORS for which we must thank the Omnipresent
One!

If He had taken us out of Egypt but not given them their punishments
That would have been good enough!

If He had given them their punishments but not taken it out on their gods
That would have been good enough!

---

night). When redemption will finally come to the Jewish people it may come in the darkest hour. But when we have the light of the Torah to guide us, even in the middle of the night we will be able to overcome darkness and see the light.

OPEN ORTHODOX DISCUSSION 4

DAYEINU: NO MORE AGUNOT

I met Tamar on a beautiful Sunday afternoon. At that time she was a twenty-seven-year-old graduate of Yeshiva University's Stern College and the mother of a three-year-old child. Although she was surrounded by family, friends, and literally hundreds of supporters she had tears in her eyes.

She said to me, "I never thought it could happen to me. If it could happen to me, then it could happen to anyone."

Tamar is very brave. She spoke out publicly and defiantly in the face of the terrible ordeal she was going through. For many years she had been an agunah, or a "chained woman." By this we do not mean that she was physically chained, but psychologically, emotionally, and legally chained. Despite the fact that she and her husband had been civilly divorced for several years, he refused to give her a *get* (a Jewish divorce) and therefore she was not permitted to remarry.

I have been a rabbi long enough to know that when a contested divorce is taking place there are at least two different sides to the story. But when either party withholds a *get* and uses that as leverage, then until that matter is settled there is only one side. Period. Otherwise we are effectively giving the spouse veto power over any court's decision. Just as we would not tolerate physical coercion, we cannot tolerate emotional coercion. The withholding of a *get* so that it can be used as leverage is a form of emotional abuse.

Once there is no chance for reconciliation a *get* should be given immediately.

כַּמָּה מַעֲלוֹת טוֹבוֹת לַמָּקוֹם עָלֵינוּ:

אִלּוּ הוֹצִיאָנוּ מִמִּצְרַיִם,
וְלֹא עָשָׂה בָהֶם שְׁפָטִים, דַּיֵּנוּ.
אִלּוּ עָשָׂה בָהֶם שְׁפָטִים,
וְלֹא עָשָׂה בֵאלֹהֵיהֶם, דַּיֵּנוּ.

---

obscuring. The plague of *choshekh* reminds all of us that the most powerful ideas are the ones that are willing to sprout up in the dark. The most powerful ideas in human history were brought forth not by the advanced civilization of Egypt, but by the counterculture spirituality of Moshe Rabbeinu.

Kedushat Levi (10:21) points out that this is why there is a crucial difference when it comes to this plague. With respect to the plague of hail it says that the Jewish people "did not have hail." But here the Torah doesn't say that the Jewish people didn't have darkness. Rather it says that the Jewish people had light, "*hayah or b'moshvotam*." For the Jewish people to avoid the plague of darkness it was not enough to simply not have darkness, rather they needed light.

The Jewish people needed real light to guide them – the light of Torah and mitzvot. This is why right after the plague of darkness the Jewish people are given their first mitzvot: Rosh Chodesh, *korban Pesach,* and *brit milah*. Without these commandments we too would not have had real light. We would have been fooled by the Egyptian neon lights.

This is true on a historical-national level, but it is also true on a personal level. How many of us go around looking for light in our lives in all the wrong places. We are sidetracked by what appears to be light, but what in reality is actually just another shade of darkness. The real light in this world is the light of Torah and the light of Hashem and the light of following His path. When the Egyptians were struggling with *choshekh* the Jewish people had the light of mitzvot. Some Jews died in this plague, but others were busy preparing for the redemption. This is the unbelievable power of spirituality and of having a connection to Hashem: There was physical darkness in the air, but those who had a relationship with God saw the darkness as inspiring and not as debilitating. For the Jews there was light in the face of darkness, "*hayah or b'moshvotam*."

The plague of the firstborn struck *ba'chatzi halailah* (in the middle of the

If He had taken it out on their gods but not killed their firstborn
That would have been good enough!
If He had killed their firstborn but not handed us their wealth
That would have been good enough!
If He had handed us their wealth but not parted the sea for us
That would have been good enough!
If He had parted the sea for us but not brought us through it dry
That would have been good enough!

---

a smokescreen in support of the husband. None of those rabbis attended the rally for Tamar. Their passivity was in fact a stand in favor of the status quo.

We must take the opposite approach. We must get involved. Don't say, "We cannot take a stand on this matter." What is at stake here is not just an agunah's well-being, but the redemption of our people.

It is the awesome, spiritual power of marriage that led to the redemption of the Jewish people from Egypt. The verse says, "A man went from the house of Levi and married a daughter of Levi" (Shemot 2:1). It is from this union, between Amram and Yokheved, that the great Moshe Rabbeinu, the redeemer of our people, was born.

But the verse itself is difficult. The commentators notice that the word "*vayelekh*" (went) is unusual in this context. Explains the great Nachmanides, quoting the Midrash: The word *vayelekh* speaks to the greatness of their act. Pharaoh had just issued a decree that every Jewish boy who was born was to be killed. In this context, Moshe's parents decided to get married and have children even thought their actions entailed a great risk.

Nachmanides says that the very act of *vayelekh* was "an act of greatness because it was an act of defiance to Pharaoh's decree." And Nachmanides adds: "Through this courageous act of defiance the Israelites were ultimately redeemed from Egypt."

According to Nachmanides, the very redemption of our people was contingent on a brave commitment to marriage and childbirth. But this positive idea comes with a negative contrast. When someone acts in a way that destroys the core of marriage, when a recalcitrant husband chains a woman and prevents her from remarrying, he is destroying our ability for redemption as a community. It is not just the agunah who is denied freedom and redemption.

אִלּוּ עָשָׂה בֵאלֹהֵיהֶם,
וְלֹא הָרַג אֶת־בְּכוֹרֵיהֶם, דַּיֵּנוּ.
אִלּוּ הָרַג אֶת־בְּכוֹרֵיהֶם,
וְלֹא נָתַן לָנוּ אֶת־מָמוֹנָם, דַּיֵּנוּ.
אִלּוּ נָתַן לָנוּ אֶת־מָמוֹנָם,
וְלֹא קָרַע לָנוּ אֶת־הַיָּם, דַּיֵּנוּ.
אִלּוּ קָרַע לָנוּ אֶת־הַיָּם,
וְלֹא הֶעֱבִירָנוּ בְתוֹכוֹ בֶּחָרָבָה, דַּיֵּנוּ.

The *get* cannot be used as a leverage to gain more money or better terms of a divorce settlement. To do such a thing is a desecration of God's name.

Make no mistake about it, being emotionally and psychologically chained can be just as enslaving as being physically chained. The Torah (Shemot 1:13) says that the Egyptians enslaved the Jews *b'farekh*. The word *farekh* is usually translated as hard labor, as in work *hamefarekhet et haguf*, that destroys the body.

But the Midrash (Shemot Rabbah 1:11) interprets the word as "*peh rakh*, a soft tongue." In other words, Pharaoh enslaved the Israelites with deception and manipulation. The slavery of Egypt was an emotional and psychological slavery as well as a physical one.

And that is what every agunah faces. She is emotionally and psychologically enslaved by her husband and is unable to free herself and move on with her life.

By Jewish law the only way an agunah can remarry, short of the death of her husband, is if her husband gives her a *get* of his own free will. Yet Rambam rules that we should physically encourage the husband to give the *get* until he says he is doing so of his own volition (*Mishneh Torah*, Hilkhot Geirushin 2:20).

Today, of course, we cannot and should not use physical attacks as a method of coercion; it is illegal and inappropriate. Nonetheless, we must not remain passive. First and foremost, when we hear of an agunah situation in our own community, we as a community and as individuals must get involved.

Although I went to the rally on behalf of Tamar I was not joined by all the other rabbis in the community. Three other rabbis issued a statement to the effect that they were not taking a stand on the matter. But they did take a stand. By issuing such a statement on the eve of the rally, they participated in

If He had brought us through it dry but not sunk our enemies in it
That would have been good enough!

If He had sunk our enemies in it but not provided for us in the wilderness for forty years
That would have been good enough!

If He had provided for us in the wilderness for forty years but not fed us manna
That would have been good enough!

If He had fed us the manna but not given us the Sabbath
That would have been good enough!

So what was so special about this incident?

Ramban (2:16) teaches us how to interpret this passage. He explains that every day the shepherds were bullying and abusing these seven daughters and stealing their water. Moshe's greatness was that not only did he return the water to its rightful owners, but he also helped them draw new water. Not only did he fix the injustice of the situation, but he also did an act of outright kindness to sustain them going forward.

Moshe then went on to marry one of these daughters, thereby becoming a source of protection for the family for the future. Moshe's greatness was that he didn't settle for fixing a specific injustice, he moved the community so that there would be less injustices.

We see a similar idea in the actions of the midwives, Shifrah and Puah. Pharaoh had commanded these women to kill the Jewish babies. In response, these Jewish midwives saved the babies, "and they allowed the children to live" (1:17).

Rashi, commenting on the words "they allowed the children to live," elaborates on the midwives' actions: not only did the midwives save the lives of these babies, they went one step further and provided the babies with nourishment. Even though the midwives were unable to fully annul the decree, they did not simply try to save the babies. They did as much as they could to lessen the injustice of the situation.

When there is an environment of injustice in the community, it is not enough to simply correct the injustice. We must work to change the culture that allows such an incident to happen.

It wasn't enough for Moshe to simply return the water to the seven Midianite daughters; he also needed to draw new water for them. It wasn't enough for Shifrah and Puah to save the lives of the newborn babies; they also had to

אִלּוּ הֶעֱבִירָנוּ בְתוֹכוֹ בֶחָרָבָה,
וְלֹא שִׁקַּע צָרֵינוּ בְּתוֹכוֹ, דַּיֵּנוּ.
אִלּוּ שִׁקַּע צָרֵינוּ בְּתוֹכוֹ,
וְלֹא סִפֵּק צָרְכֵּנוּ בַּמִּדְבָּר אַרְבָּעִים שָׁנָה, דַּיֵּנוּ.
אִלּוּ סִפֵּק צָרְכֵּנוּ בַּמִּדְבָּר אַרְבָּעִים שָׁנָה,
וְלֹא הֶאֱכִילָנוּ אֶת־הַמָּן, דַּיֵּנוּ.
אִלּוּ הֶאֱכִילָנוּ אֶת־הַמָּן,
וְלֹא נָתַן לָנוּ אֶת־הַשַּׁבָּת, דַּיֵּנוּ.

Whenever any woman in a community is chained, we are all being chained; we are all denied redemption.

As important as it is to advocate for particular agunot, that alone is not enough. It is necessary but insufficient action.

Famously, Moshe intervenes twice on behalf of his brothers. First he notices that an Egyptian is beating an Israelite. When Moshe sees this, "he strikes the Egyptian" (Shemot 2:12) and kills him. Moshe then sees two Israelites fighting with each other. Here, too, he intervenes, but this time his actions are exposed to Pharaoh and he needs to flee into exile.

By this point Moshe has twice acted courageously. But he is still not picked by Hashem to be the redeemer of His people. Moshe is not yet worthy to receive a revelation from God. His actions were noble, but they weren't enough to cause redemption. Moshe runs into the wilderness of Midian. According to Ramban (2:24), he was in the wilderness for at least sixty years!

For sixty years Moshe wasn't worthy of redeeming the people despite the fact that he had gotten involved in their troubles. Something more was required. The Torah doesn't mention the intervening sixty years of his life, because it was only at their end that Moshe became worthy of standing in God's presence, receiving revelation and effectuating redemption. It was only after the following incident that he saw the burning bush and merited to be Moshe Rabbeinu.

The first thing the Torah mentions after sixty years of Moshe's life is that he helped seven Midianite women get their water from a well. Says the Torah: "As these [seven daughters] were beginning to fill their troughs and water their father's sheep, other shepherds came and tried to chase them away. Moshe got up and came to their aid and then watered their sheep" (Shemot 2:16–17).

If He had given us the Sabbath but not drawn us near to Him at Mount Sinai — That would have been good enough!

If He had drawn us near to Him at Mount Sinai but not given us the Torah — That would have been good enough!

If He had given us the Torah but not brought us into the Land of Israel — That would have been good enough!

If He had brought us into the Land of Israel but not built us the House of His Choosing — That would have been good enough!

HOW MANY TIMES more then, do we owe thanks for to the Omnipresent for taking us out of Egypt, and giving them their just deserts, and taking it out on their gods, and killing their firstborn, and handing us their wealth, and splitting the sea for us, and bringing us through it dry, and sinking our oppressors in it, and providing for us in the wilderness for forty years, and feeding us manna, and giving us the Sabbath, and drawing us near to Him at Mount Sinai, and giving us the Torah, and bringing us into the Land of Israel, and building us the House of His Choosing for the expiation of all our sins.

---

you think that the community should create an accepted standard of not attending a wedding in which there is no rabbinic prenuptial agreement? What steps should the Jewish community take to ensure widespread use of prenuptial agreements?

3. Why do you think that the Torah mandated that the *get* needs to be given by the husband to the wife?

THE WOMEN WHO SERVED AT THE ENTRANCE TO THE TENT

Women of the Wall is a group of women that gathers on Rosh Chodesh to pray at the Kotel. There has been much controversy about this group and some of its members have been arrested for wearing *tallitot* at the Kotel. The chief rabbi of the Kotel has said publically that he views this group as wrong.

Despite our strong desire to support the State of Israel and refrain from public criticism of a country that is under constant attack, it is essential that we raise our voices on behalf of religious freedom. The more religious freedom

אִלּוּ נָתַן לָנוּ אֶת־הַשַּׁבָּת,
וְלֹא קֵרְבָנוּ לִפְנֵי הַר סִינַי, דַּיֵּנוּ.
אִלּוּ קֵרְבָנוּ לִפְנֵי הַר סִינַי,
וְלֹא נָתַן לָנוּ אֶת־הַתּוֹרָה, דַּיֵּנוּ.
אִלּוּ נָתַן לָנוּ אֶת־הַתּוֹרָה,
וְלֹא הִכְנִיסָנוּ לְאֶרֶץ יִשְׂרָאֵל, דַּיֵּנוּ.
אִלּוּ הִכְנִיסָנוּ לְאֶרֶץ יִשְׂרָאֵל,
וְלֹא בָנָה לָנוּ אֶת־בֵּית הַבְּחִירָה, דַּיֵּנוּ.

עַל אַחַת כַּמָּה וְכַמָּה טוֹבָה כְפוּלָה וּמְכֻפֶּלֶת לַמָּקוֹם עָלֵינוּ: שֶׁהוֹצִיאָנוּ מִמִּצְרַיִם, וְעָשָׂה בָהֶם שְׁפָטִים, וְעָשָׂה בֵאלֹהֵיהֶם, וְהָרַג אֶת־בְּכוֹרֵיהֶם, וְנָתַן לָנוּ אֶת־מָמוֹנָם, וְקָרַע לָנוּ אֶת־הַיָּם, וְהֶעֱבִירָנוּ בְתוֹכוֹ בֶּחָרָבָה, וְשִׁקַּע צָרֵינוּ בְּתוֹכוֹ, וְסִפֵּק צָרְכֵּנוּ בַּמִּדְבָּר אַרְבָּעִים שָׁנָה, וְהֶאֱכִילָנוּ אֶת־הַמָּן, וְנָתַן לָנוּ אֶת־הַשַּׁבָּת, וְקֵרְבָנוּ לִפְנֵי הַר סִינַי, וְנָתַן לָנוּ אֶת־הַתּוֹרָה, וְהִכְנִיסָנוּ לְאֶרֶץ יִשְׂרָאֵל, וּבָנָה לָנוּ אֶת־בֵּית הַבְּחִירָה, לְכַפֵּר עַל־כָּל־עֲוֹנוֹתֵינוּ.

---

provide sustenance for the infants. And for us, too, it is not enough to just correct the injustice for one agunah; we must change the environment of our entire community.

When there is an agunah in our community, we are all chained and deprived of redemption. Such a violation of human rights cannot be corrected solely by ensuring that this specific woman receive a *get*; we need to reach out beyond her case and seek to aid the plight of all agunot around the country. We need to advocate for systemic changes that will affect the entire Jewish community.

Questions for the Seder Table

1. One solution to the agunah crisis is that everyone should get married with a rabbinically approved prenuptial agreement. Do you have one? Why or why not?
2. In order to encourage the use of the rabbinic prenuptial agreement, do

RABBAN GAMLIEL used to say: Whoever has not mentioned these three things on Passover has not fulfilled his obligation:

THE PASSOVER OFFERING MATZAH BITTER HERBS

> There were women among the Jewish people who served God and departed from the physical desires of the world, and they gave their mirrors as a gift, since they no longer had a need for physical beauty. Rather, they came every day to the entrance of the Ohel Moed to pray and hear the words of the commandments.

Ibn Ezra offers the radical explanation that these women were a group of religious ascetics who separated from men and swore off physical, intimate pleasures.

We see similar comments in the medieval French commentator Chizkuni. He writes that these women gathered at the Ohel Moed "to pray and hear praises of God from the *kohanim* and *leviim*."

Likewise, the late-medieval commentator Seforno writes that these mirrors were gifts from women who gathered at the Ohel Moed in order to "hear the words of the Living God ... and these spiritual women despised their jewelry and donated their mirrors to the Mishkan in order to demonstrate that they no longer have need of their jewelry."

The reason why these commentators all take this approach is probably because of another biblical text that indicates that there was a group of women who gathered at the Mishkan in order to pray as a group. This is the implication of 1 Samuel 2:22, which states: "The sons of Eli slept with the women who served [*nashim hatzovot*] at the entrance to the Ohel Moed."

Thus we see that the straightforward explanation of the phrase *marot hatzovot* is that there was a group of women who took upon themselves the responsibility of gathering in prayer outside the Mishkan. Although the Women of the Wall are not exactly the same thing as the women who donated the *marot hatzovot* to the Mishkan, we can see in their actions that they are the spiritual descendants of these holy women who gathered at the entrance to the Tent in order to call out in prayer to God.

Women of the Wall is an international group of women from across the denominations, yet they have always followed an Orthodox interpretation of halakhah. All of their actions at the Wall can find support within traditional Orthodox texts. They are a courageous group acting in the spirit of the women who donated the *marot hatzovot*.

רַבָּן גַּמְלִיאֵל הָיָה אוֹמֵר: כָּל שֶׁלֹּא אָמַר שְׁלשָׁה דְבָרִים אֵלּוּ בַּפֶּסַח, לֹא יָצָא יְדֵי חוֹבָתוֹ, וְאֵלּוּ הֵן:

פֶּסַח, מַצָּה, וּמָרוֹר.

---

that exists at the Wall, the stronger Israel will be. There is a divine mandate for all people to worship on God's holy mountain, as Yeshayahu states, "My house shall be a house of prayer for all nations" (56:7). Therefore, everyone should be allowed to worship at the Wall and the Temple Mount and all the holy sites of Israel, whether those sites are currently under the authority of Jews, Muslims, or Christians.

Separate from the question of religious freedom, the Women of the Wall should be supported in their desire to pray before Hashem at the site of our ancestors. Women praying at the Wall do not represent a deviation from the tradition of our ancestors, but rather a consistent affirmation of that tradition.

In parashat Vayakhel we read that Betzalel formed the copper washstand for the Mishkan "*b'marot hatzovot asher tzavu petach Ohel Moed*" (from the mirrors of the women who gathered at the entrance to the Ohel Moed; Shemot 38:8). The phrase *marot hatzovot* is an unusual one for the Torah and does not appear elsewhere in the Five Books of the Torah. Rashi (ad loc.) cites a well-known midrash, which explains that these words refer to copper mirrors that women brought to donate for the building of the Mishkan. Moshe was at first reluctant to take these mirrors since he thought that they were used for "the evil inclination." So Hashem said to Moshe, "These mirrors are more precious to Me than all the other donations to the Mishkan."

When the Jewish people were in the depths of their slavery in Egypt, the men were so exhausted from their slave labor that they were uninterested in marital relations. However, their wives used the mirrors in a flirtatious manner and inspired their husbands to have more children. So these are the *marot,* the mirrors, *hatzovot,* that produced legions of people. These are the mirrors that were responsible for the survival of the Jewish people. For this reason Hashem said that the mirrors should make up the entire copper washstand.

This beautiful midrash has a lot of symbolic meaning and it is often taught as the explanation of the words *marot hatzovot.* But let us not confuse it with the *peshat,* the straightforward explanation of these words. Avraham Ibn Ezra writes:

THE PASSOVER OFFERING which our ancestors ate when the Temple was standing – what was the reason for it? Because the Blessed Holy One passed over our ancestors' houses in Egypt, as it is said (Shemot 12:27): "You shall say: 'It is a Passover sacrifice to God, because He passed over the Houses of the Children of Israel in Egypt when He smote the Egyptians but spared our houses.' And the people bowed down and prostrated themselves."

---

other holidays were instituted in the merit of our patriarchs, not our matriarchs. But, says an ancient midrash, then the men sinned by making not only one golden calf, but twelve golden calves. Therefore the women were given a holiday for each of the twelve calves that they refrained from worshipping. Thus, the women were given the holiday of Rosh Chodesh – one for each month of the year – and so their reward was spread out over the course of the year.

Recently, my sister in Israel pointed out to me that it is ironic that this is one of the few cases in our tradition where we ignore an ancient *minhag*. She argued that women should have vacation days for all those twelve days and that if this were a male holiday, the custom would be more widely emphasized.

An alternative explanation of why Rosh Chodesh is a woman's holiday is suggested by the medieval commentary of the Tosafists known as Daat Zekenim (35:22). Daat Zekenim cites a verse in Vayakhel that states "*Vayavo'u haanashim al hanashim*," which literally means "and the men came over the women." Rashi says that the word *al* in this context just means the men came with the women to give their donations to the Mishkan. But Daat Zekenim suggests that it means that the men came forcibly to take the jewelry from their wives. However, to everyone's surprise the women ran to give the jewelry. Because the woman gave their precious possessions with great joy, they were forever associated with the building of the Mishkan. Daat Zekenim thus concludes that since the Mishkan was finished on Rosh Chodesh Nissan, Hashem gave the women the mitzvah of Rosh Chodesh as a special reward.

In the merit of the pure motives of those holy women whose motivations were doubted by the men of society, Jewish women were given the mitzvah of Rosh Chodesh for all time.

Seforno notes that unlike the two Batei Mikdash, the Mishkan itself was never destroyed. Perhaps it was never destroyed in the merit of all of the sacred women, the *tzovot*, who were praying with pure devotion at the entrance to the Ohel Moed.

פֶּסַח שֶׁהָיוּ אֲבוֹתֵינוּ אוֹכְלִים, בִּזְמַן שֶׁבֵּית הַמִּקְדָּשׁ הָיָה קַיָּם, עַל שׁוּם מָה? עַל שׁוּם שֶׁפָּסַח הַקָּדוֹשׁ בָּרוּךְ הוּא, עַל בָּתֵּי אֲבוֹתֵינוּ בְּמִצְרַיִם, שֶׁנֶּאֱמַר: וַאֲמַרְתֶּם זֶבַח פֶּסַח הוּא לַיְיָ, אֲשֶׁר פָּסַח עַל בָּתֵּי בְנֵי יִשְׂרָאֵל בְּמִצְרַיִם בְּנָגְפּוֹ אֶת־מִצְרַיִם, וְאֶת־בָּתֵּינוּ הִצִּיל. וַיִּקֹּד הָעָם וַיִּשְׁתַּחֲווּ.

Some people who care deeply about me have tried to dissuade me from public support of this group. They question the motives of the Women of the Wall. They say that they are doing it for publicity and are just trying to convince well-meaning folks to join with them even though they are not sincere in their devotion. They say, "If these women are so sincere then where are they the other twenty-nine days of the month?"

Of course it is possible that I am naïve, but my general response is that I do not question people's religious motives. How are we to know whose motives are pure and whose are not? For example, if we were going to question people's motives then maybe it is not the women's motives that should be questioned, but rather the motives of the people who are shutting out these women from the Wall?

Here, too, I think that tradition is on the side of the Women of the Wall. Rosh Chodesh is an especially significant mitzvah, as it was the very first mitzvah given to the Jewish people. Thus it is important to note that the *Shulchan Arukh* writes that this mitzvah is given especially to women: "It is a good custom among those women who have the practice not to do work on Rosh Chodesh" (Orach Chaim 417). Many great authorities view this prohibition of work for women on Rosh Chodesh as a halakhah that we should follow because "these women were commanded in this practice from their ancient matriarchs" (citation in Biur Halakhah ad loc., and see there further for a full listing of the authorities that support this custom).

How did Rosh Chodesh come to be a woman's holiday in the first place? The *Tur Shulchan Arukh* (417) of Rabbi Yaakov ben Asher cites a midrash that women were given the reward of guarding Rosh Chodesh more than men because the women did not participate in the sin of the golden calf. When Aharon asked the men to bring their wives' jewelry, the women refused. The men then gave Aharon their own jewelry.

The Tur then cites the opinion of his brother Rabbi Yehudah, who questioned why specifically Rosh Chodesh was given to the women. He writes that the

Point to the matzot and say:

THIS MATZAH that we eat – what is the reason for it? Because the dough of our ancestors had not yet leavened when the King of Kings, the Blessed Holy One, revealed Himself to them and redeemed them, as it is said

---

yours [in your possession] shall be seen [*v'lo yera'eh lekhah chametz*], and no leavening of yours shall be seen throughout all of your borders."

2. There is a second biblical prohibition called *bal yimatzei.* According to Shemot 12:19, "For seven days, leaven shall not be found [*se'or lo yimatzei*] in your houses."
3. There is a positive biblical commandment to destroy our chametz on the eve of Pesach. This is known as the mitzvah of *tashbitu.* The Torah (Shemot 12:15) states: "For seven days you shall eat unleavened cakes, *but on the preceding day you shall clear away all leaven from your houses* [*akh bayom harishon* tashbitu *se'or mibateichem*], for whoever eats leaven from the first day until the seventh day – that soul shall be cut off from Israel."

In a religion where there is a prohibition against unnecessary destruction it is noteworthy that we are commanded to destroy perfectly good food. When else do we search for something throughout our homes and then destroy it by burning it in the streets? In this respect, *bedikat chametz* and *biur chametz* are unique mitzvot.

There is a dispute in the Talmud (*Pesachim* 21a) concerning the proper way to destroy chametz. According to the rabbis, there is no specific way to destroy the chametz; one can even crush it up and throw it to the wind. However, Rabbi Yehudah rules that the only way to destroy chametz is by burning it.

What is the reason behind Rabbi Yehudah's requirement to burn the chametz? And what are the implications of this ruling for our own observance of Pesach?

Practically speaking, removing chametz from one's possession involves a three-step process:

1. *bedikat chametz* – searching for chametz
2. *bitul chametz* – nullifying the chametz
3. *biur chametz* – burning the chametz

The opening line in tractate *Pesachim* teaches us about the requirement to search our homes for chametz:

Point to the matzot and say:

מַצָּה זוֹ שֶׁאָנוּ אוֹכְלִים, עַל שׁוּם מָה? עַל שׁוּם שֶׁלֹּא הִסְפִּיק בְּצֵקָם שֶׁל אֲבוֹתֵינוּ לְהַחֲמִיץ, עַד שֶׁנִּגְלָה עֲלֵיהֶם מֶלֶךְ מַלְכֵי הַמְּלָכִים, הַקָּדוֹשׁ

PREPARING SPIRITUALLY FOR PESACH: REMOVING AND DESTROYING THE CHAMETZ WITHIN

As a young boy the search for chametz (*bedikat chametz*) was one of the highlights of the year. My siblings and I would hide the ten pieces of bread and my father would look for them by the light of the candle. My father would make a big show of the search for chametz. We always had a feather, a spoon, and a candle, and every piece of chametz that my father found was cause for a big celebration. When my father found some chametz that we had not even hidden it would delight us even more. Three decades later I still remember those evenings fondly.

I also fondly remember the burning of the chametz (*biur chametz*). We would always burn the chametz in our front yard on the eve of Pesach. Usually that went off without incident. We would put the chametz in a brown paper bag on top of our refrigerator and burn it the next day. One time a certain member of my family brought out the brown paper bag to burn our chametz. Unfortunately, that year there were two brown paper bags on top of our refrigerator: one containing the chametz and the other containing my mother's jewelry. My mother had thought that a good place to hide the jewelry was in a brown paper bag. As a result, instead of burning the chametz we burned the jewelry. That too is an image that is seared in my mind.

As a little boy, I was impressed by the pageantry and the fire, but as adults we must search for deeper meaning and symbolism. Above all, we must search for the lessons that we should incorporate into our Pesach holiday.

The message of *bedikat chametz* and *biur chametz* is very simple. The purpose of our elaborate searches for chametz and our burning of that chametz *is to rid ourselves of our spiritual faults in preparation for the holiday of Pesach, the holiday of our redemption.*

There are two prohibitions against owning chametz on Pesach, and there is one positive commandment to destroy chametz on the eve of Pesach:

1. There is a prohibition of *bal yera'eh*. According to the Torah (Shemot 13:7): "Unleavened cakes shall be eaten during the seven days, and no leaven of

(Shemot 12:39): "And the dough they had brought along out of Egypt they baked into unleavened cakes, for there was no leaven, because they had been driven out of Egypt and had had no time to tarry; they had not even prepared any provision for themselves."

---

parallel the soul-searching that we engage in before Yom Kippur. The physicality of the search for chametz must inspire us to perform a spiritual search us well.

The halakhah mandates that we "check for chametz by the light of the candle, in holes and cracks and every place that one enters with chametz." So, too, we must check every part of our souls – the cracks and the crevices – by the spiritual light of the candle.

If we study the laws of *bedikat chametz,* we will notice that they can be read in two ways: on a literal, physical level, and on a deeper, spiritual level, referring to a search of our own souls and our own spiritual progress.

Yet conducting a search is not sufficient. After we search for the chametz of our souls we must nullify and declare nonexistent any sinful habits. Following that we burn our chametz – we symbolically destroy our sinful habits.

These three steps of *bedikah, bitul,* and *biur* are all understood in both a literal and symbolic fashion by our rabbis. Too often, we focus on their literal meaning and forget about the symbolism behind the act.

The idea that chametz represents the *yetzer hara* is based upon a Talmudic text:

> Rabbi Alexandri, on concluding his prayer, used to add the following: Sovereign of the Universe, it is known full well to You that our will is to perform Your will, and what prevents us? The yeast in the dough and the subjection to the foreign powers. May it be Your will to deliver us from their hands, so that we may return to perform the statutes of Your will with a perfect heart. (*Berakhot* 17a)

The idea that the search for chametz is actually a spiritual activity intended to search out the sins of our souls is also seen in a Talmudic text. Tosefta *Pesachim* teaches:

> On the night [*or*] of the fourteenth we search for chametz by the light of the flame. We do not check by the light of the sun nor by the light of the moon but only by the light of the flame, for searching by the light of the flame is best. Even though there is no proof of this there is a hint to this as it states, "And it shall come to pass at that time that I will search Jerusalem with

בָּרוּךְ הוּא, וּגְאָלָם, שֶׁנֶּאֱמַר: וַיֹּאפוּ אֶת־הַבָּצֵק, אֲשֶׁר הוֹצִיאוּ מִמִּצְרַיִם, עֻגֹת מַצּוֹת, כִּי לֹא חָמֵץ. כִּי גֹרְשׁוּ מִמִּצְרַיִם, וְלֹא יָכְלוּ לְהִתְמַהְמֵהַּ, וְגַם צֵדָה לֹא עָשׂוּ לָהֶם.

> On the evening of the fourteenth a search [*bedikah*] is made for leaven by the light of a lamp. (*Pesachim* 2a, Mishnah)

Why does the Talmud requires a search for chametz? Rashi (2a) writes that a search is necessary so that one does "not violate *bal yera'eh u'val yimatzei*."

What is the deeper meaning behind the search for and destruction of chametz? It is rare that the Torah requires us to search for and destroy a prohibited item, and forbids us from even owning it. For example, we are not forbidden to own a piece of nonkosher meat. Even though we are forbidden to derive benefit from a food item that contains meat and milk, there is no prohibition against owning the meat and milk together.

Rav Menachem Kasher (*Haggadah Sheleimah* [Machon Torah Sheleimah, 1967], appendix 7) raises this question and offers a novel approach to understanding the prohibitions of owning or even seeing chametz. He argues that the closest comparison to the prohibition of chametz is the prohibition of idolatry (*avodah zarah*).

Rav Kasher notes six similarities between the prohibitions of chametz and *avodah zarah*:

1. Owning either of them is forbidden.
2. They both need to be burnt.
3. They are both prohibited with respect to deriving any benefit.
4. They both have a prohibition even with respect to a miniscule amount.
5. Nullification works in both cases.
6. Both prohibitions require a search.

Thus, there is a strong connection between the prohibitions of chametz and *avodah zarah*. It is clear from this that our obligation to burn our chametz arises not simply from a need to physically eradicate the presence of chametz from our lives but also from a need to metaphysically eradicate sins from within us.

The connection of chametz to *avodah zarah* teaches us that the removal of the physical chametz from our domain is supposed to inspire us to perform a spiritual purging of the chametz in our souls. Our Pesach "cleaning" should

Point to the bitter herbs and say:

THIS BITTER HERB that we eat – what is the reason for it? Because the Egyptians embittered the lives of our ancestors in Egypt, as it is said (Shemot 1:14): "They embittered their lives with hard labor at clay and brick-making, and all sorts of work in the fields – with all the tasks at which they ruthlessly worked them."

---

bread is called "the staff of life." The need to destroy our chametz is a reminder to destroy the ever-present *avodah zarah* in our lives.

As we continue from *bedikat chametz* to *biur chametz*, our thoughts of *teshuvah* should accompany us. Although technically speaking one can destroy the chametz in any fashion, the ideal way is by burning it. The reason we are ideally supposed to burn the chametz and not simply flush it down the toilet is because burning allows us to see the chametz as a symbol of idolatry.

The burning of the chametz also provides us with a physical ritual in order to help us recognize that Pesach is about turning over a new leaf. Rabbi Yaakov Zvi Mecklenberg (d. 1865, Germany) writes about the spiritual destruction necessitated by the Torah's command to destroy our chametz:

> *Tashbitu*: Since the Torah does not state *teva'aru*, like it says elsewhere (*biarti hakodesh*), it seems that the rabbis derived from here that destruction is in the heart. Thus, the *tashbitu* of the verse is not a physical act but a mental act! (*Haktav v'Hakabbalah*, Shemot 12:15)

Thus, in Rabbi Mecklenberg's opinion one only fulfills the biblical mitzvah of destroying chametz by mentally destroying our chametz. We need to do both. We need to destroy our chametz both mentally and physically.

In our synagogue, before throwing the bread into the fire we first write down a negative character trait on a piece of paper and drop it into the flames. When we burn the chametz we should go all in. We should totally invest ourselves in the burning. By physically burning our chametz we are also symbolically burning our *yetzer hara*, and as the fire blazes we all sing, "Hashem give us a good *yetzer* to do Your will."

After we burn our chametz to the sounds of uplifting spiritual music we recite the following prayer:

> May it be your will, Hashem, our God, and God of our ancestors, that just as I destroy the chametz from my house and from my domain, so too may

Point to the bitter herbs and say:

מָרוֹר זֶה שֶׁאָנוּ אוֹכְלִים, עַל שׁוּם מָה? עַל שׁוּם שֶׁמֵּרְרוּ הַמִּצְרִים אֶת־חַיֵּי אֲבוֹתֵינוּ בְּמִצְרַיִם, שֶׁנֶּאֱמַר: וַיְמָרְרוּ אֶת־חַיֵּיהֶם בַּעֲבֹדָה קָשָׁה, בְּחֹמֶר וּבִלְבֵנִים, וּבְכָל־עֲבֹדָה בַּשָּׂדֶה, אֵת כָּל־עֲבֹדָתָם, אֲשֶׁר עָבְדוּ בָהֶם בְּפָרֶךְ.

---

lamps" (Tzephanyah 1:12). And it states, "The spirit of man is the lamp of God, searching all the inward parts" (Mishlei 20:27). (Tosefta *Pesachim* 1:1)

By comparing our souls to light, the Tosefta teaches that the search for chametz is meant to parallel an inner soul-searching.

Both the Tosefta and the corresponding passage in tractate *Pesachim* begin with the words "*or l'arba'ah asar*" (on the night of the fourteenth). The Talmud wonders why the word *or* is used to mean "night," as opposed to the word "*leil*." Here too, we assume that the purpose is to provide a spiritual meaning to a physical ritual. The goal is to search our homes with the light of the Torah. Every single aspect of our lives must be searched, not just for chametz, but also for sins.

Not only is the *bedikah* assumed to have spiritual meaning, but the *biur* as well. The Shlah Hakadosh (d. 1630) states: "It is known that the *yetzer hara* is the disgusting chametz, the yeast of the dough. The only way to destroy the chametz is by burning it. If you encounter this horrible creature drag him to the *beit midrash*" (Shlah, Tractate *Pesachim*, Matzah Ashirah, s.v. *chametz*). The search for and destruction of chametz has a higher purpose beyond the mere ritual. It serves to help us destroy the *yetzer hara* inside us. When we perform the *bedikah*, *bitul*, and *biur*, we must not only do so in a halakhically correct manner but also think about our spiritual goals.

How can we help reach our spiritual goals for Pesach?

First, we should all take a few moments before the *bedikah* to remember the relationship between chametz and idolatry. We should then ask ourselves: What is my own personal idolatry? What should I try to remove from my heart?

Anything that detracts and distracts us from our focus on God is actually *avodah zarah*. *Avodah zarah* is often not a foreign entity that we get seduced by after a romantic encounter. It is usually one of the most common elements in our life – money, ego, power – that we allow to distract us from our spiritual goals. That is why it is very helpful to compare *avodah zarah* to chametz. Chametz is one of the most ubiquitous elements in the world. This is why

IN EVERY GENERATION, every person is to consider himself as having personally come out of Egypt, as it is said (Shemot 13:8): "And you shall tell your son on that day, saying: This commemorates what God did for me when I went out of Egypt." For the Blessed Holy One did not redeem our ancestors alone; He also redeemed us along with them, as it is said (Devarim 6:23): "And He brought us out of there, in order to take us to give us the land concerning which He had made a vow to our ancestors."

---

affect us? I doubt that many people really feel like they were just liberated from slavery. So what is this holiday all about?

The Torah instructs us to remember the day we left Egypt all the days of our lives (Devarim 16:3). Commenting on the word *all* (*kol*), Ben Zoma teaches us that we must remember the Exodus every single moment – day and night. It has to always be in our consciousness. In an unredeemed world, this makes sense. We must always remember what it was like to be enslaved in Egypt. As we await the messianic redemption, we should recall the greatness of God in bringing about our redemption from Egypt.

But the sages interpret the word *kol* to allude to the messianic era. Why should we bother to remember the Exodus in the messianic era, whenever it will come? After all, in the messianic era we will have achieved the full redemption. We will have reached our goal. Why keep remembering the redemption from Egypt during the messianic era? The Egyptian redemption will be replaced like we replace a used car. Who talks about their old car once they get a new car?

In fact, the Talmud in *Berakhot* (12b) asks this very question: *V'khi mazkirin yetziat Mitzrayim bi'yemot haMashiach*? Will we really bother to recall the exodus from Egypt when we are enjoying the redemption of the messianic world?

A friend suffering from cancer answered this question for me. He explained that when he was sick in his hospital bed during the darkest days of his cancer – that was when he felt closest to God. It was in those very dark moments that he finally had clarity about the important things in life. He saw the endless distractions that occupy our lives for what they were: mere distractions that prevent us from uniting with God. During those moments, he finally achieved a deep relationship with God.

Those moments, when my friend lay in his hospital bed, were almost like his messianic era. As Rambam explains, the messianic era is marked by recognition

בְּכָל־דּוֹר וָדוֹר חַיָּב אָדָם לִרְאוֹת אֶת־עַצְמוֹ, כְּאִלּוּ הוּא יָצָא מִמִּצְרָיִם, שֶׁנֶּאֱמַר: וְהִגַּדְתָּ לְבִנְךָ בַּיּוֹם הַהוּא לֵאמֹר: בַּעֲבוּר זֶה עָשָׂה יְיָ לִי, בְּצֵאתִי מִמִּצְרָיִם. לֹא אֶת־אֲבוֹתֵינוּ בִּלְבָד, גָּאַל הַקָּדוֹשׁ בָּרוּךְ הוּא, אֶלָּא אַף אוֹתָנוּ גָּאַל עִמָּהֶם, שֶׁנֶּאֱמַר: וְאוֹתָנוּ הוֹצִיא מִשָּׁם, לְמַעַן הָבִיא אֹתָנוּ, לָתֶת לָנוּ אֶת־הָאָרֶץ אֲשֶׁר נִשְׁבַּע לַאֲבֹתֵינוּ.

You destroy all of the external forces, and may You remove the impure spirits from the earth. May You destroy the evil spirit that is within us, and may You give us a strong will! And may the evil influences be burned like smoke and may they be destroyed from the earth in the same way in which You destroyed Egypt and their gods in those days. (Prayer following *biur chametz*, found in many *machzorim*)

CHANGED FOREVER

On my left wrist I wear a bracelet with the words "Changed Forever." The bracelet is a gift from our neighbor Michel Martin, who got the bracelet while attending the tenth anniversary of the bombing of the Murrah Federal Building in Oklahoma City, which took place on April 19, 1995.

"Changed forever," Michel taught me. "Isn't that the message of Passover?"

If it were only so! If we only allowed ourselves to be changed just a little bit by the bombing in Oklahoma City! How many of us even thought about the anniversary of that bombing for more than a minute?

The essential teaching of the Exodus story is to be changed forever by events like the Oklahoma City bombing. Let's remember that the Exodus story isn't just the story of our redemption; it's the story of our enslavement and then our redemption. As we sit here today in the lap of luxury, we're supposed to remember that we were once slaves, that we once experienced pain and that we cannot forget that pain. The pain that we felt in Egypt was supposed to change us forever, to sensitize us to the plight of others – of the "broken people" in our own community and all around us in the world.

Yet as we go through Pesach, how many of us really feel changed? Do we feel the pain of "slaves" around us any more deeply? Does the holiday really

Raise the cup of wine, cover the matzot, and say:

THAT IS WHY we are duty bound to thank, praise, laud, glorify, exalt, extol, bless, acclaim, and adore Him Who performed all these wonders for our ancestors and us: He brought us from slavery to freedom, from sorrow to joy, from mourning to holiday, and from darkness to great light, and from bondage to redemption. So let us declaim a new song to Him. Halleluyah.

Put down the cup and uncover the matzot

PRAISE – O God's servants – praise the Name of God. Blessed be the Name of God now and forever. From the sun's rising place to its setting place let the Name of God be praised. High above all the nations is God, our God: enthroned so high yet deigning to look so low; raising the wretched out of the dust, lifting the poor off the dungheap, to give them a place among the high and mighty – among the high and mighty of His people; making the barren recluse a happy mother of children. Halleluyah. (Tehillim 113)

The pain of Egypt will not be forgotten, but it will no longer be as prominent. Center stage will be held by our more recent hurdles. As Yirmiyahu states, the day will come when we no longer bless the God Who redeemed us from Egypt, but the God Who redeemed us from bondage to the other nations (23:7–8).

When we leave a situation of pain and redemption our task is to seek another challenge. Sometimes struggles and challenges find people. The world considers those people unlucky – but they at least are cognizant of their struggles. In any case, no one specific struggle lasts forever.

Our challenge is to continue to seek out new struggles – a new personal Egypt, a new personal Babylon – so that we can have even greater redemptions. Our challenge is to avoid resting on our laurels; instead, we must take our past struggles and let them guide us in discovering more direct paths to God.

Ramchal (Rabbi Moshe Chaim Luzzatto, eighteenth century) explains this idea in his work *Mesilat Yesharim* (ch. 23): people always push themselves financially, professionally and materialistically to be like people who have more wealth or a better job or a nicer house; so too we must always push ourselves spiritually to be like people who we view as more spiritual or closer to God. We can do this by never being complacent about our spiritual life, by always seeking out new and greater challenges.

Raise the cup of wine, cover the matzot, and say:

לְפִיכָךְ אֲנַחְנוּ חַיָּבִים לְהוֹדוֹת, לְהַלֵּל, לְשַׁבֵּחַ, לְפָאֵר, לְרוֹמֵם, לְהַדֵּר, לְבָרֵךְ, לְעַלֵּה וּלְקַלֵּס, לְמִי שֶׁעָשָׂה לַאֲבוֹתֵינוּ וְלָנוּ אֶת־כָּל־הַנִּסִּים הָאֵלּוּ. הוֹצִיאָנוּ מֵעַבְדוּת לְחֵרוּת, מִיָּגוֹן לְשִׂמְחָה, וּמֵאֵבֶל לְיוֹם טוֹב, וּמֵאֲפֵלָה לְאוֹר גָּדוֹל, וּמִשִּׁעְבּוּד לִגְאֻלָּה. וְנֹאמַר לְפָנָיו שִׁירָה חֲדָשָׁה. הַלְלוּיָהּ.

Put down the cup and uncover the matzot

הַלְלוּיָהּ. הַלְלוּ עַבְדֵי יְיָ. הַלְלוּ אֶת־שֵׁם יְיָ. יְהִי שֵׁם יְיָ מְבֹרָךְ מֵעַתָּה וְעַד עוֹלָם. מִמִּזְרַח שֶׁמֶשׁ עַד מְבוֹאוֹ, מְהֻלָּל שֵׁם יְיָ. רָם עַל־כָּל־גּוֹיִם יְיָ, עַל הַשָּׁמַיִם כְּבוֹדוֹ. מִי כַּיְיָ אֱלֹהֵינוּ, הַמַּגְבִּיהִי לָשָׁבֶת, הַמַּשְׁפִּילִי לִרְאוֹת בַּשָּׁמַיִם וּבָאָרֶץ. מְקִימִי מֵעָפָר דָּל. מֵאַשְׁפֹּת יָרִים אֶבְיוֹן. לְהוֹשִׁיבִי עִם־נְדִיבִים, עִם נְדִיבֵי עַמּוֹ. מוֹשִׁיבִי עֲקֶרֶת הַבַּיִת, אֵם הַבָּנִים שְׂמֵחָה. הַלְלוּיָהּ.

---

of truth and understanding of God. In the hospital bed, my friend had the truth – he had a messianic epiphany.

However, when this same friend was able to get out of the hospital and resume his life, he lost that deep connection to God. He was once again, like we all are, caught up in the mundane activities of life; his clear focus and connection to God were lost.

This is the challenge of the Exodus story. When we are in the middle of our struggle – the middle of our slavery, the middle of our pain, the middle of our grief for a loved one – we can sometimes see God much more clearly and powerfully.

But as we move on how do we retain that connection? How do we stay connected to God once we have been redeemed; when have cleared our hurdle, how do we continue to see God? How do we stay forever changed by past struggles?

On the one hand we must mention it every single day and night. But that won't be enough; it will become rote. There is another necessary step.

The Talmud answers its own question: we will recall the Exodus story even during the messianic era, but the principal redemption will be the final one.

WHEN ISRAEL CAME OUT of Egypt, the House of Yaakov from a strange-languaged people – Judah became His sanctuary, Israel His dominion. The sea saw and fled; the Jordan turned back. The mountains skipped liked rams, the hills like young sheep. What is it, sea; why do you run? Jordan – why do you turn back? Why, mountains, do you skip like rams, you hills like young sheep? Dance, earth, when the Lord appears, when Yaakov's God shows, Who turned the rock into a pool of water, the flint-rock into a gushing fountain! (Tehillim 114)

All the participants lift their cups of wine, and say (on a Saturday night add the words in parentheses):

BE BLESSED, God, our God, King of the universe, Who redeemed us and redeemed our ancestors from Egypt and enabled us to live to this night to eat matzah and bitter herbs. In the same way, God, our God and God of our ancestors, let us live until the other set-times and festivals approach us – let us reach them in peace, rejoicing in the rebuilding of Your service, and partaking of the sacrifices and the Passover offerings (the Passover offerings and the sacrifices), whose blood shall reach the walls of Your alter propitiously, and we will thank You with a new song for our redemption and the emancipation of our souls. Be blessed, God, Who redeemed Israel.

Say the following blessing and drink the second cup, reclining:

Behold, I am prepared and ready to recite Kiddush over wine, and to fulfill the commandment of the second of the four cups, for the sake of the unity of the Holy One, blessed is He, and His Presence, through Him Who is hidden and inscrutable, in the name of all Israel. May the pleasantness of my Lord, our G-d, be upon us – may He establish our work, the works of our hands may He establish.

BE BLESSED, GOD, OUR GOD, KING OF THE UNIVERSE, CREATOR OF THE FRUIT OF THE VINE.

THE TRANSFORMATIVE NATURE OF THE FOUR CUPS

The drinking of the four cups is one of the most treasured rituals of the Seder so it is important to understand its symbolism in depth. It is a rabbinic mitzvah, with the earliest source appearing in the Mishnah:

> On the eve of Pesach close to the time of Minchah a person may not eat until it becomes dark. And even the poorest man may not eat until he

בְּצֵאת יִשְׂרָאֵל מִמִּצְרָיִם, בֵּית יַעֲקֹב מֵעַם לֹעֵז, הָיְתָה יְהוּדָה לְקָדְשׁוֹ, יִשְׂרָאֵל מַמְשְׁלוֹתָיו. הַיָּם רָאָה וַיָּנֹס, הַיַּרְדֵּן יִסֹּב לְאָחוֹר. הֶהָרִים רָקְדוּ כְאֵילִים, גְּבָעוֹת כִּבְנֵי־צֹאן. מַה־לְּךָ הַיָּם כִּי תָנוּס, הַיַּרְדֵּן תִּסֹּב לְאָחוֹר. הֶהָרִים תִּרְקְדוּ כְאֵילִים, גְּבָעוֹת כִּבְנֵי־צֹאן. מִלִּפְנֵי אָדוֹן חוּלִי אָרֶץ, מִלִּפְנֵי אֱלוֹהַּ יַעֲקֹב. הַהֹפְכִי הַצּוּר אֲגַם־מָיִם, חַלָּמִישׁ לְמַעְיְנוֹ־מָיִם.

All the participants lift their cups of wine, and say (on a Saturday night add the words in parentheses):

בָּרוּךְ אַתָּה יְיָ, אֱלֹהֵינוּ מֶלֶךְ הָעוֹלָם, אֲשֶׁר גְּאָלָנוּ וְגָאַל אֶת־אֲבוֹתֵינוּ מִמִּצְרַיִם, וְהִגִּיעָנוּ לַלַּיְלָה הַזֶּה, לֶאֱכָל־בּוֹ מַצָּה וּמָרוֹר. כֵּן, יְיָ אֱלֹהֵינוּ וֵאלֹהֵי אֲבוֹתֵינוּ, יַגִּיעֵנוּ לְמוֹעֲדִים וְלִרְגָלִים אֲחֵרִים, הַבָּאִים לִקְרָאתֵנוּ לְשָׁלוֹם. שְׂמֵחִים בְּבִנְיַן עִירֶךָ, וְשָׂשִׂים בַּעֲבוֹדָתֶךָ, וְנֹאכַל שָׁם מִן הַזְּבָחִים וּמִן הַפְּסָחִים (מִן הַפְּסָחִים וּמִן הַזְּבָחִים), אֲשֶׁר יַגִּיעַ דָּמָם, עַל קִיר מִזְבַּחֲךָ לְרָצוֹן, וְנוֹדֶה לְּךָ שִׁיר חָדָשׁ עַל גְּאֻלָּתֵנוּ, וְעַל פְּדוּת נַפְשֵׁנוּ. בָּרוּךְ אַתָּה יְיָ, גָּאַל יִשְׂרָאֵל.

Say the following blessing and drink the second cup, reclining:

הִנְנִי מוּכָן וּמְזֻמָּן לְקַיֵּם מִצְוַת כּוֹס שְׁנִיָּה מֵאַרְבַּע כּוֹסוֹת לְשֵׁם יִחוּד קוּדְשָׁא בְּרִיךְ הוּא וּשְׁכִינְתֵּיהּ עַל־יְדֵי הַהוּא טָמִיר וְנֶעְלָם בְּשֵׁם כָּל־יִשְׂרָאֵל. וִיהִי נֹעַם אֲדֹנָי אֱלֹהֵינוּ עָלֵינוּ, וּמַעֲשֵׂה יָדֵינוּ כּוֹנְנָה עָלֵינוּ, וּמַעֲשֵׂה יָדֵינוּ כּוֹנְנֵהוּ:

בָּרוּךְ אַתָּה יְיָ, אֱלֹהֵינוּ מֶלֶךְ הָעוֹלָם,
בּוֹרֵא פְּרִי הַגָּפֶן.

The early Chasidim understood this best. Whenever they got too comfortable with their lives, they used to wander around in a self-imposed exile. We must always seek the challenge.

We will not be able to guard the sacred experience of our present struggles forever. We will not always be able to feel its raw emotion in our daily lives. But we can take it with us to our next challenge in life. And we can continue using it as we climb toward God. Only then can we truly be changed forever.

The authorities also disagree over whether grape juice might be drunk instead of wine. The *Shulchan Arukh* (472:10) states that one who generally doesn't drink wine because it harms his health or because he dislikes it must force himself to drink in order to fulfill the mitzvah of four cups. Rav Moshe Feinstein likewise ruled that one should use wine rather than grape juice in order to demonstrate freedom (Rabbi David Feinstein, *Kol Dodi* Haggadah). Rambam, on the other hand, writes that the four cups should be mixed so that the drinking is pleasant for the individual (*Mishneh Torah*, Hilkhot Chametz u'Matzah 7:9.) Based on this, Rav Soloveitchik instructed people who dislike wine to drink grape juice, since taste is subjective (Hershel Schachter, *Nefesh HaRav* [Jerusalem, 1994], 185).

What do these halakhot teach us about the nature of the four cups? How do we conceptualize this mitzvah? One approach is that the four cups of wine are intended to bring joy and happiness to our lives on the night we celebrate the anniversary of our exodus from Egypt. Wine is often associated with happiness in Judaism. According to Rashbam, the obligation of rejoicing on Yom Tov is fulfilled through the mitzvah of drinking wine (commentary to Pesachim 99b, s.v. *v'afilu ani.*). Therefore, the mitzvah of the four cups may represent a special mitzvah of rejoicing. As the Michtam writes, "The mitzvah of the four cups was instituted on this night to enable us to rejoice, corresponding to the four statements of redemption" (Michtam, *Pesachim*, beginning of tenth chapter, cited by Rabbi Menachem Genack, "The Four Cups of Wine," *Chavrusa* [March 2003], page 3). While this explanation has a lot of merit, it doesn't explain why there is a dispute over some of the laws, both in the Talmud and in the medieval and modern authorities.

There is an analysis of this topic that is taught by the Brisker Rav (1886–1959). The Brisker Rav explained that there are two ways to conceptualize this mitzvah. One approach is that there are four independent parts of the Seder that we want to elevate in importance. We therefore make a blessing on wine around these parts in order to demonstrate their significance. In many areas of Jewish law the addition of wine to a ritual adds significance to the ritual (e.g., Kiddush, Havdalah, *brit milah*, wedding). Thus, on Seder night, we make a blessing over wine when we recite the Kiddush, when we tell the story of the Haggadah, when we recite Birkat Hamazon, and when we sing Hallel at the conclusion of the Seder. In this formulation the four cups serve the same function as Kiddush on Friday night: just as Kiddush – the blessing sanctifying the day – is recited over wine in order to give greater significance to the Kiddush, we drink a cup of wine at four points in the Seder to highlight those moments of transition.

> reclines. And they must not give him less than four cups of wine, even if he is supported from the charity platter. (*Pesachim* 99b, Mishnah)

The Mishnah states that we must drink at least four cups but it does not say why we have to drink the cups.

Based upon the Jerusalem Talmud, Rashi (Bavli, *Pesachim* 99b) links the four cups to the four expressions of redemption that are stated with respect to the exodus from Egypt in Shemot 6:6–7: *v'hotzeiti, v'hitzalti, v'gaalti, v'lakachti*. The Jerusalem Talmud actually offered four reasons for this practice, and Rashi recorded only the first. The *Haggadah Torah Shelemah* of Rav Kasher records more than twenty reasons for why we drink four cups of wine on Passover night – a clear indication that there is no one overwhelmingly correct reason.

Not only is the reason for drinking four cups obscure, but some of the laws relating to this mitzvah are unique. The Babylonian Talmud (108), for example, notes that a poor person must borrow money to perform the mitzvah of the four cups properly, despite the fact that for most positive commandments one is not obligated to impoverish oneself by spending more than 20 percent of one's net worth.

So, too, the Talmud (ibid.) questions whether it is permissible to drink the four cups one after another, rather than at the four specified points of the Seder. Rav answers that one who does so will have fulfilled the obligation to drink the four cups, but not the obligation to act in the manner of freedom. The fact that the Talmud states that a person can technically fulfill the mitzvah of drinking four cups but still miss an essential part of the mitzvah (the sensation of feeling free) implies that at its core this mitzvah is supposed to affect us in a different manner than the other mitzvot.

Furthermore, Rabbi Yehudah teaches that we should give nuts to the children instead of wine because, as the Ran explains, children don't enjoy wine. What does this law teach us about the core idea of the mitzvah of drinking four cups?

When we move beyond the Talmud, we encounter a series of halakhic disputes that deepen the confusion surrounding the four cups. For example, though Tosafot writes that only a cheekful of each cup need be drunk (*Pesachim* 108a, s.v. *ruba*), the Rambam and the *Shulchan Arukh* rule that the majority of each cup must be drunk (*Mishneh Torah*, Hilkhot Chametz u'Matzah 7:9; *Shulchan Arukh* 472:9). In addition, the Talmud indicated that it is permissible to drink the four cups one after another (see *Pesachim* 108a, and Rashbam s.v. *bevat achat*), whereas the *Shulchan Arukh* (472:8) rules that in order to fulfill the mitzvah one must drink the four cups in the order of the Seder.

> First, "I led you out from the burden of Egypt" [*v'hotzeiti*] – this refers to the release from bricks and mortars, the part of slavery that ended during the plague of wild animals [see Shemot 8:25]. But still they were under the power of slavery until the plague of hail, at which point the Egyptians began to honor the Israelites [see 9:35]. And regarding this stage it is written, "I saved you from their servitude" [*v'hitzalti*]. But still they were under the domain of the kingdom and Pharaoh. So at the plague of the firstborn they became free, as it is written, "I redeemed" [*v'gaalti*]. And following that Hashem elevated them to the level of "I took you as a nation" [*v'lakachti*]. The four cups were established to commemorate this since there is no other food that changes the face and behavior of a person like drinking wine, since it gladdens the heart and lifts the spirit....
>
> "And you will know that I am Hashem" [*vi'yedaatem*]: This is another promise. It is a fifth expression of praise. You will elevate yourself so much until you reach the level of "and you will know," i.e., a level of cleaving to and knowledge of Hashem. It is clear that this level will take place at a later time than the earlier levels. This will be from the time of Mount Sinai and onward.
>
> It is important to note that this promise is not going to be for all of the Jewish people. For it is impossible that there can be a nation in which every single person is on such a high level that they are cleaving to God. Rather it means that there will be many people on this high level.... This is why there is a fifth cup that corresponds to the expression "you will know," and since there is not an absolute obligation for every individual to achieve this level therefore this cup is [an optional] mitzvah and not an obligation. (*Haamek Davar*, Shemot 6:6–7)

Since wine is a mood changer, we use wine at the Seder to help us appreciate the different moods and levels of redemption that the people went through. Wine helps us pass from abject slavery to physical freedom, to honor, and eventually to becoming Hashem's nation.

But the key is the fifth possible mood. That mood shifts us from the passive level of absorbing and appreciating God's miracles into a level of fulfilling the ultimate redemption. The highest level of redemption is not when we receive God's gifts, but when we achieve a level of knowledge of God. *Vi'yedaatem*: the more we know God, the more we are redeemed by Him.

Only four cups are generally drunk on Seder night – not five. But the halakhic literature discusses the possibility of a fifth cup. Rambam argues that one may choose to drink five cups but that there is not a strict obligation to do

The wine is not intended to bring to us a unique feeling required for the holiday of Pesach; instead, its goal is to emphasize the four main parts of the Seder.

The alternative approach suggested by the Brisker Rav is that these four cups constitute an independent mitzvah, which has its own transformational goals. There are numerous distinctions in halakhah that can arise depending upon how we conceptualize the mitzvah of the four cups. Here are two distinctions:

1. For Kiddush on Friday night, only a cheekful of wine needs to be drunk in order to fulfill one's obligation. Thus, Tosafot's view that one only needs to drink a cheekful of wine for each of the four cups is consistent with the view that the four cups are like Kiddush on Friday night. In contrast, Rambam's opinion that one should drink a majority of the cup is in line with the view that the four cups constitute an independent mitzvah, different from that of Kiddush.
2. Tosafot (99b) writes that theoretically not everyone at the table needs to drink a cup; it is sufficient for the Seder leader to drink and everyone else to say amen. This, too, is like Kiddush on Friday night. In contrast, Rambam holds that every single person must drink from the cup and therefore he is consistent with the opinion that the mitzvah of the four cups is a unique law with a transformational goal (*Mishneh Torah,* Hilkhot Chametz u'Matzah 7:7).

Rabbi Naftali Tzvi Yehudah Berlin (the "Netziv," 1816–1893, Lithuania) adopts the approach that the mitzvah of the four cups has a transformational goal. In his commentary *Haamek Davar* he implies that the four cups are a tool to help us internalize what it means to go through the various stages of redemption necessary to ascend from slavery to spiritual freedom.

Many people have heard of the custom of walking around the Seder table with matzah on one's shoulder in order to dramatize the Seder story. According to the Netziv, the four cups serve a similar function – except that the four cups are not only intended to help us understand how the Israelites left Egypt but also to aid our spiritual transformation and elevation:

> It is difficult to comprehend how a simple slave could rise within a short time to the level of the Israelites who stood at Mount Sinai and received the Torah and witnessed the Revelation. Thus, [the story] is expounded to elevate the mind and the body little by little. So, too, this is how the Israelites elevated themselves in Egypt.
>
> This is the explanation behind the four expressions of redemption:

Rav Efraim Oshry, the rabbi of the Kovno ghetto, was approached with the following question:

> I was asked how to fulfill the rabbinical commandment to drink four cups of wine, since no wine was available. The famine in the ghetto was growing worse from day to day, and the only common drink available was tea sweetened with saccharin. And even that could be obtained only with great difficulty. I was asked if one could fulfill the commandment by drinking four cups of this saccharine sweetened tea.
>
> Response: I ruled that since in the ghetto sweetened tea was considered a popular drink it was permissible to use it for the four cups.…
>
> In order to inspire the Jews with hope that redemption was not far off, and also to fulfill the requirement of the halakhah, my students went house to house knocking on people's doors and made the tea available to as many students as possible. (*Mimaamakim* 3:51–55)

Just imagine how depressing it must have been to go into Pesach in the Kovno ghetto. No wine for the four cups. But then a knock comes at the door and for some it was the first step toward redemption; it was the sign that even without wine they could be drinking the four cups. The power of the four cups lies in our mindset on Seder night.

so (*Mishneh Torah,* Hilkhot Chametz u'Matzah 8:10), while Rabbi Eliezer of Worms (thirteenth century) writes that the Great Hallel (psalm 136) should be recited over the fifth cup, and it should be drunk – but without leaning (*Rokeiach* 283). Since we lean to symbolize freedom, it is generally understood that the fifth cup represents a stage that has not yet been (fully) realized. Most scholars assume that the fifth cup relates to *v'heveiti,* "and I will bring you into the land [of Israel]" (Shemot 6:8). In the words of the Daat Zekenim, a biblical commentary from the Tosafist school, "If a servant was freed by his master and [the master] gave him a cup in his hand but didn't give him a place to live, then what good is it? So too, if God did not bring us to the land of Israel what good would the Exodus be?"

The Netziv agrees that the fifth cup indicates a state that has not been fully realized; he agrees that the fifth cup is not obligatory. But according to the Netziv, the fifth cup relates to a level in which we turn our redemption from the passive to the active – from a level in which God redeems us, to an active level in which we cleave to God. This is a level that cannot be commanded and for this reason it is very much desirable, but still optional, as it is reserved for a small percentage of the Jewish people.

The implications of the Netziv's approach is that as we drink the four cups we should be asking ourselves: What stage of redemption were the Jewish people at? We should be looking at the Pesach story and considering how the Israelites developed from slaves to prophets. More than that, we should be using the Pesach story and Seder night to ask ourselves: What stage are we at in our redemption process?

The four cups are an experiential mitzvah. The cups are intended to help us appreciate the spiritual growth that we have achieved since last Pesach, and more recently since Rosh Hashanah. Pesach night comes exactly six months after Sukkot for a reason. We should be looking at Pesach night as an opportunity for spiritual growth. Many of us left Rosh Hashanah and Yom Kippur and Sukkot thinking we were going to make huge spiritual strides this year. Pesach is the holiday of redemption. It is the time of year when we should be asking ourselves: If we were in Egypt would we have been redeemed? Are we ready for redemption? Are we meeting our spiritual benchmarks?

The four cups of wine are not about wine, but about spiritual growth. We drink the wine in order to set in front of ourselves the benchmarks of success that we will need in order to achieve a true redemption through cleaving to God. Even if we can't achieve the highest level this year, we should be actively engaged in climbing the spiritual ladder.

QUESTIONS ON RACHTZAH

1. How are the hands of the rabbis being washed?
2. Why are the rabbis sitting at individual tables?
3. Why do they each have their own Seder plates?
4. They were all sitting together at night. Why?

Extra credit: What are the names of the five rabbis who stayed up discussing the Exodus from Egypt until early morning? *Hint*: Look in the Haggadah a few paragraphs after the Mah Nishtanah.

RACHTZAH

Rinse the hands and say the following blessing:

Be blessed, God, our God, King of the universe, Who has sanctified us by His commandments and commanded us concerning the rinsing of the hands.

רָחְצָה

Rinse the hands and say the following blessing:

בָּרוּךְ אַתָּה יְיָ, אֱלֹהֵינוּ מֶלֶךְ הָעוֹלָם, אֲשֶׁר קִדְּשָׁנוּ בְּמִצְוֹתָיו, וְצִוָּנוּ עַל נְטִילַת יָדָיִם.

QUESTIONS FOR MOTZI MATZAH

1. What happened right before Motzi Matzah?
2. What is removed from the matzah holder?
3. How many blessings are said over the matzot?
4. What are they?

Extra credit: What is the difference between the two blessings?

MOTZI

Pick up the three matzot from the Seder tray and say the following blessing:

Be blessed, God, our God, King of the universe, Who brings forth bread from the earth.

MATZAH

Replace the bottom matzah. Everybody gets a piece of the top and middle matzot. Say the following blessing and eat, reclining. (Some first dip the matzah in charoset.)

Be blessed, God, our God, King of the universe, Who sanctified us with His commandments and commanded us concerning the eating of matzah.

מוֹצִיא

Pick up the three matzot from the Seder tray and say the following blessing:

בָּרוּךְ אַתָּה יְיָ, אֱלֹהֵינוּ מֶלֶךְ הָעוֹלָם, הַמּוֹצִיא לֶחֶם מִן הָאָרֶץ.

מַצָּה

Replace the bottom matzah. Everybody gets a piece of the top and middle matzot. Say the following blessing and eat, reclining. (Some first dip the matzah in charoset.)

בָּרוּךְ אַתָּה יְיָ, אֱלֹהֵינוּ מֶלֶךְ הָעוֹלָם, אֲשֶׁר קִדְּשָׁנוּ בְּמִצְוֹתָיו, וְצִוָּנוּ עַל אֲכִילַת מַצָּה.

QUESTIONS FOR MAROR

1. What is maror?
2. Why do we eat maror at the Seder?
3. Why is this picture used to depict maror?
4. Why is there a pyramid in the background?

MAROR

Everybody dips some bitter herb in charoset, says the following blessing, and eats sitting up.

Be blessed, God, our God, King of the universe, Who sanctified us with His commandments and commanded us concerning the eating of maror.

Rambam writes: "We soak figs or dates and cook them and crush them until they are soft. Then we knead them with vinegar. Afterwards we add spikenard or hyssop without grinding them" (Commentary to the Mishnah, *Pesachim* 10:3).

Dr. Susan Weingarten, an Israeli scholar who studies the history of food and Judaism and has a special focus on the history of charoset, has found more than sixty unique charoset recipes (cited by Joan Nathan, http://tabletmag.com/

מָרוֹר

Everybody dips some bitter herb in charoset, says the following blessing, and eats sitting up.

בָּרוּךְ אַתָּה יְיָ, אֱלֹהֵינוּ מֶלֶךְ הָעוֹלָם, אֲשֶׁר קִדְּשָׁנוּ בְּמִצְוֹתָיו, וְצִוָּנוּ עַל אֲכִילַת מָרוֹר.

UNDERSTANDING CHAROSET

We often think of Rambam (Maimonides) as a great scholar of Jewish law and philosophy, but in his commentary to the Mishnah he shows us that he also has a talent for cooking. The Rambam there records a recipe for the ritual food that we have at the Seder known as charoset.

concerned about *kappa* in the maror and therefore we can conclude that it is no longer the reason why we eat charoset at our Seder today.

On the other hand, according to Rabbi Elazar bar Tzadok who says that charoset is a mitzvah, how is it a mitzvah? Nowhere in the Torah does it mention charoset! We must conclude that it is a rabbinic mitzvah and that when we dip the charoset in the maror the act carries with it a great deal of symbolism.

The Babylonian Talmud (*Pesachim* 116a) offers two different possibilities concerning the symbolism behind the mitzvah of charoset and the Jerusalem Talmud offers a third reason. One explanation of the Babylonian Talmud is that the charoset reminds us of the clay that the Israelites worked with in Egypt. The Jerusalem Talmud tells us that charoset is symbolic of blood.

The Babylonian Talmud's second answer suggests that the charoset is a reminder to us of the "*tapuach* tree." (*Tapuach* in biblical Hebrew refers to a citrus tree, i.e., an *etrog*.) Rashi explains that in Egypt the enslaved men would come home from the fields exhausted and uninterested in intimacy. However, their holy wives would inspire them as they sat under the *tapuach* tree.

Why is this story so important that it be told at the Seder?

This story is a reminder of the heroism of the enslaved Israelite men and women. When we hear the word *hero* we don't necessarily think of a wife inspiring her husband, but that is the message of the charoset. The Israelites were being brutally enslaved. Slavery is as much psychological as it is physical. When people are enslaved the simple act of holding their heads up high and believing in a bright future is often the first step and the necessary step to breaking the chains of their captors. This act of the Israelites in Egypt in deciding to create more children even while they were being enslaved themselves was an act of great defiance which paved the way to redemption from Egypt.

Perhaps the charoset is a reminder to include the spiritual heroism of the Israelites in the telling of the Exodus story. With all the focus in the Torah on the greatness of Moshe, on the plagues, and on the miracles of God, perhaps there was a concern that the hidden, day-to-day heroism of the people might get shortchanged. The charoset reminds us that they were brave in their spiritual resistance and did not give up their souls to slavery. We should never forget their spiritual resistance to the Egyptian leadership.

Rabbi Yisrael Meir Lau, the former chief rabbi of Israel, survived Buchenwald as a seven-year-old child. He writes of the heroism of the imprisoned Jews enslaved by Nazis in the ghetto and then in the concentration camps. When we jewish-life-and-religion/29257/paste-test). Many of these recipes are recorded in rabbinic literature. Some are only recorded in popular folklore.

Interestingly, a charoset made out of pears and pomegranates is discussed as early as the fifteenth century by a great Ashkenazic rabbi named Rabbi Israel Isserlein (1390–1460). He was the leading Ashkenazic rabbi of the time and the author of the classic work *Terumat Hadeshen*.

Rabbi Isserlein's student, Rabbi Yosef ben Moshe, writes in his work *Leket Yosher* (page 83) that Rabbi Isserlein taught that it is a mitzvah to put into the charoset "pomegranates and all fruits mentioned in Shir Hashirim, but he was not sure why pears are put into charoset. Nevertheless one should not change the custom." And Rabbi Yosef adds that his own father had told him to put pears into charoset in order to give it the color of mortar. Rabbi Yosef suggests that Rabbi Isserlein required the charoset to be thick like mortar but not necessarily to be the color of mortar.

Despite the abundance of recipes, many of which are intricate and contain exotic fruits and spices, the great code of Jewish law known as the *Shulchan Arukh* teaches that we are *not* actually supposed to eat the charoset. The *Shulchan Arukh* (475:1) writes that we must take an olive-size portion of maror, dip it entirely in charoset, but then shake off the charoset before eating the maror so as not to nullify the bitterness of the maror. This doesn't mean that we can't eat any charoset on Seder night. It just means that we can't eat it with maror or matzah in a ritual manner.

In truth, though, there is a long tradition of not eating the charoset at all, even in a nonritual manner. The early fourteenth-century Italian work *Shibolei Haleket* writes that the custom is to put little pieces of brick and cement into the charoset in order to remind us of the mortar that our ancestors used in Egypt.

If we don't eat the charoset in a ritual manner, why do we have it at the Seder?

The Talmud in tractate *Pesachim* (116a) records two different approaches to charoset. The first is the majority, anonymous opinion of the *tanna kamma* that charoset is *not* a mitzvah, and the second is the minority opinion of Rabbi Elazar bar Tzadok that charoset *is* a mitzvah.

If according to the *tanna kamma* charoset is not even a mitzvah then why do have it at our Seder and why do we dip the maror in the charoset? The Talmud records the explanation of Rav Ami who says that we have charoset to protect against "*kappa*." It is unclear what exactly *kappa* is and what danger it poses. In any event, the *Shulchan Aruch Harav* (47:11) notes that these days we are not

GUEST VOICE: RACHEL LIEBERMAN

One of the principles of Open Orthodoxy is that we need to be open to learning Torah from many different sources. Rachel Lieberman is the program director at JOFA, the Jewish Orthodox Feminist Alliance. She shares some feminist traditions for the Seder. Whether or not you choose to incorporate them it is appropriate to think about these new traditions and to appreciate the spiritual value inherent within them.

WOMEN AT THE SEDER TABLE

At our family's Seder, we incorporate a number of nontraditional elements and customs that pay homage to women's roles in the Passover story. The four customs I will discuss are: welcoming Miriam the Prophetess along with Elijah the Prophet with songs and dances, placing a Miriam's Cup on the Seder table, decorating the table with mirrors, and adding an orange to the Seder plate.

We recognize Miriam the Prophetess along with Elijah the Prophet. After the Israelites crossed the Red Sea, the Torah cites Miriam as a prophetess: "And Miriam the prophetess, the sister of Aharon, took a timbrel in her hand; and all the women went out after her with timbrels and with dances" (Shemot 15:20). Rashi (ad loc.) gives two explanations for why Miriam was called a prophetess. The first is that before Moshe was born, she prophesied that her mother would give birth to a son who would redeem the Israelites. The second has to do with the fact that Miriam and the women brought timbrels out of Egypt with them. This suggests their foreknowledge that God would perform miracles for the Israelites and would redeem them from Egypt – thus creating a need for the timbrels.

We also place a "Miriam's Cup" filled with water on the Seder table, next to the "Elijah's Cup" filled with wine. Miriam's legacy is linked to water. Rashi explains that the well that followed the Israelites in the desert for forty years was due to the merit of Miriam. It was only upon her death that the well dried up (Rashi to Bamidbar 20:2). The Ikar Siftei Chakhamim (ad loc.) explains that Miriam merited this well because she watched over Moshe when he was a baby, after he was cast off in a basket in the Nile, and waited to see what would happen to him. Miriam's name, which means "bitter sea," refers to the well that hydrated the Israelites throughout their forty years in the desert and to her song with the women at the sea. It is appropriate to recognize this contribution throughout the Seder. The Miriam's Cup on the Seder table allows us to remember Miriam as it prompts us to discuss her contribution to the Exodus story.

When we open the door for Elijah, after singing "Eliyahu Hanavi" and think of resistance to the Nazis we often make the mistake of focusing on who took up arms and fired shots against the Nazis. Rabbi Lau discusses another type of resistance that is no less brave. This was the resistance of the men and women who strove for spirituality in the midst of their darkness.

Rabbi Lau relates that as a five-year-old boy, he and his mother were hiding in an attic in the ghetto while the Nazis were looking for them. His mother had foreseen this, and had baked her son's favorite honey cookies to distract him. Rabbi Lau writes that the taste of those cookies have remained with him throughout his life. "The memory of them is my consolation in trying situations; they are the drop of honey with which I sweeten bitter days" (*Out of the Depths: The Story of a Child of Buchenwald Who Returned Home At Last* [New York: Sterling, 2011], 14). When we see our sweet charoset at our Seder let us think about those honey cookies. Let us think about the quiet bravery and spirituality of Rabbi Lau's mother, Rabbanit Chaya Lau.

As a mere child in Buchenwald, Rabbi Lau was isolated from his older brother Naphtali and placed in a different part of the camp. Rabbi Lau relates that beginning months before Pesach, Naphtali and his friends would trade three potatoes for the daily bread ration and then hide the potatoes until Pesach so that they would not have to eat bread. Rabbi Lau tells of how the Jews celebrated Seder night in Buchenwald:

> Over and over they sang the holiday song *Karev Yom* from memory: "The day is approaching that will be neither day nor night / He has placed guards over your city all day and all night / The darkness of the night will be lit like the light of day." They had no Haggadah and no matzah. Still, among them there was no leavened food to be seen – only potatoes. (*Out of the Depths*, 59)

The Jews of Buchenwald might not have had matzah or a Haggadah, but with their heroic spirituality in the face of evil they had charoset.

As we mentioned, the fruit in the charoset comes from Shir Hashirim, the great biblical love song of God and the Jewish people. In Buchenwald, as the holy prisoners practiced their heroic spirituality they were making their own charoset, and in doing so they were singing their own love song to God. In the midst of the darkest days of Buchenwald they were telling Hashem that they loved Him.

origins. The popularity of this tradition shows the longing in many families for the inclusion of women in our Passover narratives, and in the communal leadership of the broader Jewish community. Now that women rabbis are prevalent in liberal Jewish communities, and Maharats and other female communal leaders are taking their places in the Orthodox community, I believe that it is even more important for us to add an orange to our Seder plates. It is essential for us to continue to emphasize – and to normalize – the presence and contributions of women in the rabbinate.

The inclusion of women is still new and groundbreaking, and we cannot take those strides for granted. The orange reminds us to continue to advocate for the equality of women in all aspects of communal and ritual leadership. And now that I've learned more about the origin of Heschel's tradition, I would like to add a new tradition to our family's Seder: spitting out the seeds. The inclusion of women in leadership and ritual is not a smooth process. It is coupled with challenges and with adversity. By eating the orange and spitting out the seeds, we should all remember that the inclusion of women is just the first step. The next step is the rooting out of institutionalized sexism, sexual harassment, and the erasure of women in our texts, in our God language, in all levels of our communities. We must work to make the community a more inclusive and affirming place for all involved.

The Passover Seder poses a unique opportunity for individuals and families to take greater control over their ritual life. The Seder is a ritual that we observe at home, away from rabbinic authorities and from community leaders. In our homes, at our Seders, we have the opportunity to be flexible, to personalize the Seder according to the needs of our family and our guests. This is a great opportunity to customize the experience and to experiment with new traditions. I encourage you to work with your family and Seder guests to explore what innovations, new rituals, and texts might be appropriate for your Seder. Passover is also about telling ancient stories that resonate with us today. Make sure that this year's Seder reflects your modern values of equity and inclusion. In order to be redeemed from slavery, a moment in time when the Jewish people were so broken, we needed to utilize the talents and the leadership of all members of the community – men and women alike. Hopefully that sentiment will continue to resonate with us throughout the ages.

reciting the paragraph "Pour Out Your Wrath," we sing Debbie Friedman's "Miriam's Song," dancing with timbrels:

> And Miriam the prophet took her timbrel in her hand,
> And all the women followed her just as she had planned,
> And Miriam raised her voice in song –
> She sang with praise and might
> We've just lived through a miracle: We're going to dance tonight!

Another tradition that we have incorporated in our Seder involves the adornment of the table with mirrors. Mirrors are yet an additional reminder of women's role in the survival of the Israelites in Egypt. Rashi explains that due to the backbreaking work of slavery, many of the Jewish men were too exhausted to have marital relations with their wives and perpetuate the Jewish people. The women knew that it was essential to continue the Jewish people and used the copper mirrors to beautify themselves and to entice their husbands. This helped their husbands to desire them, thus perpetuating the Jewish people (Rashi to Shemot 38:8).

Perhaps the most common feminist tradition that we incorporate is that of placing an orange on the Seder plate, or on the Seder table. The story goes that a prominent rabbi was asked, "When will Judaism accept women as rabbis," to which he replied, incredulously, "A woman belongs on the *bimah* like an orange belongs on the Seder plate." Susannah Heschel, a prominent Jewish feminist who is credited with starting this tradition, contests this origin story and explains that she started the custom of placing an orange on the Seder table as an affirmation and recognition of gay and lesbian Jews and their contributions to the Jewish community. At Heschel's Seder table, guests would eat a segment of the orange and spit out the seeds as a sign of spitting out homophobia and the challenges to marginalized Jews. Heschel decries what she calls a misappropriation of her story, upset that the tradition she created was attributed to a man and that the reference to gay and lesbian Jews was erased. She also argues that the custom has been devalued now that women rabbis are ubiquitous in the liberal denominations and it is no longer a courageous act to welcome them (Susannah Heschel, "An Orange on Plate for Women – and Spit Out Seeds of Hate," *Jewish Daily Forward*, March 22, 2013).

Given Heschel's account of her reasons for placing the orange on the Seder table, it is ironic to see this apparent appropriation of a feminist custom. However I would argue that the widespread adoption of this custom transcends its

QUESTIONS FOR KOREKH

1. What does Korekh refer to?
2. Why do we eat it?
3. Who eats it?
4. When do we eat it?

KOREKH

Using the bottom matzah from the tray, everybody makes a maror sandwich, says the following passages, and eats reclining.

IN REMEMBRANCE of the Temple, according to Hillel the Elder. This is what Hillel did when the Temple was standing: he would wrap together the portion of the Passover offering, the matzah, and the maror and eat them together, in order to do what is said (Bamidbar 9:11): "On matzot and bitter herbs they shall eat it."

כּוֹרֵךְ

Using the bottom matzah from the tray, everybody makes a maror sandwich, says the following passages, and eats reclining.

זֵכֶר לְמִקְדָּשׁ כְּהִלֵּל. כֵּן עָשָׂה הִלֵּל בִּזְמַן שֶׁבֵּית הַמִּקְדָּשׁ הָיָה קַיָּם: הָיָה כּוֹרֵךְ פֶּסַח מַצָּה וּמָרוֹר וְאוֹכֵל בְּיַחַד, לְקַיֵּם מַה שֶּׁנֶּאֱמַר: עַל־מַצּוֹת וּמְרֹרִים יֹאכְלֻהוּ.

QUESTIONS FOR SHULCHAN OREKH

1. What is Shulchan Orekh?
2. Why do we serve hard-boiled eggs at the Seder?
3. Why do we have saltwater on the table?
4. Do we invite guests to join us at the Seder? Why?

SHULCHAN OREKH

Remove the Seder tray from the table and eat the festival meal.

שֻׁלְחָן עוֹרֵךְ

Remove the Seder tray from the table and eat the festival meal.

QUESTIONS FOR TZAFUN

1. What happens in the part of the Seder called Tzafun?
2. Who has the *afikoman*?
3. How does the leader of the Seder get the *afikoman* back?
4. What is eaten after the *afikoman*?

TZAFUN

Put the tray back on the table, give everybody a piece of matzah from the large section put away for the afikoman, say the following passage, and eat reclining.

This piece of matzah is eaten in remembrance of the Pesach offering.

What's strange is the answer given to this son. The Haggadah answers: *Ein maftirin achar hapesach afikoman,* which is usually translated as "One should not eat any dessert [*afikoman*] after eating the Paschal Lamb." The response to the Wise Son is perplexing – he asked a very general question and the Haggadah responded with the most specific answer possible.

In order to really understand the Haggadah's answer we have to understand

צָפוּן

Put the tray back on the table, give everybody a piece of matzah from the large section put away for the afikoman, say the following passage, and eat reclining.

This piece of matzah is eaten in remembrance of the Pesach offering.

THE MEANING OF THE *AFIKOMAN*

The Wise Son – what does he say? "What are these testimonies, laws and rulings that Hashem our God has commanded you?"

The Wise Son asks a straightforward question. In fact, it's a good question. The son wants to know the laws and teachings of the Torah.

QUESTIONS FOR BAREKH

1. What does the word *barekh* mean?
2. The last words in the Birkat Hamazon (Grace after Meals) are on the top of the picture. They are a prayer that God give strength to His people and bless them with peace. Why do we need to say this?
3. The words on the bottom of the picture ask God for a day that is all good. It is said on the holidays of Pesach, Shavuot, and Sukkot. What is meant by "all good"?
4. Why did the artist choose a woman for this picture and why is she surrounded by nature?

---

different dinner parties and eat dessert and drink till they were drunk (Saul Lieberman, *Hayerushalmi Kifshuto*, 521).

This was the *epikomaizon* – a wild, communal party that followed dinner, at which every excess was permitted. There was tons of food, wine, and mingling. And the custom was not to go to just one *epikomaizon*, but to attend many *epikomaiza* in one evening. People would go from party to party to party.

This explains the Haggadah's response to the Wise Son. The son had asked about the laws of Judaism and the Haggadah responded: *Ein maftirin achar hapesach afikoman*, after eating the holy Paschal Lamb, don't finish off your evening by attending an *epikomaizon* party. Instead, say our rabbis (and here

what the word *afikoman* literally means. The Talmud itself (*Pesachim* 119b) also debates the etymology of this word. According to Rav, the word *afikoman* means "*shelo ye'akru mi'chavurah l'chavurah*" (one should not wander from group to group). According to Shmuel, *afikoman* means "*ordilaiei li, v'guzlaiei l'Abba*" (mushrooms for me and pigeons for Abba).

Professor Saul Lieberman explains that the word *afikoman* is really the Greek word *epikoman,* or *epikomaizon*. The *epikomaizon* was an event that would traditionally follow a meal in Hellenistic society. Today when we finish eating we go home and go to sleep. In ancient Greece the practice was to follow each meal with an *epikomaizon,* at which the diners would wander around to

BAREKH

Fill the third cup.

WHEN THE LORD returned the captives of Zion, we were like people in a dream. Then was our mouth filled with laughter, and our tongue with exultation: then said they among the nations, The Lord has done great things for them. The Lord has done great things for us; so we rejoiced! Bring back our captives, O Lord, as the streams in the south. They that sow in tears shall reap in joy. Though he goes on his way weeping, bearing the store of seed, he shall come back with joy, bearing his sheaves. (Tehillim 126)

If at least three males past Bar Mitzvah are present, the person conducting the Seder or a male appointed by him lifts his cup of wine and leads the saying of Grace after Meals.

Leader: My masters, let us bless.

Others: Let God's Name be blessed now and forever.

Leader: Let God's Name be blessed now and forever. By permission of (the host and of) our masters and my teachers, let us bless Him (*or, if ten adults, males over Bar Mitzvah age are present,* "our God") of Whose fare we have eaten.

Others: Blessed be He (*or, if ten adult males are present,* "our God") of Whose fare we have eaten and on Whose bounty we live.

Leader: Blessed be He (*or, if ten adult males are present,* "our God") of Whose fare we have eaten and on Whose bounty we live.

Others and Leader: Blessed is He and blessed is His Name.

All say:

BE BLESSED, God, our God, King of the universe, Who feeds the entire world of His bounty – with grace, with loving kindness, mercifully. He gives food to all flesh, for His loving kindness is eternal. And because of his great goodness we have never lacked food, and may we never lack it. For His great Name's sake – for He is a God Who feeds and provides for all, and is good to all, and prepares food for all His creatures that He has created. Be blessed, God, Who feeds all.

בָּרֵךְ

Fill the third cup.

שִׁיר הַמַּעֲלוֹת, בְּשׁוּב יְיָ אֶת שִׁיבַת צִיּוֹן הָיִינוּ כְּחֹלְמִים. אָז יִמָּלֵא שְׂחוֹק פִּינוּ וּלְשׁוֹנֵנוּ רִנָּה, אָז יֹאמְרוּ בַגּוֹיִם הִגְדִּיל יְיָ לַעֲשׂוֹת עִם אֵלֶּה. הִגְדִּיל יְיָ לַעֲשׂוֹת עִמָּנוּ הָיִינוּ שְׂמֵחִים. שׁוּבָה יְיָ אֶת שְׁבִיתֵנוּ כַּאֲפִיקִים בַּנֶּגֶב. הַזֹּרְעִים בְּדִמְעָה בְּרִנָּה יִקְצֹרוּ. הָלוֹךְ יֵלֵךְ וּבָכֹה נֹשֵׂא מֶשֶׁךְ הַזָּרַע, בֹּא יָבֹא בְרִנָּה נֹשֵׂא אֲלֻמֹּתָיו.

If at least three males past Bar Mitzvah are present, the person conducting the Seder or a male appointed by him lifts his cup of wine and leads the saying of Grace after Meals.

Leader רַבּוֹתַי נְבָרֵךְ!

Others יְהִי שֵׁם יְיָ מְבֹרָךְ מֵעַתָּה וְעַד עוֹלָם.

Leader יְהִי שֵׁם יְיָ מְבֹרָךְ מֵעַתָּה וְעַד עוֹלָם. בִּרְשׁוּת מָרָנָן וְרַבָּנָן וְרַבּוֹתַי, נְבָרֵךְ (אֱלֹהֵינוּ) שֶׁאָכַלְנוּ מִשֶּׁלּוֹ.

Others בָּרוּךְ (אֱלֹהֵינוּ) שֶׁאָכַלְנוּ מִשֶּׁלּוֹ וּבְטוּבוֹ חָיִינוּ.

Leader בָּרוּךְ (אֱלֹהֵינוּ) שֶׁאָכַלְנוּ מִשֶּׁלּוֹ וּבְטוּבוֹ חָיִינוּ.

Others and Leader בָּרוּךְ הוּא וּבָרוּךְ שְׁמוֹ.

All say:

בָּרוּךְ אַתָּה יְיָ, אֱלֹהֵינוּ מֶלֶךְ הָעוֹלָם, הַזָּן אֶת הָעוֹלָם כֻּלּוֹ בְּטוּבוֹ בְּחֵן בְּחֶסֶד וּבְרַחֲמִים, הוּא נוֹתֵן לֶחֶם לְכָל בָּשָׂר כִּי לְעוֹלָם חַסְדּוֹ. וּבְטוּבוֹ הַגָּדוֹל תָּמִיד לֹא חָסַר לָנוּ, וְאַל יֶחְסַר לָנוּ מָזוֹן לְעוֹלָם וָעֶד. בַּעֲבוּר שְׁמוֹ הַגָּדוֹל, כִּי הוּא אֵל זָן וּמְפַרְנֵס לַכֹּל וּמֵטִיב לַכֹּל, וּמֵכִין מָזוֹן לְכָל בְּרִיּוֹתָיו אֲשֶׁר בָּרָא. בָּרוּךְ אַתָּה יְיָ, הַזָּן אֶת הַכֹּל.

---

we quote the version of the text that appears in the Tosefta for tractate *Pesachim* [10:8], which gives a more complete account of the Wise Son's question), "*Chayav adam laasok b'hilkhot haPesach kol halailah*" (One is obligated to be involved in studying the laws of Pesach for the whole evening).

/cont. p. 123

WE THANK You, God, our God, for allotting to our ancestors a desirable, goodly and ample land, and for bringing us out of the land of Egypt, for emancipating us from a land of slavery, for sealing Your covenant in our flesh, for teaching us Your Torah, for making Your statutes known to us, for bestowing life, grace, loving kindness upon us, and for feeding us and supplying us with food continually, every day, at all times, and at every hour.

FOR ALL THIS, God, our God, we thank You and bless You. May Your Name be blessed by every living thing always, forever. As it is written (Devarim 8:10): "When you have eaten your fill, you shall bless God, your God, for the goodly land He has given you." Be blessed, God, for the land and for the food.

HAVE MERCY, God, our God, on Israel your people, on Jerusalem Your city, on Zion the dwelling place of your glory, on the kingdom of the House of David Your anointed one, and on the great and holy house that is called by Your name. Our God, our Father, our Shepherd – pasture us, feed us, provide for us, and sustain us, and give us relief – and give us speedy relief, God, our God, from all our troubles. Do not, we beg You, God, our God, cause us to become dependent on the handouts of mortals or on their loans, but only on Your hand – full, open, bountiful and generous – so that we shall never be ashamed or be put to shame.

If Passover falls on Shabbat, say the following passage.

Let it be Your will, God, our God, that we shall be strengthened by performing Your commandments – especially by observing this seventh day, this great and holy Sabbath, for this day is great and holy before You, to pause and rest on it lovingly as it was Your pleasure to command. And let it be your will, God, our God, that there shall be no cause for trouble, sorrow, or sighing on our day of rest. And show us, God, our God, Zion Your city comforted and Jerusalem Your holy city rebuilt, for You are the Giver of salvation and the Giver of consolation.

If an *epikomaizon* party is forbidden on Pesach, it should also be forbidden the whole year. Why does the Haggadah teach us that these types of parties are specifically forbidden on Pesach?

The reason for singling out Pesach is that Pesach symbolizes the birth of our nation. Pesach is the holiday in which we celebrate our freedom and our

נוֹדֶה לְּךָ יְיָ אֱלֹהֵינוּ עַל שֶׁהִנְחַלְתָּ לַאֲבוֹתֵינוּ, אֶרֶץ חֶמְדָּה טוֹבָה וּרְחָבָה, וְעַל שֶׁהוֹצֵאתָנוּ יְיָ אֱלֹהֵינוּ מֵאֶרֶץ מִצְרַיִם, וּפְדִיתָנוּ מִבֵּית עֲבָדִים, וְעַל בְּרִיתְךָ שֶׁחָתַמְתָּ בִּבְשָׂרֵנוּ, וְעַל תּוֹרָתְךָ שֶׁלִּמַּדְתָּנוּ, וְעַל חֻקֶּיךָ שֶׁהוֹדַעְתָּנוּ, וְעַל חַיִּים חֵן וָחֶסֶד שֶׁחוֹנַנְתָּנוּ, וְעַל אֲכִילַת מָזוֹן שָׁאַתָּה זָן וּמְפַרְנֵס אוֹתָנוּ תָּמִיד, בְּכָל יוֹם וּבְכָל עֵת וּבְכָל שָׁעָה.

וְעַל הַכֹּל יְיָ אֱלֹהֵינוּ אֲנַחְנוּ מוֹדִים לָךְ, וּמְבָרְכִים אוֹתָךְ, יִתְבָּרַךְ שִׁמְךָ בְּפִי כָּל חַי תָּמִיד לְעוֹלָם וָעֶד. כַּכָּתוּב, וְאָכַלְתָּ וְשָׂבָעְתָּ, וּבֵרַכְתָּ אֶת יְיָ אֱלֹהֶיךָ עַל הָאָרֶץ הַטֹּבָה אֲשֶׁר נָתַן לָךְ. בָּרוּךְ אַתָּה יְיָ, עַל הָאָרֶץ וְעַל הַמָּזוֹן.

רַחֵם נָא יְיָ אֱלֹהֵינוּ, עַל יִשְׂרָאֵל עַמֶּךָ, וְעַל יְרוּשָׁלַיִם עִירֶךָ, וְעַל צִיּוֹן מִשְׁכַּן כְּבוֹדֶךָ, וְעַל מַלְכוּת בֵּית דָּוִד מְשִׁיחֶךָ, וְעַל הַבַּיִת הַגָּדוֹל וְהַקָּדוֹשׁ שֶׁנִּקְרָא שִׁמְךָ עָלָיו. אֱלֹהֵינוּ, אָבִינוּ, רְעֵנוּ, זוּנֵנוּ, פַּרְנְסֵנוּ, וְכַלְכְּלֵנוּ, וְהַרְוִיחֵנוּ, וְהַרְוַח לָנוּ יְיָ אֱלֹהֵינוּ מְהֵרָה מִכָּל צָרוֹתֵינוּ. וְנָא, אַל תַּצְרִיכֵנוּ יְיָ אֱלֹהֵינוּ, לֹא לִידֵי מַתְּנַת בָּשָׂר וָדָם, וְלֹא לִידֵי הַלְוָאָתָם. כִּי אִם לְיָדְךָ הַמְּלֵאָה, הַפְּתוּחָה, הַקְּדוֹשָׁה וְהָרְחָבָה, שֶׁלֹּא נֵבוֹשׁ וְלֹא נִכָּלֵם לְעוֹלָם וָעֶד.

If Passover falls on Shabbat, say the following passage.

רְצֵה וְהַחֲלִיצֵנוּ יְיָ אֱלֹהֵינוּ בְּמִצְוֹתֶיךָ וּבְמִצְוַת יוֹם הַשְּׁבִיעִי הַשַּׁבָּת הַגָּדוֹל וְהַקָּדוֹשׁ הַזֶּה. כִּי יוֹם זֶה גָּדוֹל וְקָדוֹשׁ הוּא לְפָנֶיךָ, לִשְׁבָּת בּוֹ וְלָנוּחַ בּוֹ בְּאַהֲבָה כְּמִצְוַת רְצוֹנֶךָ. וּבִרְצוֹנְךָ הָנִיחַ לָנוּ יְיָ אֱלֹהֵינוּ, שֶׁלֹּא תְהֵא צָרָה וְיָגוֹן וַאֲנָחָה בְּיוֹם מְנוּחָתֵנוּ. וְהַרְאֵנוּ יְיָ אֱלֹהֵינוּ בְּנֶחָמַת צִיּוֹן עִירֶךָ, וּבְבִנְיַן יְרוּשָׁלַיִם עִיר קָדְשֶׁךָ, כִּי אַתָּה הוּא בַּעַל הַיְשׁוּעוֹת וּבַעַל הַנֶּחָמוֹת.

In other words, the answer to the Wise Son is: You want to know what the laws of Judaism are? Well, the answer is don't celebrate the holiday of Pesach by going to these *epikomaizon* parties, instead focus on studying the word of God and the laws of the Torah all evening long.

OUR GOD and God of our fathers: let the remembrance and mindfulness of us, the remembrance of our ancestors, the remembrance of Jerusalem Your holy city, and the remembrance of Your entire people the House of Israel come to You, reach You, be seen by You, be favored by You, be heard by You, minded by You and remembered by You to our relief, to our benefit, for grace, for loving kindness and for mercy, for life and for peace, on this Matzot Festival Day. On this day, God, our God, remember us for good, be mindful of us on it for blessing, and preserve us on it for a good life. And be so merciful as to grace us with the promise of salvation and mercy, and have mercy on us and save us. For to You our eyes are turned, for You are a gracious and merciful God King.

AND REBUILD Jerusalem the holy city speedily in our days. Be blessed, God, Rebuilder – in His mercy – of Jerusalem. Amen.

BE BLESSED, God, our God, King of the universe, the God Who is our Father, our King, our Mighty One, our Creator, our Redeemer, our Maker, our Holy One, the Holy One of Yaakov, our Shepherd – Israel's Shepherd – the King Who is good and does good to all, Who every day did good, does good, will do good to all of us; who bestowed, bestows and will bestow favors on us forever: grace, loving kindness, mercy and relief, succor and prosperity, blessing and salvation, consolation, maintenance and sustenance, and life, and peace, and all that is good; and may He never let us lack for any good thing.

THE MERCIFUL – forever may He reign over us. The Merciful – may He be blessed in Heaven and on earth. The Merciful – may He be praised for all generation, and may He glory in us forever and for all time, and take pride in us forever and for all eternity. The Merciful – may He grant us honorable sustenance. The Merciful – may He break the yoke from our neck and may He lead us proud and erect back to our land. The Merciful – may He send ample blessing on this house and on this table at which we have eaten. The Merciful – may He send us the prophet Eliyahu so fondly remembered, to bring us good tidings, salvations, and consolations.

Haggadah to act differently. We should not respond to the birth of our nation with an extra-long party, but with an extra-long study session. We should seize

אֱלֹהֵינוּ וֵאלֹהֵי אֲבוֹתֵינוּ, יַעֲלֶה וְיָבֹא וְיַגִּיעַ, וְיֵרָאֶה, וְיֵרָצֶה, וְיִשָּׁמַע, וְיִפָּקֵד, וְיִזָּכֵר זִכְרוֹנֵנוּ וּפִקְדוֹנֵנוּ, וְזִכְרוֹן אֲבוֹתֵינוּ, וְזִכְרוֹן מָשִׁיחַ בֶּן דָּוִד עַבְדֶּךָ, וְזִכְרוֹן יְרוּשָׁלַיִם עִיר קָדְשֶׁךָ, וְזִכְרוֹן כָּל עַמְּךָ בֵּית יִשְׂרָאֵל לְפָנֶיךָ, לִפְלֵיטָה לְטוֹבָה לְחֵן וּלְחֶסֶד וּלְרַחֲמִים, לְחַיִּים וּלְשָׁלוֹם בְּיוֹם חַג הַמַּצּוֹת הַזֶּה. זָכְרֵנוּ יְיָ אֱלֹהֵינוּ בּוֹ לְטוֹבָה, וּפָקְדֵנוּ בוֹ לִבְרָכָה, וְהוֹשִׁיעֵנוּ בוֹ לְחַיִּים. וּבִדְבַר יְשׁוּעָה וְרַחֲמִים, חוּס וְחָנֵּנוּ, וְרַחֵם עָלֵינוּ וְהוֹשִׁיעֵנוּ, כִּי אֵלֶיךָ עֵינֵינוּ, כִּי אֵל מֶלֶךְ חַנּוּן וְרַחוּם אָתָּה.

וּבְנֵה יְרוּשָׁלַיִם עִיר הַקֹּדֶשׁ בִּמְהֵרָה בְיָמֵינוּ. בָּרוּךְ אַתָּה יְיָ, בּוֹנֵה בְרַחֲמָיו יְרוּשָׁלָיִם. אָמֵן.

בָּרוּךְ אַתָּה יְיָ אֱלֹהֵינוּ מֶלֶךְ הָעוֹלָם, הָאֵל אָבִינוּ, מַלְכֵּנוּ, אַדִּירֵנוּ בּוֹרְאֵנוּ, גּוֹאֲלֵנוּ, יוֹצְרֵנוּ, קְדוֹשֵׁנוּ קְדוֹשׁ יַעֲקֹב, רוֹעֵנוּ רוֹעֵה יִשְׂרָאֵל. הַמֶּלֶךְ הַטּוֹב, וְהַמֵּטִיב לַכֹּל, שֶׁבְּכָל יוֹם וָיוֹם הוּא הֵטִיב, הוּא מֵטִיב, הוּא יֵיטִיב לָנוּ. הוּא גְמָלָנוּ, הוּא גוֹמְלֵנוּ, הוּא יִגְמְלֵנוּ לָעַד, לְחֵן וּלְחֶסֶד וּלְרַחֲמִים וּלְרֶוַח הַצָּלָה וְהַצְלָחָה בְּרָכָה וִישׁוּעָה, נֶחָמָה, פַּרְנָסָה וְכַלְכָּלָה, וְרַחֲמִים, וְחַיִּים וְשָׁלוֹם, וְכָל טוֹב, וּמִכָּל טוּב לְעוֹלָם אַל יְחַסְּרֵנוּ.

הָרַחֲמָן, הוּא יִמְלוֹךְ עָלֵינוּ לְעוֹלָם וָעֶד. הָרַחֲמָן, הוּא יִתְבָּרַךְ בַּשָּׁמַיִם וּבָאָרֶץ. הָרַחֲמָן, הוּא יִשְׁתַּבַּח לְדוֹר דּוֹרִים, וְיִתְפָּאַר בָּנוּ לָעַד וּלְנֵצַח נְצָחִים, וְיִתְהַדַּר בָּנוּ לָעַד וּלְעוֹלְמֵי עוֹלָמִים. הָרַחֲמָן, הוּא יְפַרְנְסֵנוּ בְּכָבוֹד. הָרַחֲמָן, הוּא יִשְׁבּוֹר עֻלֵּנוּ מֵעַל צַוָּארֵנוּ וְהוּא יוֹלִיכֵנוּ קוֹמְמִיּוּת לְאַרְצֵנוּ. הָרַחֲמָן, הוּא יִשְׁלַח לָנוּ בְּרָכָה מְרֻבָּה בַּבַּיִת הַזֶּה, וְעַל שֻׁלְחָן זֶה שֶׁאָכַלְנוּ עָלָיו. הָרַחֲמָן, הוּא יִשְׁלַח לָנוּ אֶת אֵלִיָּהוּ הַנָּבִיא זָכוּר לַטּוֹב, וִיבַשֶּׂר לָנוּ בְּשׂוֹרוֹת טוֹבוֹת יְשׁוּעוֹת וְנֶחָמוֹת.

---

independence – it's our July Fourth. Other nations celebrate their freedom with huge, extravagant, and wild parties. We, on the other hand, are told by the

Children at their parents' table say:

The Merciful – may He bless my father my teacher, and my mother my teacher – them and their household and their children and all that is theirs,

Adults at their own table say the appropriate part/s of the following:

The Merciful – may He bless me (and my wife/husband, and my progeny, and all that is mine);

Guests say:

The Merciful – may He bless the master of this house and his wife the mistress of this house, them and their children and all that is theirs.

And all others seated at this table, us and all that is ours. Just as our fathers Avraham, Yitzchak, and Yaakov were blessed with all, of all, all, so may He bless us, all of us together, with a perfect blessing; and let us say: Amen.

ON HIGH may there be invoked for them and for us such merit as will be a safeguard of peace, and so that we may carry a blessing from God and justice from our Saving-God, and so that we may "win favor and approbation from God and from people." (Mishlei 3:4)

Say the following only on Shabbat.

The Merciful – may He grant us the Day-That-Is-All-Sabbath and the repose of the Life-That-Is-to-Be.

On all days continue as follows.

The Merciful – may He bequeath to us a Day-That-Is-All-Good. The Merciful – may He judge us worthy of the messianic era and the life of the World-That-Is-to-Be. "He Who gives His king great victories, Who deals graciously with His anointed one – with David and his descendants forever." (2 Shmuel 22:51) "He who keeps His high spheres in harmony" (Iyov 25:2) – may He grant harmony to us and to all Israel. Now say: Amen.

We should respond to the birth of our nation with study and spiritual contemplation, not physical celebrations of our happiness.

Children at their parents' table say:

הָרַחֲמָן, הוּא יְבָרֵךְ אֶת אָבִי מוֹרִי בַּעַל הַבַּיִת הַזֶּה, וְאֶת אִמִּי מוֹרָתִי בַּעֲלַת הַבַּיִת הַזֶּה,

Adults at their own table say the appropriate part/s of the following:

הָרַחֲמָן, הוּא יְבָרֵךְ אוֹתִי (וְאֶת אִשְׁתִּי/בַּעֲלִי, וְאֶת זַרְעִי, וְאֶת כָּל אֲשֶׁר לִי),

Guests say:

הָרַחֲמָן, הוּא יְבָרֵךְ אֶת בַּעַל הַבַּיִת הַזֶּה, וְאֶת אִשְׁתּוֹ בַּעֲלַת הַבַּיִת הַזֶּה.

אוֹתָם וְאֶת בֵּיתָם וְאֶת זַרְעָם וְאֶת כָּל אֲשֶׁר לָהֶם, אוֹתָנוּ וְאֶת כָּל אֲשֶׁר לָנוּ, כְּמוֹ שֶׁנִּתְבָּרְכוּ אֲבוֹתֵינוּ, אַבְרָהָם יִצְחָק וְיַעֲקֹב: בַּכֹּל, מִכֹּל, כֹּל. כֵּן יְבָרֵךְ אוֹתָנוּ כֻּלָּנוּ יַחַד, בִּבְרָכָה שְׁלֵמָה, וְנֹאמַר אָמֵן.

בַּמָּרוֹם יְלַמְּדוּ עֲלֵיהֶם וְעָלֵינוּ זְכוּת, שֶׁתְּהֵא לְמִשְׁמֶרֶת שָׁלוֹם, וְנִשָּׂא בְרָכָה מֵאֵת יְיָ וּצְדָקָה מֵאֱלֹהֵי יִשְׁעֵנוּ, וְנִמְצָא חֵן וְשֵׂכֶל טוֹב בְּעֵינֵי אֱלֹהִים וְאָדָם.

Say the following only on Shabbat.

הָרַחֲמָן, הוּא יַנְחִילֵנוּ יוֹם שֶׁכֻּלּוֹ שַׁבָּת וּמְנוּחָה לְחַיֵּי הָעוֹלָמִים.

On all days continue as follows.

הָרַחֲמָן, הוּא יַנְחִילֵנוּ יוֹם שֶׁכֻּלּוֹ טוֹב. הָרַחֲמָן, הוּא יְזַכֵּנוּ לִימוֹת הַמָּשִׁיחַ וּלְחַיֵּי הָעוֹלָם הַבָּא. מִגְדּוֹל יְשׁוּעוֹת מַלְכּוֹ, וְעֹשֶׂה חֶסֶד לִמְשִׁיחוֹ לְדָוִד וּלְזַרְעוֹ עַד עוֹלָם. עֹשֶׂה שָׁלוֹם בִּמְרוֹמָיו, הוּא יַעֲשֶׂה שָׁלוֹם, עָלֵינוּ וְעַל כָּל יִשְׂרָאֵל, וְאִמְרוּ אָמֵן.

---

the moment to study God's word all night and understand what it means to be free, and what the responsibilities of being an independent nation are.

"**FEAR** God, you, His holy ones; for those who fear Him want for nothing." (Tehillim 34:10) "Lions have been reduced to starvation; those who seek God lack no good thing." (Tehillim 34:11) "Give thanks to God, for He is good; for His loving kindness endures forever." (Tehillim 118:1) "You give openhandedly, filling the need of every living creature." (Tehillim 145:16) "Blessed is he who trusts in God and rests his confidence in God." (Yirmiyahu 17:7) "I was a lad and now am old, and never have I seen a righteous person forsaken, his children begging bread." (Tehillim 37:35) "May God grant His people strength, may God bless His people with well-being." (Tehillim 29:11)

Say the following blessing and drink the third cup, reclining.

Behold, I am prepared and ready to recite Kiddush over wine, and to fulfill the commandment of the third of the four cups, for the sake of the unity of the Holy One, blessed is He, and His Presence, through Him Who is hidden and inscrutable, in the name of all Israel.

BE BLESSED, GOD, OUR GOD, KING OF THE UNIVERSE, CREATOR OF THE FRUIT OF THE VINE.

Fill Eliyahu's cup, open the front door, and say:

POUR OUT Your wrath on the nations that know You not and on the kingdoms that do not invoke Your Name. For they have devoured Yaakov and laid waste his homestead. (Tehillim 79:6–7) Pour out Your fury on them and let Your blazing anger overtake them. (Tehillim 69:25) Pursue them in anger and exterminate them from under God's skies. (Eikhah 3:66)

Close the door. Fill the fourth cup.

---

being persecuted and attacked for our message and our very existence. It is not addressed, God forbid, at righteous Gentiles or those who had benign tolerance for the Jewish people in their midst. But it does call the Jews together to stand up for their own dignity, to be unashamed at opening the door and declaring to the world that the Jewish people is here to stay. The last words, "destroy them from under the heavens of God," focuses the reader on casting out the bad, to enable the good – the Jews – to praise God and bring God's

יְראוּ אֶת יְיָ קְדֹשָׁיו, כִּי אֵין מַחְסוֹר לִירֵאָיו. כְּפִירִים רָשׁוּ וְרָעֵבוּ, וְדוֹרְשֵׁי יְיָ לֹא יַחְסְרוּ כָל טוֹב. הוֹדוּ לַייָ כִּי טוֹב, כִּי לְעוֹלָם חַסְדּוֹ. פּוֹתֵחַ אֶת יָדֶךָ, וּמַשְׂבִּיעַ לְכָל חַי רָצוֹן. בָּרוּךְ הַגֶּבֶר אֲשֶׁר יִבְטַח בַּייָ, וְהָיָה יְיָ מִבְטַחוֹ. נַעַר הָיִיתִי גַּם זָקַנְתִּי וְלֹא רָאִיתִי צַדִּיק נֶעֱזָב, וְזַרְעוֹ מְבַקֶּשׁ לָחֶם. יְיָ עֹז לְעַמּוֹ יִתֵּן, יְיָ יְבָרֵךְ אֶת עַמּוֹ בַשָּׁלוֹם.

Say the following blessing and drink the third cup, reclining.

הִנְנִי מוּכָן וּמְזֻמָּן לְקַיֵּם מִצְוַת כּוֹס שְׁלִישִׁית מֵאַרְבַּע כּוֹסוֹת לְשֵׁם יִחוּד קוּדְשָׁא בְּרִיךְ הוּא וּשְׁכִינְתֵּיהּ עַל־יְדֵי הַהוּא טָמִיר וְנֶעְלָם בְּשֵׁם כָּל־יִשְׂרָאֵל.

בָּרוּךְ אַתָּה יְיָ, אֱלֹהֵינוּ מֶלֶךְ הָעוֹלָם,
בּוֹרֵא פְּרִי הַגָּפֶן.

Fill Eliyahu's cup, open the front door, and say:

שְׁפֹךְ חֲמָתְךָ אֶל־הַגּוֹיִם, אֲשֶׁר לֹא יְדָעוּךָ וְעַל־מַמְלָכוֹת אֲשֶׁר בְּשִׁמְךָ לֹא קָרָאוּ. כִּי אָכַל אֶת־יַעֲקֹב, וְאֶת־נָוֵהוּ הֵשַׁמּוּ. שְׁפָךְ־עֲלֵיהֶם זַעְמֶךָ, וַחֲרוֹן אַפְּךָ יַשִּׂיגֵם. תִּרְדֹּף בְּאַף וְתַשְׁמִידֵם, מִתַּחַת שְׁמֵי יְיָ.

Close the door. Fill the fourth cup.

GUEST VOICE: RABBI ASHER LOPATIN

Rabbi Asher Lopatin is the president of the Yeshivat Chovevei Torah Rabbinical School. The mission of Yeshivat Chovevei Torah is to "to recruit, professionally train, and place rabbis throughout the world who will lead the Jewish people and shape their communities' spiritual and intellectual character in consonance with modern and open Orthodox values and commitments" (www.yctorah.org).

FROM SHEFOKH CHAMATEKHA TO NISHMAT: AN EVOLUTION FROM THE PARTICULAR TO THE UNIVERSAL

The traditional beginning of the fourth cup of wine is reciting "Shefokh Chamatekha" (Pour Out Your Wrath) as the door is opened. This prayer, based on biblical verses, releases all the frustrations Jews have had over the years at

QUESTIONS FOR HALLEL

1. What does the word *hallel* mean?
2. Why does this picture show the splitting of the sea?
3. Why didn't the Jews drown in the water?
4. How did the Jews have the courage to go between walls of water, a sight they had never seen before?

---

people traditionally use to praise God move us away from a particularist praise of God and instead call on all nations to praise God. As Tehillim 117:1 says, "All nations praise God!" There is still plenty of particularism in the Hallel, but it

presence into the world. And off we go with Hallel – the chapters of singing praise and glory to God.

Yet something fascinating happens along the way: the psalms that the Jewish

HALLEL

NOT TO US, God, not to us, but to Your Name bring glory, for the sake of Your loving kindness, of Your constancy. Why should the nations say: "Where, then, is their God?" – when our God is in heaven, doing whatever He wishes. Their idols are silver and gold, the work of human hands. They have a mouth but speak not; eyes they have but they do not see. They have ears but they do not hear; nose they have but they smell not; hands – but they do not feel; feet – but they do not walk; their throat cannot utter a sound. Their makers become like them, and so do all who trust in them. Israel trusts in God – He is their help and shield. The House of Aharon trusts in God – He is their help and shield. The God-fearers trust in God – He is their help and shield. (Tehillim 115:1–11)

GOD REMEMBERS US – HE WILL BLESS: He will bless the House of Israel. He will bless the House of Aharon. He will bless the God-fearers – the small and the great alike. May God give you increase – you and your children. Blessed are you of God, Maker of the heavens and earth. The heavens are God's heavens, but the earth He gave to man. Not the dead praise God, not those who go down to the Realm-of-Silence. But we shall bless God, now and forever. Halleluyah. (Tehillim 115:12–18)

God of everyone. Though the Haggadah and Passover are very much about the reality and the dreams of the Jewish people, and though we have the right and the responsibility to celebrate our particular existence, at some point we must lead by breaking through this particularistic prism and seeing the global picture, the universal aspect of the world that God created.

The culmination of this section is the beautiful song Nishmat, which begins with the words "the soul of every being shall bless Your name," and ends with "the King, the God, Who gives life to all the worlds." What a journey from Shefokh Chamatekha – God, go get our enemies and destroy them so that we can serve you! – to *Chei ha'olamim* – God, help us make this world alive in the way that serves You, that brings glory to Your plan for creation; help us enable all the individual nations to come together so that every creature blesses You!

הַלֵּל

לֹא לָנוּ יְיָ לֹא לָנוּ כִּי לְשִׁמְךָ תֵּן כָּבוֹד, עַל חַסְדְּךָ עַל אֲמִתֶּךָ. לָמָּה יֹאמְרוּ הַגּוֹיִם, אַיֵּה נָא אֱלֹהֵיהֶם, וֵאלֹהֵינוּ בַשָּׁמָיִם, כֹּל אֲשֶׁר חָפֵץ עָשָׂה. עֲצַבֵּיהֶם כֶּסֶף וְזָהָב, מַעֲשֵׂה יְדֵי אָדָם. פֶּה לָהֶם וְלֹא יְדַבֵּרוּ, עֵינַיִם לָהֶם וְלֹא יִרְאוּ. אָזְנַיִם לָהֶם וְלֹא יִשְׁמָעוּ, אַף לָהֶם וְלֹא יְרִיחוּן. יְדֵיהֶם וְלֹא יְמִישׁוּן, רַגְלֵיהֶם וְלֹא יְהַלֵּכוּ, לֹא יֶהְגּוּ בִּגְרוֹנָם. כְּמוֹהֶם יִהְיוּ עֹשֵׂיהֶם, כֹּל אֲשֶׁר בֹּטֵחַ בָּהֶם. יִשְׂרָאֵל בְּטַח בַּייָ, עֶזְרָם וּמָגִנָּם הוּא. בֵּית אַהֲרֹן בִּטְחוּ בַייָ, עֶזְרָם וּמָגִנָּם הוּא. יִרְאֵי יְיָ בִּטְחוּ בַייָ, עֶזְרָם וּמָגִנָּם הוּא.

יְיָ זְכָרָנוּ יְבָרֵךְ, יְבָרֵךְ אֶת בֵּית יִשְׂרָאֵל, יְבָרֵךְ אֶת בֵּית אַהֲרֹן. יְבָרֵךְ יִרְאֵי יְיָ, הַקְּטַנִּים עִם הַגְּדֹלִים. יֹסֵף יְיָ עֲלֵיכֶם, עֲלֵיכֶם וְעַל בְּנֵיכֶם. בְּרוּכִים אַתֶּם לַייָ, עֹשֵׂה שָׁמַיִם וָאָרֶץ. הַשָּׁמַיִם שָׁמַיִם לַייָ, וְהָאָרֶץ נָתַן לִבְנֵי אָדָם. לֹא הַמֵּתִים יְהַלְלוּ יָהּ, וְלֹא כָּל יֹרְדֵי דוּמָה. וַאֲנַחְנוּ נְבָרֵךְ יָהּ, מֵעַתָּה וְעַד עוֹלָם, הַלְלוּיָהּ.

---

is mixed with an understanding that God wants praise from everyone: "Let Israel say, 'God's kindness endures forever.' ... Let all who fear God say, 'God's kindness endures forever'" (Tehillim 118:2, 4).

The Haggadah then takes us further on the journey from particularism to universalism with the "Great Hallel" – psalm 136. This psalm focuses on the trajectory of the Jewish people through history. It starts with recounting the creation of the world, indicating that the world was created for the Jewish people. Then it mentions the battles of the Jews against their enemies – reminiscent of Shefokh Chamatekha. But then the psalm ends with a new vision of creation and the world: the world is not just about one people and God is not just about one people. Our rabbis tell us that this psalm is so holy because it yanks us from a particularist slumber to understanding that God has to feed the entire world – not just the Jews! We end this psalm with "Praise to the God of the heavens!" – not the God of the Jews or of Israel, but the

I YEARN that God should hear my supplicating voice, that He should bend His ear to me whenever in my lifetime I cry out. The coils of death are taking me in their grip, the torments of Hell are overtaking me, trouble and anguish are my lot. So I call out in God's Name: "Please, God, save my life!" Gracious is God, and just; our God is merciful, God protects the simple; when I am down and out He will save me. Rest again, my soul, for God has been good to you. For You have rescued me from death, my eyes from weeping, my feet from stumbling. I will walk in God's presence in the realm of the living. I trusted [in God] even when I thought I was finished, when I was at my wit's end, when in my desperation I said: "All people are untrustworthy." (Tehillim 116:1–11)

HOW CAN I REPAY God for all his bounties to me? I will raise the cup of salvation and invoke God's Name. I will pay my vows to God in the presence of all His people. Grievous in God's eyes is the death of His faithful ones. Please, God – I am indeed Your servant; I am Your servant, son of Your maidservant; You have loosed my bonds. To You, I will bring a Thanks-offering, and I will invoke God's Name. I will pay my vows to God in the presence of His entire people. In the courts of God's House in the heart of Jerusalem. Halleluyah. (Tehillim 116:12–19)

---

before Moshe, there was a rebellion. There would have been no Moshe without this rebellion.

In chapter 1 of Shemot Pharaoh commands the midwives Shifrah and Puah, "When the Hebrew women give birth…if it is a boy, then kill him" (1:16). Shifrah and Puah bravely resist. Instead of fearing Pharaoh, they feared God. They allowed the baby boys to live.

It seems possible from the text that one of the boys who was allowed to live as a result of the midwives' bravery was Moshe himself. In other words, had there been no Shifrah and Puah there might have been no Moshe. Indeed, the Torah declares that God looked with great favor upon Shifrah and Puah: God blessed them with houses (1:21). According to Rashi (ad loc.), this means that Hashem blessed the midwives with priestly and royal descendants. From these two women came *kohanim, leviim,* and kings.

These two midwives were the inspiration for the revolution from Egypt.

אָהַבְתִּי כִּי יִשְׁמַע יְיָ, אֶת קוֹלִי תַּחֲנוּנָי. כִּי הִטָּה אָזְנוֹ לִי וּבְיָמַי אֶקְרָא. אֲפָפוּנִי חֶבְלֵי מָוֶת, וּמְצָרֵי שְׁאוֹל מְצָאוּנִי, צָרָה וְיָגוֹן אֶמְצָא. וּבְשֵׁם יְיָ אֶקְרָא, אָנָּה יְיָ מַלְּטָה נַפְשִׁי. חַנּוּן יְיָ וְצַדִּיק, וֵאלֹהֵינוּ מְרַחֵם. שֹׁמֵר פְּתָאִים יְיָ דַּלּוֹתִי וְלִי יְהוֹשִׁיעַ. שׁוּבִי נַפְשִׁי לִמְנוּחָיְכִי, כִּי יְיָ גָּמַל עָלָיְכִי. כִּי חִלַּצְתָּ נַפְשִׁי מִמָּוֶת, אֶת עֵינִי מִן דִּמְעָה, אֶת רַגְלִי מִדֶּחִי. אֶתְהַלֵּךְ לִפְנֵי יְיָ, בְּאַרְצוֹת הַחַיִּים. הֶאֱמַנְתִּי כִּי אֲדַבֵּר, אֲנִי עָנִיתִי מְאֹד. אֲנִי אָמַרְתִּי בְחָפְזִי, כָּל הָאָדָם כֹּזֵב.

מָה אָשִׁיב לַיְיָ, כָּל תַּגְמוּלוֹהִי עָלָי. כּוֹס יְשׁוּעוֹת אֶשָּׂא, וּבְשֵׁם יְיָ אֶקְרָא. נְדָרַי לַיְיָ אֲשַׁלֵּם, נֶגְדָה נָּא לְכָל עַמּוֹ. יָקָר בְּעֵינֵי יְיָ הַמָּוְתָה לַחֲסִידָיו. אָנָּה יְיָ כִּי אֲנִי עַבְדֶּךָ, אֲנִי עַבְדְּךָ, בֶּן אֲמָתֶךָ, פִּתַּחְתָּ לְמוֹסֵרָי. לְךָ אֶזְבַּח זֶבַח תּוֹדָה וּבְשֵׁם יְיָ אֶקְרָא. נְדָרַי לַיְיָ אֲשַׁלֵּם נֶגְדָה נָּא לְכָל עַמּוֹ. בְּחַצְרוֹת בֵּית יְיָ בְּתוֹכֵכִי יְרוּשָׁלָיִם הַלְלוּיָהּ.

That is the journey of the Jewish people. Never to forget the need for Shefokh Chamatekha, but to know that the goal is Nishmat. Our goal is to nourish the world with inspiration and freedom, for the particular to inspire the universal. Let us all head out on this journey toward the messianic era.

DR. MARTIN LUTHER KING JR. DAY IS A JEWISH HOLIDAY

Our synagogue often celebrates Martin Luther King Jr. Day. We have invited churches into our synagogue to celebrate together with us. There are those who are critical of this – after all, it's not a holiday on the Jewish calendar. Why would a Jewish synagogue celebrate a non-Jewish holiday in conjunction with a church?

The Torah's introduction to the Exodus story is perhaps the most appropriate place to look to for insight on this issue. The spirit of Dr. King can be seen in these first chapters of Shemot, and they guide us in understanding how a synagogue should relate to Martin Luther King Jr. Day.

When does the revolution from Egypt begin? Who is the first hero? Even

Praise God, all you nations; laud Him, all peoples. For great is His loving kindness towards us, and God's constancy is everlasting. Halleluyah.
(Tehillim 117)

Give thanks to God, for He is good — For His grace endures forever.
Say it now, Israel — For His grace endures forever.
Say it now, House of Aharon — For His grace endures forever.
Say it now, God-fearers — For His grace endures forever.
(Tehillim 118:1–4)

IN MY DISTRESS I called on God; He answered by setting me free. God is with me; I have no fear: What can people do to me? God is with me helping me, so I shall gloat over my enemies. It is better to trust in God than to trust in people. It is better to trust in God than to trust in the great. All the nations have beset me; but in God's Name I will surely rout them. They surround me on all sides; but in God's Name I will surely rout them. They surround me like bees at the honeycomb; they attack me like flames at the stubble; but in God's Name I will surely rout them. They wanted to knock me down, but God helped me. God is my strength and my power, and He has become my salvation. Joyous shouts of deliverance resound in the tents of the righteous: God's right hand is triumphant. I shall not die – I shall live, and proclaim God's works. God chastened me severely, but He did not hand me over to death. Open the gates of victory to me: I would enter them, I would give thanks to God. This is God's gate – the victors enter through it. (Tehillim 118:5–20)

---

were able to look beyond their own immediate needs and even the needs of their own family; they acted bravely for another family and another nation.

The lesson of the Shifrah and Puah story is that in order for the Children of Israel to be liberated there needed to be brave and caring people who acted for "the other." Shifrah and Puah didn't look the other way to save themselves; they didn't put their loyalty to their boss before their loyalty to God. They didn't do the safe thing; they did the right thing.

The importance of standing up for people outside one's own community

הַלְלוּ אֶת יְיָ, כָּל גּוֹיִם, שַׁבְּחוּהוּ כָּל הָאֻמִּים.
כִּי גָבַר עָלֵינוּ חַסְדּוֹ, וֶאֱמֶת יְיָ לְעוֹלָם הַלְלוּיָהּ.

הוֹדוּ לַייָ כִּי טוֹב,	כִּי לְעוֹלָם חַסְדּוֹ.
יֹאמַר נָא יִשְׂרָאֵל,	כִּי לְעוֹלָם חַסְדּוֹ.
יֹאמְרוּ נָא בֵית אַהֲרֹן,	כִּי לְעוֹלָם חַסְדּוֹ.
יֹאמְרוּ נָא יִרְאֵי יְיָ,	כִּי לְעוֹלָם חַסְדּוֹ.

מִן הַמֵּצַר קָרָאתִי יָּהּ, עָנָנִי בַמֶּרְחָב יָהּ. יְיָ לִי לֹא אִירָא, מַה יַּעֲשֶׂה לִי אָדָם. יְיָ לִי בְּעֹזְרָי, וַאֲנִי אֶרְאֶה בְשֹׂנְאָי. טוֹב לַחֲסוֹת בַּייָ, מִבְּטֹחַ בָּאָדָם. טוֹב לַחֲסוֹת בַּייָ, מִבְּטֹחַ בִּנְדִיבִים. כָּל גּוֹיִם סְבָבוּנִי, בְּשֵׁם יְיָ כִּי אֲמִילַם. סַבּוּנִי גַם סְבָבוּנִי, בְּשֵׁם יְיָ כִּי אֲמִילַם. סַבּוּנִי כִדְבֹרִים דֹּעֲכוּ כְּאֵשׁ קוֹצִים, בְּשֵׁם יְיָ כִּי אֲמִילַם. דָּחֹה דְחִיתַנִי לִנְפֹּל, וַייָ עֲזָרָנִי. עָזִּי וְזִמְרָת יָהּ, וַיְהִי לִי לִישׁוּעָה. קוֹל רִנָּה וִישׁוּעָה בְּאָהֳלֵי צַדִּיקִים, יְמִין יְיָ עֹשָׂה חָיִל. יְמִין יְיָ רוֹמֵמָה, יְמִין יְיָ עֹשָׂה חָיִל. לֹא אָמוּת כִּי אֶחְיֶה, וַאֲסַפֵּר מַעֲשֵׂי יָהּ. יַסֹּר יִסְּרַנִּי יָּהּ, וְלַמָּוֶת לֹא נְתָנָנִי. פִּתְחוּ לִי שַׁעֲרֵי צֶדֶק, אָבֹא בָם אוֹדֶה יָהּ. זֶה הַשַּׁעַר לַייָ, צַדִּיקִים יָבֹאוּ בוֹ.

They allowed for the birth of Moshe. In return God blessed these midwives with the highest honor. From these midwives came the leaders of Israel.

Who were these midwives? Rashi teaches that they were really Yokheved, the mother of Moshe, and Miriam, the sister of Moshe. This is difficult to understand, since why then does the Torah call them Shifrah and Puah.

In fact, the names Shifrah and Puah sound like they are Egyptian names. Thus, a second approach offered in the first century by Josephus and in the nineteenth century by Malbim argues that Shifrah and Puah were really Egyptian women. This approach seems much more in tune with the literal text of the Torah. According to this, the first act of resistance on behalf of the Hebrews was done not by Hebrews but by Egyptians. These Egyptian women

I THANK YOU for You have answered me, and You have become my salvation. I thank You for You have answered me, and You have become my salvation. The stone that the builders rejected has become the chief cornerstone. The stone that the builders rejected has become the chief cornerstone. This is God's doing: it is marvelous in our eyes. This is God's doing: it is marvelous in our eyes. This is the day on which God acted: let us exult and rejoice on it. This is the day on which God acted: let us exult and rejoice on it. (Tehillim 118:21–24)

Please, God, deliver us!
Please, God, deliver us!
Please, God, let us prosper!
Please, God, let us prosper!
(Tehillim 118:25)

May all who enter be blessed in God's Name; we bless you from God's House. May all who enter be blessed in God's Name; we bless you from God's House. God is God, and He has given us light; blind the Festival Offering with branches to the altar's horns. God is God, and He has given us light; blind the Festival Offering with branches to the altar's horns. You are my God and I will thank You, my God – and I will extol You. You are my God and I will thank You, my God – and I will extol You. Give thanks to God, for He is good; His grace endures forever. Give thanks to God, for He is good; His grace endures forever. (Tehillim 118:126–129)

People often say, "Anything that distracts from our main mission must be avoided. Don't take up the cause of others because it will prevent us from focusing on our own needs." This approach is a mistake. In order to best fulfill our own needs we must also be cognizant of the needs of others.

Dr. Martin Luther King Jr. acted with great bravery and courage for blacks in this country. He put his own body on the line. He spoke truth to power. He inspired and he fought. But what separates him from many other great leaders is that he was able to transcend his own personal cause.

אוֹדְךָ כִּי עֲנִיתָנִי, וַתְּהִי לִי לִישׁוּעָה. אוֹדְךָ כִּי עֲנִיתָנִי, וַתְּהִי לִי לִישׁוּעָה. אֶבֶן מָאֲסוּ הַבּוֹנִים, הָיְתָה לְרֹאשׁ פִּנָּה. אֶבֶן מָאֲסוּ הַבּוֹנִים, הָיְתָה לְרֹאשׁ פִּנָּה. מֵאֵת יְיָ הָיְתָה זֹּאת, הִיא נִפְלָאת בְּעֵינֵינוּ. מֵאֵת יְיָ הָיְתָה זֹּאת, הִיא נִפְלָאת בְּעֵינֵינוּ. זֶה הַיּוֹם עָשָׂה יְיָ, נָגִילָה וְנִשְׂמְחָה בוֹ. זֶה הַיּוֹם עָשָׂה יְיָ נָגִילָה וְנִשְׂמְחָה בוֹ.

אָנָּא יְיָ הוֹשִׁיעָה נָּא.
אָנָּא יְיָ הוֹשִׁיעָה נָּא.
אָנָּא יְיָ הַצְלִיחָה נָא.
אָנָּא יְיָ הַצְלִיחָה נָא.

בָּרוּךְ הַבָּא בְּשֵׁם יְיָ, בֵּרַכְנוּכֶם מִבֵּית יְיָ. בָּרוּךְ הַבָּא בְּשֵׁם יְיָ, בֵּרַכְנוּכֶם מִבֵּית יְיָ. אֵל יְיָ וַיָּאֶר לָנוּ, אִסְרוּ חַג בַּעֲבֹתִים עַד קַרְנוֹת הַמִּזְבֵּחַ. אֵל יְיָ וַיָּאֶר לָנוּ, אִסְרוּ חַג בַּעֲבֹתִים, עַד קַרְנוֹת הַמִּזְבֵּחַ. אֵלִי אַתָּה וְאוֹדֶךָּ אֱלֹהַי אֲרוֹמְמֶךָּ. אֵלִי אַתָּה וְאוֹדֶךָּ אֱלֹהַי אֲרוֹמְמֶךָּ. הוֹדוּ לַיְיָ כִּי טוֹב, כִּי לְעוֹלָם חַסְדּוֹ. הוֹדוּ לַיְיָ כִּי טוֹב, כִּי לְעוֹלָם חַסְדּוֹ.

---

relates to the very character of Moshe. Why was Moshe selected to be the leader of the Jewish people? What do we know about Moshe's life?

The first thing Moshe does as an adult is to stand up for an Israelite who was being beaten by an Egyptian. He smites the Egyptian down. But after that, he is still not selected as a leader. Then, Moshe interferes when he sees two Israelites quarreling, but he is still not selected as a leader. He then runs to the land of Midian and steps in when he sees the daughters of Yitro being oppressed by the shepherds. Then – and only then – is he selected as our leader. Only once Moshe has shown the ability to look beyond his own narrow cause is he deemed worthy of being our liberator.

The lesson of Moshe's selection as our leader is in line with what we learned from the story of Shifrah and Puah. In order to achieve redemption one must look beyond the immediate needs of your own people.

GIVE THANKS to God, for He is good; His grace endures forever. Give thanks to God-of-all-the-Gods; His grace endures forever. Give thanks to Lord-of-all-the-lords; His grace endures forever. To Him Who alone works great marvels; His grace endures forever. To Him Who made the heavens with wisdom; His grace endures forever. To Him Who laid the earth on the waters; His grace endures forever. To Him Who made great lights; His grace endures forever. The sun to rule by day; His grace endures forever. The moon and stars to rule by night; His grace endures forever. To Him Who struck Egypt through their firstborn; His grace endures forever. And brought Israel out of their midst; His grace endures forever. With a strong hand and an outstretched arm; His grace endures forever. To Him Who split apart the Reed Sea; His grace endures forever. And led Israel right through it; His grace endures forever. But hurled Pharaoh and his host into the Reed Sea; His grace endures forever. To Him Who led His people through the wilderness; His grace endures forever. To Him Who struck down mighty kings; His grace endures forever. And also slew great potentates; His grace endures forever. Sihon king of the Amorites; His grace endures forever. And Og king of Bashan; His grace endures forever. And then He bequeathed their land; His grace endures forever. To His servant Israel to have; His grace endures forever. Who remembered us when we were down and out; His grace endures forever. And rescued us from our enemies; His grace endures forever. Who supplies food to all flesh; His grace endures forever. Thank the God-of-all-Heavens; His grace endures forever. (Tehillim 136)

There is a third lesson in the Exodus story that relates directly to the teachings of Dr. King. The lesson is simple: If we are silent when we see evil it will not be long before such evil will rear its ugly head upon us.

Pharaoh first decreed that the baby boys of the Hebrew women should be killed. But then Pharaoh saw that his own people tolerated this evil. He then commanded "all his people": "Any male that is born should be cast into the sea" (1:22). Rashi points out Pharaoh was no longer only persecuting the Israelite babies; he was now killing his own people! The decree had started out against one group but eventually spread to encompass the Egyptians as well.

When one sees evil in the world one must speak out. An injustice against anyone is an injustice against everyone. The Torah teaches that these are not

הוֹדוּ לַייָ כִּי טוֹב, כִּי לְעוֹלָם חַסְדּוֹ. הוֹדוּ לֵאלֹהֵי הָאֱלֹהִים, כִּי לְעוֹלָם חַסְדּוֹ. הוֹדוּ לַאֲדֹנֵי הָאֲדֹנִים, כִּי לְעוֹלָם חַסְדּוֹ. לְעֹשֵׂה נִפְלָאוֹת גְּדֹלוֹת לְבַדּוֹ, כִּי לְעוֹלָם חַסְדּוֹ. לְעֹשֵׂה הַשָּׁמַיִם בִּתְבוּנָה, כִּי לְעוֹלָם חַסְדּוֹ. לְרוֹקַע הָאָרֶץ עַל הַמָּיִם, כִּי לְעוֹלָם חַסְדּוֹ. לְעֹשֵׂה אוֹרִים גְּדֹלִים, כִּי לְעוֹלָם חַסְדּוֹ. אֶת הַשֶּׁמֶשׁ לְמֶמְשֶׁלֶת בַּיּוֹם, כִּי לְעוֹלָם חַסְדּוֹ. אֶת הַיָּרֵחַ וְכוֹכָבִים לְמֶמְשְׁלוֹת בַּלָּיְלָה, כִּי לְעוֹלָם חַסְדּוֹ. לְמַכֵּה מִצְרַיִם בִּבְכוֹרֵיהֶם, כִּי לְעוֹלָם חַסְדּוֹ. וַיּוֹצֵא יִשְׂרָאֵל מִתּוֹכָם, כִּי לְעוֹלָם חַסְדּוֹ. בְּיָד חֲזָקָה וּבִזְרוֹעַ נְטוּיָה, כִּי לְעוֹלָם חַסְדּוֹ. לְגֹזֵר יַם סוּף לִגְזָרִים, כִּי לְעוֹלָם חַסְדּוֹ. וְהֶעֱבִיר יִשְׂרָאֵל בְּתוֹכוֹ, כִּי לְעוֹלָם חַסְדּוֹ. וְנִעֵר פַּרְעֹה וְחֵילוֹ בְיַם סוּף, כִּי לְעוֹלָם חַסְדּוֹ. לְמוֹלִיךְ עַמּוֹ בַּמִּדְבָּר, כִּי לְעוֹלָם חַסְדּוֹ. לְמַכֵּה מְלָכִים גְּדֹלִים, כִּי לְעוֹלָם חַסְדּוֹ. וַיַּהֲרֹג מְלָכִים אַדִּירִים, כִּי לְעוֹלָם חַסְדּוֹ. לְסִיחוֹן מֶלֶךְ הָאֱמֹרִי, כִּי לְעוֹלָם חַסְדּוֹ. וּלְעוֹג מֶלֶךְ הַבָּשָׁן, כִּי לְעוֹלָם חַסְדּוֹ. וְנָתַן אַרְצָם לְנַחֲלָה, כִּי לְעוֹלָם חַסְדּוֹ. נַחֲלָה לְיִשְׂרָאֵל עַבְדּוֹ, כִּי לְעוֹלָם חַסְדּוֹ. שֶׁבְּשִׁפְלֵנוּ זָכַר לָנוּ, כִּי לְעוֹלָם חַסְדּוֹ. וַיִּפְרְקֵנוּ מִצָּרֵינוּ, כִּי לְעוֹלָם חַסְדּוֹ. נוֹתֵן לֶחֶם לְכָל בָּשָׂר, כִּי לְעוֹלָם חַסְדּוֹ. הוֹדוּ לְאֵל הַשָּׁמָיִם, כִּי לְעוֹלָם חַסְדּוֹ.

To give some perspective: The greatest work for the Soviet Jewry movement was done by the Student Struggle for Soviet Jewry. One of its founders was Glenn Richter. Glenn shared with me that in 1965 the leaders of the Student Struggle for Soviet Jewry went to Dr. King and asked for his help in speaking out against the Soviet Union. Rabbi Avi Weiss, the leader of the group, related that Dr. King's closest advisors urged him to remain silent. They said, "It is not your cause. Stay focused." Thankfully, he did not listen to them. Instead – at a critical moment – he spoke in support. He ended up issuing a stronger statement on behalf of Soviet Jews than some Jewish groups were willing to issue at that time.

He taught us that where there is injustice anywhere, there is injustice everywhere. He taught us that the opposite of good is not evil, it is indifference.

THE BREATH of every living thing blesses Your Name, God, our God, and the spirit of all flesh glorifies and extols the memory of You, our King, always. Since ever forever God You are, and besides You we have no King who liberates and saves, redeeming, rescuing, providing and exercising mercy in every time of trouble and distress. We have no King but You. God of first and last, God of all creatures, Lord of all the born, Who is lauded with manifold praises, Who directs His universe with loving kindness and His creatures with mercy. And God does not slumber or sleep – He Who awakens the sleeping and rouses the slumbering, and gives speech to the mute and sets free the imprisoned and supports the falling and straightens the bent – to You alone we give thanks.

EVEN if our mouth were an ocean of song, and our tongue were rolling seas of exultation, our lips spacious skies of praise, our eyes radiant as the sun and the moon, our hands outspread like soaring eagles, and our feet as fleet as the hinds – with all this we would still not be able to thank You, God, our God and God of our fathers, and to bless Your Name for even one-thousands-of-a-thousandth-of-a-thousandth-of-a-ten-thousandth-of-a-myriad of all the favors You granted our ancestors and us. From Egypt You liberated us, God, our God, from slavery You emancipated us. In famine You fed us, providing plentifully. From the swords You saved us and from pestilence rescued us, from terrible, deadly

---

so long; we've been the victims of economic injustice so long – still the last hired and first fired all over this nation. And I know the temptation. I can understand from a psychological point of view why some caught up in the clutches of the injustices surrounding them almost respond with bitterness and come to the conclusion that the problem can't be solved within, and they talk about getting away from it in terms of racial separation. But even though I can understand it psychologically, I must say to you this afternoon that this isn't the way. Black supremacy is as dangerous as white supremacy. And oh, I hope you will allow me to say to you this afternoon that God is not merely interested in the freedom of black men and brown men and yellow men. God is interested in the freedom of the whole human race.

What an honor it is for Jews to celebrate the life of this man!

נִשְׁמַת כָּל חַי, תְּבָרֵךְ אֶת שִׁמְךָ יְיָ אֱלֹהֵינוּ. וְרוּחַ כָּל בָּשָׂר, תְּפָאֵר וּתְרוֹמֵם זִכְרְךָ מַלְכֵּנוּ תָּמִיד, מִן הָעוֹלָם וְעַד הָעוֹלָם אַתָּה אֵל. וּמִבַּלְעָדֶיךָ אֵין לָנוּ מֶלֶךְ גּוֹאֵל וּמוֹשִׁיעַ, פּוֹדֶה וּמַצִּיל וּמְפַרְנֵס וּמְרַחֵם, בְּכָל עֵת צָרָה וְצוּקָה, אֵין לָנוּ מֶלֶךְ אֶלָּא אָתָּה. אֱלֹהֵי הָרִאשׁוֹנִים וְהָאַחֲרוֹנִים, אֱלוֹהַּ כָּל בְּרִיּוֹת, אֲדוֹן כָּל תּוֹלָדוֹת, הַמְהֻלָּל בְּרֹב הַתִּשְׁבָּחוֹת, הַמְנַהֵג עוֹלָמוֹ בְּחֶסֶד, וּבְרִיּוֹתָיו בְּרַחֲמִים. וַיְיָ לֹא יָנוּם וְלֹא יִישָׁן. הַמְעוֹרֵר יְשֵׁנִים וְהַמֵּקִיץ נִרְדָּמִים, וְהַמֵּשִׂיחַ אִלְּמִים, וְהַמַּתִּיר אֲסוּרִים, וְהַסּוֹמֵךְ נוֹפְלִים, וְהַזּוֹקֵף כְּפוּפִים, לְךָ לְבַדְּךָ אֲנַחְנוּ מוֹדִים.

אִלּוּ פִינוּ מָלֵא שִׁירָה כַּיָּם, וּלְשׁוֹנֵנוּ רִנָּה כַּהֲמוֹן גַּלָּיו, וְשִׂפְתוֹתֵינוּ שֶׁבַח כְּמֶרְחֲבֵי רָקִיעַ, וְעֵינֵינוּ מְאִירוֹת כַּשֶּׁמֶשׁ וְכַיָּרֵחַ, וְיָדֵינוּ פְרוּשׂוֹת כְּנִשְׁרֵי שָׁמָיִם, וְרַגְלֵינוּ קַלּוֹת כָּאַיָּלוֹת, אֵין אֲנַחְנוּ מַסְפִּיקִים, לְהוֹדוֹת לְךָ יְיָ אֱלֹהֵינוּ וֵאלֹהֵי אֲבוֹתֵינוּ, וּלְבָרֵךְ אֶת שְׁמֶךָ עַל אַחַת מֵאָלֶף אֶלֶף אַלְפֵי אֲלָפִים וְרִבֵּי רְבָבוֹת פְּעָמִים, הַטּוֹבוֹת שֶׁעָשִׂיתָ עִם אֲבוֹתֵינוּ וְעִמָּנוּ. מִמִּצְרַיִם גְּאַלְתָּנוּ יְיָ אֱלֹהֵינוּ, וּמִבֵּית עֲבָדִים פְּדִיתָנוּ, בְּרָעָב

---

mere words. This is a prophecy. If injustice is not stopped it will spread like a forest fire and engulf all the bystanders.

In light of this, celebrating Martin Luther King Jr. Day is entirely consonant with the Jewish tradition; having a Martin Luther King Jr. program highlights one of Judaism's core values. Not only does such a program give honor to a brave man who fearlessly lived these lessons of the Exodus story, but it also reminds us that the lesson he taught is intertwined with the lesson of the Torah: in our quest to achieve our own redemption we must see the needs of others. Without such sight, we will forever be blinded from the presence of the Messiah.

These are the words of Dr. King on June 23, 1963. They surely apply to us as well:

We've been pushed around so long; we've been the victims of lynching mobs diseases You delivered us. Till now Your mercies have succored us, Your loving kindness has not failed us. So, God, do not ever fail us. Therefore, the limbs that You have shaped in us, and the breath and spirit that You have breathed in our nostrils, and the tongue that You have placed in our mouth – they, all of them, shall give thanks and bless and praise and glorify and exalt and revere and hallow and enthrone Your Name, our King. Indeed, every mouth shall acknowledge You, every tongue shall swear allegiance to You, every knee shall bend to You, every erect body shall prostate itself before You, all hearts shall fear You, all innards shall sing to Your Name, as it is said (Tehillim 35:10), "All my bones shall say, 'God, who is like You – rescuing the wretched from those stronger than them, the poor and the needy from their despoilers!'"

WHO IS LIKE YOU, who can be compared to You, who can equal You – great, mighty and awesome God, supreme God, Creator-of-Heaven-and-Earth?! We shall praise You, laud You, glorify You, and bless Your holy Name, as it is said (Tehillim 103:1):

"**BLESS GOD**, O my soul; all my being – bless His holy Name!" God in the vastness of Your power, great in the glory of Your Name, mighty forever, and awesome in Your awe-inspiring acts, King enthroned in a high and exalted seat – Inhabiter-of-Eternity-in-a-High-and-Holy-Place is his name. And it is written (Tehillim 33:1): "Exult in God, O your righteous; it befits the upright to acclaim Him."

BY THE MOUTH of the upright You shall be praised, and by the lips of the righteous You shall be blessed, and by the tongues of the pious You shall be exalted, and by the innards of the holy You shall be hallowed. And in the assemblies of the myriads of Your people the House of Israel shall Your Name, O our King, be glorified in joyous song in every generation.

FOR it is the duty of all creatures, God, our God and God of our fathers, to give thanks, to praise, laud, glorify, extol, honor, bless, exalt and adore You even beyond all the songs and praises of David son of Yishai Your servant, Your anointed one.

זַנְתָּנוּ, וּבְשָׂבָע כִּלְכַּלְתָּנוּ, מֵחֶרֶב הִצַּלְתָּנוּ, וּמִדֶּבֶר מִלַּטְתָּנוּ, וּמֵחֳלָיִם רָעִים וְנֶאֱמָנִים דִּלִּיתָנוּ. עַד הֵנָּה עֲזָרוּנוּ רַחֲמֶיךָ, וְלֹא עֲזָבוּנוּ חֲסָדֶיךָ, וְאַל תִּטְּשֵׁנוּ יְיָ אֱלֹהֵינוּ לָנֶצַח. עַל כֵּן אֵבָרִים שֶׁפִּלַּגְתָּ בָּנוּ, וְרוּחַ וּנְשָׁמָה שֶׁנָּפַחְתָּ בְּאַפֵּינוּ, וְלָשׁוֹן אֲשֶׁר שַׂמְתָּ בְּפִינוּ, הֵן הֵם יוֹדוּ וִיבָרְכוּ וִישַׁבְּחוּ וִיפָאֲרוּ וִירוֹמְמוּ וְיַעֲרִיצוּ וְיַקְדִּישׁוּ וְיַמְלִיכוּ אֶת שִׁמְךָ מַלְכֵּנוּ, כִּי כָל פֶּה לְךָ יוֹדֶה, וְכָל לָשׁוֹן לְךָ תִשָּׁבַע, וְכָל בֶּרֶךְ לְךָ תִכְרַע, וְכָל קוֹמָה לְפָנֶיךָ תִשְׁתַּחֲוֶה, וְכָל לְבָבוֹת יִירָאוּךָ, וְכָל קֶרֶב וּכְלָיוֹת יְזַמְּרוּ לִשְׁמֶךָ. כַּדָּבָר שֶׁכָּתוּב, כָּל עַצְמוֹתַי תֹּאמַרְנָה יְיָ מִי כָמוֹךָ. מַצִּיל עָנִי מֵחָזָק מִמֶּנּוּ, וְעָנִי וְאֶבְיוֹן מִגֹּזְלוֹ.

מִי יִדְמֶה לָּךְ, וּמִי יִשְׁוֶה לָּךְ וּמִי יַעֲרָךְ לָךְ. הָאֵל הַגָּדוֹל הַגִּבּוֹר וְהַנּוֹרָא, אֵל עֶלְיוֹן, קֹנֵה שָׁמַיִם וָאָרֶץ. נְהַלֶּלְךָ וּנְשַׁבֵּחֲךָ וּנְפָאֶרְךָ וּנְבָרֵךְ אֶת־שֵׁם קָדְשֶׁךָ. כָּאָמוּר: לְדָוִד, בָּרְכִי נַפְשִׁי אֶת יְיָ, וְכָל קְרָבַי אֶת שֵׁם קָדְשׁוֹ.

הָאֵל בְּתַעֲצֻמוֹת עֻזֶּךָ, הַגָּדוֹל בִּכְבוֹד שְׁמֶךָ. הַגִּבּוֹר לָנֶצַח וְהַנּוֹרָא בְּנוֹרְאוֹתֶיךָ. הַמֶּלֶךְ הַיּוֹשֵׁב עַל כִּסֵּא רָם וְנִשָּׂא. שׁוֹכֵן עַד, מָרוֹם וְקָדוֹשׁ שְׁמוֹ. וְכָתוּב: רַנְּנוּ צַדִּיקִים בַּייָ, לַיְשָׁרִים נָאוָה תְהִלָּה.

בְּפִי יְשָׁרִים תִּתְהַלָּל, וּבְדִבְרֵי צַדִּיקִים תִּתְבָּרַךְ, וּבִלְשׁוֹן חֲסִידִים תִּתְרוֹמָם, וּבְקֶרֶב קְדוֹשִׁים תִּתְקַדָּשׁ. וּבְמַקְהֲלוֹת רִבְבוֹת עַמְּךָ בֵּית יִשְׂרָאֵל, בְּרִנָּה יִתְפָּאַר שִׁמְךָ מַלְכֵּנוּ, בְּכָל דּוֹר וָדוֹר.

שֶׁכֵּן חוֹבַת כָּל הַיְצוּרִים, לְפָנֶיךָ יְיָ אֱלֹהֵינוּ, וֵאלֹהֵי אֲבוֹתֵינוּ, לְהוֹדוֹת לְהַלֵּל לְשַׁבֵּחַ לְפָאֵר לְרוֹמֵם לְהַדֵּר לְבָרֵךְ לְעַלֵּה וּלְקַלֵּס, עַל כָּל דִּבְרֵי שִׁירוֹת וְתִשְׁבְּחוֹת דָּוִד בֶּן יִשַׁי, עַבְדְּךָ מְשִׁיחֶךָ.

FOREVER praised in Your Name, our King – God, great and holy King in heaven and on earth. Because You are worthy – God, our God and God of our fathers – of song and laudation, praise and psalmody, power and dominion, victory, greatness and might, fame and glory, sanctity and sovereignty, blessings and thanksgiving to Your great and holy Name, for You are God, now and forever. Be blessed, God, God, King, sublime in praises, God for thanksgiving, Lord of wonders, Who prefers songs of psalmody, Sole King, God, Ever-living One.

ALL Your works shall praise You, God, our God. And Your devotees – the righteous who do Your will – and Your entire people the House of Israel shall exultantly give thanks, bless, laud, glorify, exalt, adore, hallow, and declare the kingship of Your Name, our King. For it is good to thank You, and it is fitting to sing Your Name, because now and forever You are God.

Lift the cup of wine, say the following blessing, and drink the fourth cup, reclining.

BE BLESSED, GOD, OUR GOD, KING OF THE UNIVERSE,
CREATOR OF THE FRUIT OF THE VINE.

Say the concluding blessing after wine (on the Sabbath add the words in parenthesis)

BE BLESSED, God, our God, King of the universe, for the vine and the fruit of the vine, and for the yield of the field, and for the land so lovely, so good and so spacious that You saw fit to bequeath to our ancestors to eat of its produce and sate ourselves on its bounty. Have mercy, God, our God, on Israel Your people and on Jerusalem Your city and on Zion the abode of Your glory, on Your altar and on Your shrine. Rebuild Jerusalem the holy city speedily in our days. And bring us back up to it and let us rejoice in its upbuilding, let us eat of its fruit and sate ourselves on its bounty and we will bless you for it in holiness and purity. (And may it please You to strengthen us on this Sabbath day,) And grant us joy on this Matzot Festival Day, for You, God, are good and You do good to all. We thank You for the Land and for the fruit of its vine. Be blessed, God, for the Land and for the fruit of its vine.

יִשְׁתַּבַּח שִׁמְךָ לָעַד מַלְכֵּנוּ, הָאֵל הַמֶּלֶךְ הַגָּדוֹל וְהַקָּדוֹשׁ בַּשָּׁמַיִם וּבָאָרֶץ. כִּי לְךָ נָאֶה, יְיָ אֱלֹהֵינוּ וֵאלֹהֵי אֲבוֹתֵינוּ, שִׁיר וּשְׁבָחָה, הַלֵּל וְזִמְרָה, עֹז וּמֶמְשָׁלָה, נֶצַח, גְּדֻלָּה וּגְבוּרָה, תְּהִלָּה וְתִפְאֶרֶת, קְדֻשָּׁה וּמַלְכוּת, בְּרָכוֹת וְהוֹדָאוֹת מֵעַתָּה וְעַד עוֹלָם.

יְהַלְלוּךָ יְיָ אֱלֹהֵינוּ כָּל מַעֲשֶׂיךָ, וַחֲסִידֶיךָ צַדִּיקִים עוֹשֵׂי רְצוֹנֶךָ, וְכָל עַמְּךָ בֵּית יִשְׂרָאֵל בְּרִנָּה יוֹדוּ וִיבָרְכוּ וִישַׁבְּחוּ וִיפָאֲרוּ וִירוֹמְמוּ וְיַעֲרִיצוּ וְיַקְדִּישׁוּ וְיַמְלִיכוּ אֶת שִׁמְךָ מַלְכֵּנוּ, כִּי לְךָ טוֹב לְהוֹדוֹת וּלְשִׁמְךָ נָאֶה לְזַמֵּר, כִּי מֵעוֹלָם וְעַד עוֹלָם אַתָּה אֵל. בָּרוּךְ אַתָּה יְיָ, מֶלֶךְ מְהֻלָּל בַּתִּשְׁבָּחוֹת.

Lift the cup of wine, say the following blessing, and drink the fourth cup, reclining.

בָּרוּךְ אַתָּה יְיָ, אֱלֹהֵינוּ מֶלֶךְ הָעוֹלָם,
בּוֹרֵא פְּרִי הַגָּפֶן.

Say the concluding blessing after wine (on the Sabbath add the words in parenthesis)

בָּרוּךְ אַתָּה יְיָ, אֱלֹהֵינוּ מֶלֶךְ הָעוֹלָם, עַל הַגֶּפֶן וְעַל פְּרִי הַגֶּפֶן. וְעַל תְּנוּבַת הַשָּׂדֶה, וְעַל אֶרֶץ חֶמְדָּה טוֹבָה וּרְחָבָה, שֶׁרָצִיתָ וְהִנְחַלְתָּ לַאֲבוֹתֵינוּ, לֶאֱכוֹל מִפִּרְיָהּ וְלִשְׂבּוֹעַ מִטּוּבָהּ. רַחֵם נָא יְיָ אֱלֹהֵינוּ עַל יִשְׂרָאֵל עַמֶּךָ, וְעַל יְרוּשָׁלַיִם עִירֶךָ, וְעַל צִיּוֹן מִשְׁכַּן כְּבוֹדֶךָ, וְעַל מִזְבְּחֶךָ וְעַל הֵיכָלֶךָ. וּבְנֵה יְרוּשָׁלַיִם עִיר הַקֹּדֶשׁ בִּמְהֵרָה בְיָמֵינוּ, וְהַעֲלֵנוּ לְתוֹכָהּ, וְשַׂמְּחֵנוּ בְּבִנְיָנָהּ וְנֹאכַל מִפִּרְיָהּ וְנִשְׂבַּע מִטּוּבָהּ, וּנְבָרֶכְךָ עָלֶיהָ בִּקְדֻשָּׁה וּבְטָהֳרָה (וּרְצֵה וְהַחֲלִיצֵנוּ בְּיוֹם הַשַּׁבָּת הַזֶּה) וְשַׂמְּחֵנוּ בְּיוֹם חַג הַמַּצּוֹת הַזֶּה. כִּי אַתָּה יְיָ טוֹב וּמֵטִיב לַכֹּל, וְנוֹדֶה לְּךָ עַל הָאָרֶץ וְעַל פְּרִי הַגָּפֶן. בָּרוּךְ אַתָּה יְיָ, עַל הָאָרֶץ וְעַל פְּרִי הַגָּפֶן.

QUESTIONS FOR NIRTZAH

1. What does the word *nirtzah* mean?
2. Where are the people in the picture dancing?
3. Why are they dancing?
4. Who are the dancers?

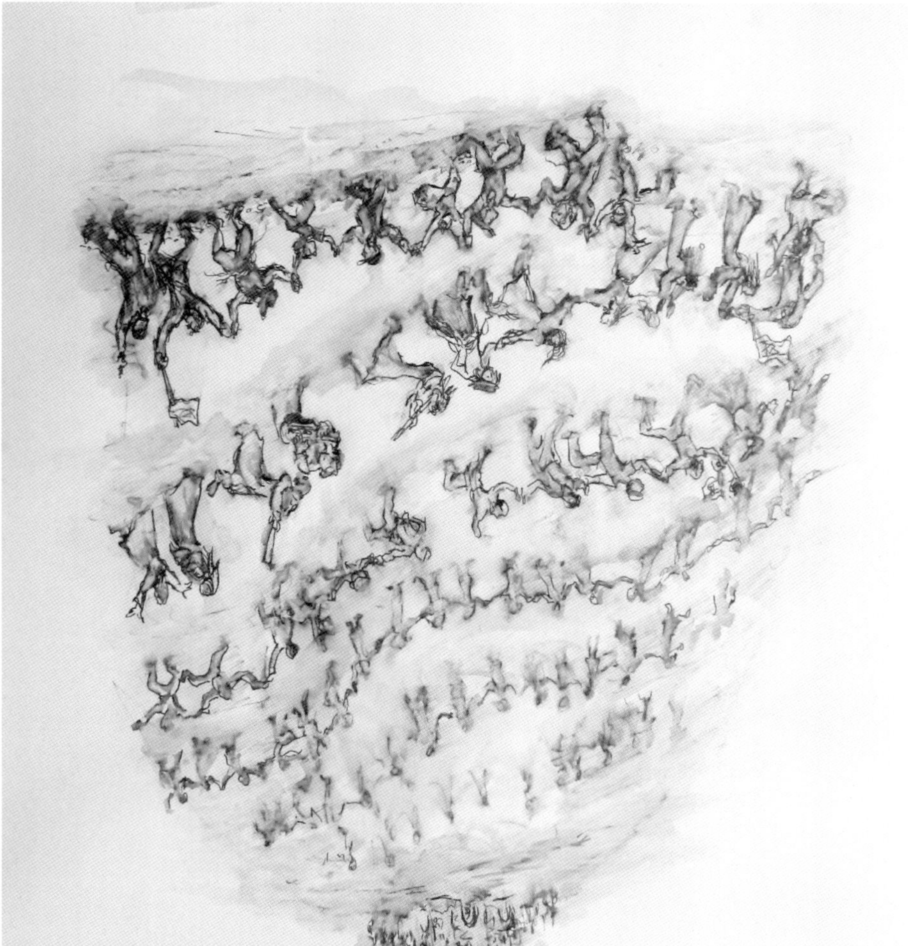

NIRTZAH

WE'VE MADE another Seder just as we were told. We followed all the rules laid down in days of old. Just as we've been privileged to do it now with care, May God grant us the chance to do it every year. Pure-one, O pure Dweller-of-the-Realm-Above: Restore Your countless people, bring them home with love; Quickly take Your vine shoots and replant them strong Back in Zion's vineyard, where they will sing Your song.

NEXT YEAR IN THE REBUILT JERUSALEM!

THE PRESENCE OF A MALE RABBINIC COURT AT THE IMMERSION OF A FEMALE CONVERT

RABBI JEFFREY S. FOX
ROSH YESHIVA, YESHIVAT MAHARAT

SUMMARY POSITION

Dear Rabbi Fox,

I want to ask a question that has emerged after extensive discussions with the men and women in our conversion course. We told the women that another woman would be in the mikveh when she immersed. We also told them that they could wear clothing that was loose fitting and that only once they were under the water would the rabbis be summoned in for just a moment to make certain that they were under water.

I was shocked by the fact that they responded to me with tears in their eyes and shaky voices explaining to me that this was difficult for them. I will always remember their tears. On top of that, here in D.C. this has become a mockery in the eyes of the world. The *Washington Post* published a lengthy article saying that the convert goes into the mikveh naked in front of the rabbi. This is in most cases not true, but the perception is very painful.

What do you recommend in this difficult situation?

Shmuel Herzfeld, Rabbi
Ruth Balinsky Friedman, Maharat
Ohev Sholom – the National Synagogue

נִרְצָה

חֲסַל סִדּוּר פֶּסַח כְּהִלְכָתוֹ, כְּכָל מִשְׁפָּטוֹ וְחֻקָּתוֹ. כַּאֲשֶׁר זָכִינוּ לְסַדֵּר אוֹתוֹ, כֵּן נִזְכֶּה לַעֲשׂוֹתוֹ. זָךְ שׁוֹכֵן מְעוֹנָה, קוֹמֵם קְהַל עֲדַת מִי מָנָה. בְּקָרוֹב נַהֵל נִטְעֵי כַנָּה, פְּדוּיִם לְצִיּוֹן בְּרִנָּה.

לְשָׁנָה הַבָּאָה בִּירוּשָׁלָיִם.

CONVERSIONS: A NEW APPROACH IS NEEDED

As part of the Exodus story the Israelites underwent a conversion process. This prepared them for receiving the Torah at Sinai, which transformed them from being Israelites to being the Jewish people. The Talmud tells us that the process that our ancestors underwent is exactly what a convert needs to do in order to become Jewish today (*Keritot* 9a). There is a dispute in the Talmud as to what exactly was the process of conversion for our ancestors in Egypt, but the Talmud rules in accordance with the opinion that our ancestors underwent both circumcision (for males) and immersion in a mikveh (*Yevamot* 46b). Consequently, all converts today must also undergo immersion in a mikveh in order to become Jewish.

The Talmud discusses the exact manner in which a woman is supposed to immerse in a mikveh in order to convert to Judaism (*Yevamot* 46b and 47b). The process is inherently difficult since the *beit din* (rabbinic court) in charge of the conversion must be made up of men, and they must be present for the conversion.

In October 2014, our synagogue finished the construction of a new mikveh. At the same time, another Orthodox rabbi in town with whom I had no connection was arrested and charged with placing a hidden camera in a mikveh in Georgetown in order to view the women who came to use that mikveh. This event caused our community to be more sensitive to all of our practices associated with mikveh, including ones that were not at all related to what this other rabbi was accused of.

That is the context for the question that Maharat Ruth Balinsky Friedman (my colleague in our congregation) and I sent to Rabbi Jeffrey Fox. (Please note that the question uses the term "I" because it reflects my personal reaction. However, the question was sent to Rabbi Fox by both of us together.)

On the first night:

IT HAPPENED AT MIDNIGHT

In times of yore You wrought most miracles at night. In the early watches of this night, You granted Avraham victory at night;
It happened at midnight.

Gerar's king You judged in a dream by night; You startled Lavan in the dark of night; Yaakov fought and bested an angel by night;
It happened at midnight.

Egypt's firstborn You smote at midnight; They could not find their wealth when they rose at night; Sisra You routed through stars of the night;
It happened at midnight.

Sancheriv's legions You devastated by night; Babylon's god was overthrown in the dark of the night; Daniel was shown the secret of Your mysteries of the night;
It happened at midnight.

Drunken Belshatzar was killed this very night; Daniel was saved from the lions' den at night; Haman wrote evil decrees in the night;
It happened at midnight.

You arose and vanquished him by Achashverosh's sleepless night; You will help those who ask: "What of the night?" You will call: "Morning follows the night";
It happened at midnight.

Speed the day that is neither day nor night; Most High, proclaim that Yours is the day and also the night; Set guards over Your city all day and all night; Make bright as day the darkness of the night;
It happened at midnight

---

1. Three male rabbis stand in the room with the mikveh and the naked woman while she immerses in the water, simply turning her back to the men.
2. Three male rabbis stand in the room with the mikveh and the woman while she immerses with a sheet or a robe of some kind covering her. There are some that use a large T-shirt, a large sheet with a hole, or simply a loose fitting robe that does not create a barrier between the woman and the water.

On the first night:

וַיְהִי בַּחֲצִי הַלַּיְלָה

וּבְכֵן "וַיְהִי בַּחֲצִי הַלַּיְלָה".

אָז רוֹב נִסִּים הִפְלֵאתָ בַּלַּיְלָה, בְּרֹאשׁ אַשְׁמוּרוֹת זֶה הַלַּיְלָה, גֵּר צֶדֶק נִצַּחְתּוֹ כְּנֶחֱלַק לוֹ לַיְלָה, וַיְהִי בַּחֲצִי הַלַּיְלָה.

דַּנְתָּ מֶלֶךְ גְּרָר בַּחֲלוֹם הַלַּיְלָה, הִפְחַדְתָּ אֲרַמִּי בְּאֶמֶשׁ לַיְלָה, וַיָּשַׂר יִשְׂרָאֵל לְמַלְאָךְ וַיּוּכַל לוֹ לַיְלָה, וַיְהִי בַּחֲצִי הַלַּיְלָה.

זֶרַע בְּכוֹרֵי פַתְרוֹס מָחַצְתָּ בַּחֲצִי הַלַּיְלָה, חֵילָם לֹא מָצְאוּ בְּקוּמָם בַּלַּיְלָה, טִיסַת נְגִיד חֲרֹשֶׁת סִלִּיתָ בְכוֹכְבֵי לַיְלָה, וַיְהִי בַּחֲצִי הַלַּיְלָה.

יָעַץ מְחָרֵף לְנוֹפֵף אִוּוּי, הוֹבַשְׁתָּ פְגָרָיו בַּלַּיְלָה, כָּרַע בֵּל וּמַצָּבוֹ בְּאִישׁוֹן לַיְלָה, לְאִישׁ חֲמוּדוֹת נִגְלָה רָז חֲזוֹת לַיְלָה, וַיְהִי בַּחֲצִי הַלַּיְלָה.

מִשְׁתַּכֵּר בִּכְלֵי קֹדֶשׁ נֶהֱרַג בּוֹ בַּלַּיְלָה, נוֹשַׁע מִבּוֹר אֲרָיוֹת פּוֹתֵר בִּעֲתוּתֵי לַיְלָה, שִׂנְאָה נָטַר אֲגָגִי וְכָתַב סְפָרִים לַיְלָה, וַיְהִי בַּחֲצִי הַלַּיְלָה.

עוֹרַרְתָּ נִצְחֲךָ עָלָיו בְּנֶדֶד שְׁנַת לַיְלָה, פּוּרָה תִדְרוֹךְ לְשׁוֹמֵר מַה מִּלַּיְלָה, צָרַח כַּשּׁוֹמֵר וְשָׂח אָתָא בֹקֶר וְגַם לַיְלָה, וַיְהִי בַּחֲצִי הַלַּיְלָה.

קָרֵב יוֹם אֲשֶׁר הוּא לֹא יוֹם וְלֹא לַיְלָה, רָם הוֹדַע כִּי לְךָ הַיּוֹם אַף לְךָ הַלַּיְלָה, שׁוֹמְרִים הַפְקֵד לְעִירְךָ כָּל הַיּוֹם וְכָל הַלַּיְלָה, תָּאִיר כְּאוֹר יוֹם חֶשְׁכַת לַיְלָה, וַיְהִי בַּחֲצִי הַלַּיְלָה.

Dear Rabbi Herzfeld and Maharat Balinsky Friedman,

The Orthodox community is deeply committed to *tzniut* as a lifestyle and not simply a rule regarding clothing. I hope to bring this value back to the forefront in this area of Jewish practice.

There are five different practices currently in place by different Orthodox *batei din* around the world:

On the second night:

THIS IS THE PASSOVER OFFERING

Thus you will say: this is the Passover offering.
Your wondrous powers You displayed on Passover; Above all festivals You set Passover; You revealed Yourself to Avraham at midnight of Passover;
And you shall say: This is the Passover offering.

At Avraham's door You knocked at high noon on Passover; He fed the angels matzot on Passover; To the cattle he ran for the ox on Passover;
And you shall say: This is the Passover offering.

The Sodomites enraged God and were burned on Passover; Lot was saved and he baked matzot on Passover; You swept Egypt as You passed through on Passover; And you shall say: This is the Passover offering.

God, You crushed the firstborn on Passover night; But Your own firstborn You spared by the sign of the blood; The Destroyer did not enter our homes on Passover; And you shall say: This is the Passover offering.

Jericho was taken on Passover; Gideon felled Midian through a barley-cake dream on Passover; Assyria's legions were consumed on Passover;
And you shall say: This is the Passover offering.

Sancheriv halted to shun the siege on Passover; A hand wrote Babylon's doom on the wall on Passover; Feasting Babylon was conquered on Passover;
And you shall say: This is the Passover offering.

Esther assembled the people for a three-day fast on Passover; You crushed Haman on a gallows tree on Passover; You will punish Edom doubly on Passover; Let Your might free us as it did then on the night of Passover;
And you shall say: This is the Passover offering.

---

5. Three male rabbis stand outside the door of the mikveh room, with the door fully closed, while listening for the splash of the water as the woman immerses, as well as the voice of the convert and the female mikveh attendant who ensures the complete submersion of the woman.

After reviewing the pertinent sources, I will offer my recommendation as to which of these five models is the most halakhically appropriate.

The role of the male rabbinic court in the conversion of a female must be situated in the broader question of the rabbinic court in conversion.

On the second night:

וַאֲמַרְתֶּם זֶבַח פֶּסַח

וּבְכֵן "וַאֲמַרְתֶּם זֶבַח פֶּסַח".

אֹמֶץ גְּבוּרוֹתֶיךָ הִפְלֵאתָ בַּפֶּסַח, בְּרֹאשׁ כָּל מוֹעֲדוֹת נִשֵּׂאתָ פֶּסַח, גִּלִּיתָ
לָאֶזְרָחִי חֲצוֹת לֵיל פֶּסַח, וַאֲמַרְתֶּם זֶבַח פֶּסַח.

דְּלָתָיו דָּפַקְתָּ כְּחֹם הַיּוֹם בַּפֶּסַח, הִסְעִיד נוֹצְצִים עֻגוֹת מַצּוֹת בַּפֶּסַח, וְאֶל
הַבָּקָר רָץ זֵכֶר לְשׁוֹר עֵרֶךְ פֶּסַח, וַאֲמַרְתֶּם זֶבַח פֶּסַח.

זֹעֲמוּ סְדוֹמִים וְלֹהֲטוּ בָּאֵשׁ בַּפֶּסַח, חֻלַּץ לוֹט מֵהֶם, וּמַצּוֹת אָפָה בְּקֵץ פֶּסַח,
טִאטֵאתָ אַדְמַת מֹף וְנֹף בְּעָבְרְךָ בַּפֶּסַח, וַאֲמַרְתֶּם זֶבַח פֶּסַח.

יָהּ, רֹאשׁ כָּל אוֹן מָחַצְתָּ בְּלֵיל שִׁמּוּר פֶּסַח, כַּבִּיר, עַל בֵּן בְּכוֹר פָּסַחְתָּ בְּדַם
פֶּסַח, לְבִלְתִּי תֵּת מַשְׁחִית לָבֹא בִּפְתָחַי בַּפֶּסַח, וַאֲמַרְתֶּם זֶבַח פֶּסַח.

מְסֻגֶּרֶת סֻגָּרָה בְּעִתּוֹתֵי פֶּסַח, נִשְׁמְדָה מִדְיָן בִּצְלִיל שְׂעוֹרֵי עֹמֶר פֶּסַח, שֹׂרְפוּ
מִשְׁמַנֵּי פּוּל וְלוּד בִּיקַד יְקוֹד פֶּסַח, וַאֲמַרְתֶּם זֶבַח פֶּסַח.

עוֹד הַיּוֹם בְּנֹב לַעֲמוֹד, עַד גָּעָה עוֹנַת פֶּסַח, פַּס יָד כָּתְבָה לְקַעֲקֵעַ צוּל
בַּפֶּסַח, צָפֹה הַצָּפִית עָרוֹךְ הַשֻּׁלְחָן בַּפֶּסַח, וַאֲמַרְתֶּם זֶבַח פֶּסַח.

קָהָל כִּנְּסָה הֲדַסָּה צוֹם לְשַׁלֵּשׁ בַּפֶּסַח, רֹאשׁ מִבֵּית רָשָׁע מָחַצְתָּ בְּעֵץ חֲמִשִּׁים
בַּפֶּסַח, שְׁתֵּי אֵלֶּה רֶגַע, תָּבִיא לְעוּצִית בַּפֶּסַח, תָּעֹז יָדְךָ וְתָרוּם יְמִינְךָ, כְּלֵיל
הִתְקַדֵּשׁ חַג פֶּסַח, וַאֲמַרְתֶּם זֶבַח פֶּסַח.

---

3. Three male rabbis stand outside the door of the mikveh room, with the door ajar so that they can see the back of the woman's head while she immerses in the water, thus ensuring that her head is completely submerged. The woman in this case is not wearing a robe or garment of any kind.
4. Three male rabbis stand outside the door of the mikveh room, with the door ajar so that they can see the back of the woman's head while she immerses in the water, thus ensuring that her head is completely submerged. The woman in this case is wearing a robe or garment.

On both nights continue:

IT IS FITTING TO PRAISE HIM

August in kingship, rightfully chosen
His angel-legions say to Him: "Yours, only Yours, Yours alone,
O Lord, is the kingship!" It is fitting to praise Him.
Preeminent in kingship, truly resplendent,
His faithful say to Him: "Yours, only Yours, Yours alone,
O Lord, is the kingship!" It is fitting to praise Him.
Pristine in kingship, truly powerful,
His disciples say to Him: "Yours, only Yours, Yours alone,
O Lord, is the kingship!" It is fitting to praise Him.
Exalted in kingship, truly awe-inspiring,
His heavenly courtiers say to Him: "Yours, only Yours, Yours alone,
O Lord, is the kingship!" It is fitting to praise Him.
Humble in kingship, truly liberating,
His upright say to Him: "Yours, only Yours, Yours alone,
O Lord, is the kingship!" It is fitting to praise Him.
Holy in kingship, truly merciful,
His angels say to Him: "Yours, only Yours, Yours alone,
O Lord, is the kingship!" It is fitting to praise Him.
Mightily sovereign, truly sustaining,
His faultless ones say to Him: "Yours, only Yours, Yours alone,
O Lord, is the kingship!" It is fitting to praise Him.

---

by the rabbinic court. Rabbi Yosef Karo summarizes both positions in his *Shulchan Arukh* (Yoreh Deah 268:3). The first perspective that he quotes is the Ashkenazic position of the printed Tosafot (*Yevamot* 45b, s.v. *mi lo tavlah*) and Rabbeinu Asher (*Yevamot* 4:31) that after the fact such a conversion is kosher, even if not ideal. The second position that he quotes is that of Rambam (*Mishneh Torah*, Hilkhot Issurei Biah 13:9) and Rif (*Yevamot*

On both nights continue:

כִּי לוֹ נָאֶה, כִּי לוֹ יָאֶה.

אַדִּיר בִּמְלוּכָה, בָּחוּר כַּהֲלָכָה, גְּדוּדָיו יֹאמְרוּ לוֹ:
לְךָ וּלְךָ, לְךָ כִּי לְךָ, לְךָ אַף לְךָ, לְךָ יְיָ הַמַּמְלָכָה. כִּי לוֹ נָאֶה, כִּי לוֹ יָאֶה.

דָּגוּל בִּמְלוּכָה, הָדוּר כַּהֲלָכָה, וָתִיקָיו יֹאמְרוּ לוֹ:
לְךָ וּלְךָ, לְךָ כִּי לְךָ, לְךָ אַף לְךָ, לְךָ יְיָ הַמַּמְלָכָה. כִּי לוֹ נָאֶה, כִּי לוֹ יָאֶה.

זַכַּאי בִּמְלוּכָה, חָסִין כַּהֲלָכָה, טַפְסְרָיו יֹאמְרוּ לוֹ:
לְךָ וּלְךָ, לְךָ כִּי לְךָ, לְךָ אַף לְךָ, לְךָ יְיָ הַמַּמְלָכָה. כִּי לוֹ נָאֶה, כִּי לוֹ יָאֶה.

יָחִיד בִּמְלוּכָה, כַּבִּיר כַּהֲלָכָה, לִמּוּדָיו יֹאמְרוּ לוֹ:
לְךָ וּלְךָ, לְךָ כִּי לְךָ, לְךָ אַף לְךָ, לְךָ יְיָ הַמַּמְלָכָה. כִּי לוֹ נָאֶה, כִּי לוֹ יָאֶה.

מוֹשֵׁל בִּמְלוּכָה, נוֹרָא כַּהֲלָכָה, סְבִיבָיו יֹאמְרוּ לוֹ:
לְךָ וּלְךָ, לְךָ כִּי לְךָ, לְךָ אַף לְךָ, לְךָ יְיָ הַמַּמְלָכָה. כִּי לוֹ נָאֶה, כִּי לוֹ יָאֶה.

עָנָו בִּמְלוּכָה, פּוֹדֶה כַּהֲלָכָה, צַדִּיקָיו יֹאמְרוּ לוֹ:
לְךָ וּלְךָ, לְךָ כִּי לְךָ, לְךָ אַף לְךָ, לְךָ יְיָ הַמַּמְלָכָה. כִּי לוֹ נָאֶה, כִּי לוֹ יָאֶה.

קָדוֹשׁ בִּמְלוּכָה, רַחוּם כַּהֲלָכָה, שִׁנְאַנָּיו יֹאמְרוּ לוֹ:
לְךָ וּלְךָ, לְךָ כִּי לְךָ, לְךָ אַף לְךָ, לְךָ יְיָ הַמַּמְלָכָה. כִּי לוֹ נָאֶה, כִּי לוֹ יָאֶה.

תַּקִּיף בִּמְלוּכָה, תּוֹמֵךְ כַּהֲלָכָה, תְּמִימָיו יֹאמְרוּ לוֹ:
לְךָ וּלְךָ, לְךָ כִּי לְךָ, לְךָ אַף לְךָ, לְךָ יְיָ הַמַּמְלָכָה. כִּי לוֹ נָאֶה, כִּי לוֹ יָאֶה.

The Talmud (Bavli, *Yevamot* 47b) already recognized the importance of the need for modesty in the process, and I hope to increase our commitment to that value. This summary will serve to outline the main points of a longer *teshuvah*.

There is complex debate among the medieval commentators regarding the status of a conversion in which the immersion was not witnessed at all

AUGUST IS HE

August is He; May He rebuild His Temple very soon, in our time:
O God, build; O God, rebuild Your Temple soon.

Chosen is He, pure is He, preeminent is He;
May He rebuild His Temple very soon, in our time:
O God, build; O God, rebuild Your Temple soon.

Magnificent is He, venerable is He, refined is He, pious is He;
May He rebuild His Temple very soon, in our time:
O God, build; O God, rebuild Your Temple soon.

Pure is He, One-alone is He, mighty is He, wise is He,
King is He, awesome is He, exalted is He, powerful is He, redeemer is He, just is He; May He rebuild His Temple very soon, in our time:
O God, build; O God, rebuild Your Temple soon.

Holy is He, merciful is He, Almighty is He, potent is He;
May He rebuild His Temple very soon, in our time:
O God, build; O God, rebuild Your Temple soon.

---

witnessed by the male rabbinic court then an emergency situation (*she'at hadechak*) has been created and we may rely on less than ideal (*b'di'eved*) halakhic positions. Since the *Shulchan Arukh* accepts these approaches, there is ample support to rely on Tosafot and Rosh and not demand that the immersion be witnessed.

In addition, Rav Moshe Feinstein in a foundational responsum in 1974 (*Igrot Moshe*, Yoreh Deah 3:112) deals with a case in which there was not enough room and only one member of the male rabbinic court was able to witness the immersion. He goes on to outline a core concept in Jewish law: when the rabbinic court hears something or knows something with certainty, it is as if they witnessed that event. Rav Moshe wrote the following: שלכן בטבילה שצריך הגר לפני ב״ד סגי בשמיעת הטבילה לכו״ע, *"For in the context of immersion which requires the presence of a rabbinic court, hearing is sufficient according to all positions."*

Rav Moshe's claim is that as long as the rabbinic court has full knowledge of the immersion, all halakhic decisors must accept the validity of this

אַדִּיר הוּא

אַדִּיר הוּא, יִבְנֶה בֵיתוֹ בְּקָרוֹב, בִּמְהֵרָה בִּמְהֵרָה, בְּיָמֵינוּ בְּקָרוֹב. אֵל בְּנֵה, בְּנֵה בֵיתְךָ בְּקָרוֹב.

בָּחוּר הוּא, גָּדוֹל הוּא, דָּגוּל הוּא, יִבְנֶה בֵיתוֹ בְּקָרוֹב, בִּמְהֵרָה בִּמְהֵרָה, בְּיָמֵינוּ בְּקָרוֹב. אֵל בְּנֵה, אֵל בְּנֵה, בְּנֵה בֵיתְךָ בְּקָרוֹב.

הָדוּר הוּא, וָתִיק הוּא, זַכַּאי הוּא, חָסִיד הוּא, יִבְנֶה בֵיתוֹ בְּקָרוֹב, בִּמְהֵרָה בִּמְהֵרָה, בְּיָמֵינוּ בְּקָרוֹב. אֵל בְּנֵה, אֵל בְּנֵה, בְּנֵה בֵיתְךָ בְּקָרוֹב.

טָהוֹר הוּא, יָחִיד הוּא, כַּבִּיר הוּא, לָמוּד הוּא, מֶלֶךְ הוּא, נוֹרָא הוּא, סַגִּיב הוּא, עִזּוּז הוּא, פּוֹדֶה הוּא, צַדִּיק הוּא, יִבְנֶה בֵיתוֹ בְּקָרוֹב, בִּמְהֵרָה בִּמְהֵרָה, בְּיָמֵינוּ בְּקָרוֹב. אֵל בְּנֵה, אֵל בְּנֵה, בְּנֵה בֵיתְךָ בְּקָרוֹב.

קָדוֹשׁ הוּא, רַחוּם הוּא, שַׁדַּי הוּא, תַּקִּיף הוּא, יִבְנֶה בֵיתוֹ בְּקָרוֹב, בִּמְהֵרָה בִּמְהֵרָה, בְּיָמֵינוּ בְּקָרוֹב. אֵל בְּנֵה, אֵל בְּנֵה, בְּנֵה בֵיתְךָ בְּקָרוֹב.

15a), according to which such a person would not be permitted to marry into the Jewish community without another immersion.

According to the classic rules of *psak,* when Rav Yosef Karo presents a debate in this manner he means to decide in accordance with the first position. Therefore, we have an unusual instance in which Rabbi Yosef Karo rejected the position of Rambam and Rif in favor of Rosh and Tosafot (see also Shach 268:8 and Bach 268 s.v. *v'khol inyanav*).

There are several modern *poskim* who rely on this position in different cases. Rav Uziel (*Mishpetei Uziel,* Yoreh Deah 1:13) deals with a case in which the community mikveh is located in the non-Jewish bathhouse. Since it was difficult to imagine the male rabbinic court entering a public bathhouse, Rav Uziel said that it was permissible for three women to oversee the immersion and report back to the court. Rav Uziel was focused on the appropriate behavior of the members of the rabbinic court, something that we need to keep in mind.

There is no doubt that if a woman expresses discomfort with being

WHO KNOWS ONE?

WHO KNOWS ONE? I know one! One is our God in heaven and on earth.

WHO KNOWS TWO? I know two! Two are the Tablets of the Covenant; One is our God in heaven and on earth.

WHO KNOWS THREE? I know three! Three are the patriarchs; Two are the Tablets of the Covenant; One is our God in heaven and on earth.

WHO KNOWS FOUR? I know four! Four are the matriarchs; Three are the patriarchs; Two are the Tablets of the Covenant; One is our God in heaven and on earth.

WHO KNOWS FIVE? I know five! Five are the books of the Torah; Four are the matriarchs; Three are the patriarchs; Two are the Tablets of the Covenant; One is our God in heaven and on earth.

---

because of our own perspective, and taking into consideration the feelings of the potential converts.

Since there is no requirement to enter the room, the policy of all conversion courts should be to stand outside the door. Some may choose to leave the door open enough to see the back of the convert's head while she immerses in a robe; others may leave the door open just a crack or closed entirely and ensure that sound can reach them.

If we return to the five practices that I listed above, we can now evaluate what might be best:

1. Three male rabbis stand in the room with the mikveh and the naked woman while she immerses in the water, simply turning her back to the men.
2. The three male rabbis stand in the room with the mikveh while the woman immerses with a sheet or a robe of some kind.
3. The three male rabbis stand outside the door with the door ajar so that they can see the back of the woman's head submerge under the water while the woman is not wearing a robe or a sheet.
4. The three male rabbis stand outside the door with the door ajar so that they can see the back of the woman's head submerge under the water while she is wearing a robe or a sheet.

אֶחָד מִי יוֹדֵעַ?

אֶחָד מִי יוֹדֵעַ? אֶחָד אֲנִי יוֹדֵעַ: אֶחָד אֱלֹהֵינוּ שֶׁבַּשָּׁמַיִם וּבָאָרֶץ.

שְׁנַיִם מִי יוֹדֵעַ? שְׁנַיִם אֲנִי יוֹדֵעַ: שְׁנֵי לֻחוֹת הַבְּרִית, אֶחָד אֱלֹהֵינוּ שֶׁבַּשָּׁמַיִם וּבָאָרֶץ.

שְׁלֹשָׁה מִי יוֹדֵעַ? שְׁלֹשָׁה אֲנִי יוֹדֵעַ: שְׁלֹשָׁה אָבוֹת, שְׁנֵי לֻחוֹת הַבְּרִית, אֶחָד אֱלֹהֵינוּ שֶׁבַּשָּׁמַיִם וּבָאָרֶץ.

אַרְבַּע מִי יוֹדֵעַ? אַרְבַּע אֲנִי יוֹדֵעַ: אַרְבַּע אִמָּהוֹת, שְׁלֹשָׁה אָבוֹת, שְׁנֵי לֻחוֹת הַבְּרִית, אֶחָד אֱלֹהֵינוּ שֶׁבַּשָּׁמַיִם וּבָאָרֶץ.

חֲמִשָּׁה מִי יוֹדֵעַ? חֲמִשָּׁה אֲנִי יוֹדֵעַ: חֲמִשָּׁה חוּמְשֵׁי תוֹרָה, אַרְבַּע אִמָּהוֹת, שְׁלֹשָׁה אָבוֹת, שְׁנֵי לֻחוֹת הַבְּרִית, אֶחָד אֱלֹהֵינוּ שֶׁבַּשָּׁמַיִם וּבָאָרֶץ.

---

conversion (even those who hold according to Rambam and Rif). This is the way that Rav Moshe Klein in his *Mishnat Hager* (*siman* 45 and chapter 5:23–24, note 45) explains this core response of Rav Moshe Feinstein.

Rav Moshe's logic is compelling and can be applied to our case by allowing the door to be closed, or open just a crack, as long as sound can travel. The advantage of Rav Moshe's position is that he makes his claim for all decisors and says that it works even from the outset (*mi'l'khatchilah*). If modern rabbinic courts are not prepared to rely on Rav Moshe from the outset, we must be prepared to accept the decision of the *Shulchan Arukh* and rely on the position that the court need not witness the immersion.

The current practice of some rabbinic courts is embarrassing. There are some who enter the room with the mikveh water and do not allow the woman to cover up with a robe. This is simply unacceptable. The presence of the men in the room with the mikveh water is not required according to the *Shulchan Arukh* and Rav Moshe Feinstein. Given the importance of the value of modesty in our community, it is time for all male rabbis involved in conversion to show our shared commitment to this core value – both

WHO KNOWS SIX? I know six! Six are the orders of the Mishnah; Five are the books of the Torah; Four are the matriarchs; Three are the patriarchs; Two are the Tablets of the Covenant; One is our God in heaven and on earth.

WHO KNOWS SEVEN? I know seven! Seven are the days of the week; Six are the orders of the Mishnah; Five are the books of the Torah; Four are the matriarchs; Three are the patriarchs; Two are the Tablets of the Covenant; One is our God in heaven and on earth.

WHO KNOWS EIGHT? I know eight! Eight are the days to circumcision; Seven are the days of the week; Six are the orders of the Mishnah; Five are the books of the Torah; Four are the matriarchs; Three are the patriarchs; Two are the Tablets of the Covenant; One is our God in heaven and on earth.

WHO KNOWS NINE? I know nine! Nine are the months to childbirth; Eight are the days to circumcision; Seven are the days of the week; Six are the orders of the Mishnah; Five are the books of the Torah; Four are the matriarchs; Three are the patriarchs; Two are the Tablets of the Covenant; One is our God in heaven and on earth.

---

1. The woman is in a robe and the male *beit din* stands outside a door that is open just enough for them to witness only the back of her head while she immerses (option no. 4 above).
2. The woman is in a robe and the male *beit din* stands outside a door that is open just enough to let sound travel and could even be closed if they can hear through the closed door (option no. 5 above).
3. In a situation in which there is no door close enough for them to see her head, the male *beit din* stands a few feet away while the mikveh attendant assists the woman into the water with a robe. The men must stand with their backs to the mikveh water and ensure that they can hear the water. It is my strong preference for the men to be outside of the room and I recommend that mikvaot be built with this in mind. If that is not an option, a temporary room divider should be brought for female conversions.

Based on the approach of Rav Moshe, ensuring that the *beit din* can hear and be heard is essential. In this way the immersion can be considered to

שִׁשָּׁה מִי יוֹדֵעַ? שִׁשָּׁה אֲנִי יוֹדֵעַ: שִׁשָּׁה סִדְרֵי מִשְׁנָה, חֲמִשָּׁה חוּמְשֵׁי תוֹרָה, אַרְבַּע אִמָּהוֹת, שְׁלֹשָׁה אָבוֹת, שְׁנֵי לֻחוֹת הַבְּרִית, אֶחָד אֱלֹהֵינוּ שֶׁבַּשָּׁמַיִם וּבָאָרֶץ.

שִׁבְעָה מִי יוֹדֵעַ? שִׁבְעָה אֲנִי יוֹדֵעַ: שִׁבְעָה יְמֵי שַׁבַּתָּא, שִׁשָּׁה סִדְרֵי מִשְׁנָה, חֲמִשָּׁה חוּמְשֵׁי תוֹרָה, אַרְבַּע אִמָּהוֹת, שְׁלֹשָׁה אָבוֹת, שְׁנֵי לֻחוֹת הַבְּרִית, אֶחָד אֱלֹהֵינוּ שֶׁבַּשָּׁמַיִם וּבָאָרֶץ.

שְׁמוֹנָה מִי יוֹדֵעַ? שְׁמוֹנָה אֲנִי יוֹדֵעַ: שְׁמוֹנָה יְמֵי מִילָה, שִׁבְעָה יְמֵי שַׁבַּתָּא, שִׁשָּׁה סִדְרֵי מִשְׁנָה, חֲמִשָּׁה חוּמְשֵׁי תוֹרָה, אַרְבַּע אִמָּהוֹת, שְׁלֹשָׁה אָבוֹת, שְׁנֵי לֻחוֹת הַבְּרִית, אֶחָד אֱלֹהֵינוּ שֶׁבַּשָּׁמַיִם וּבָאָרֶץ.

תִּשְׁעָה מִי יוֹדֵעַ? תִּשְׁעָה אֲנִי יוֹדֵעַ: תִּשְׁעָה יַרְחֵי לֵדָה, שְׁמוֹנָה יְמֵי מִילָה, שִׁבְעָה יְמֵי שַׁבַּתָּא, שִׁשָּׁה סִדְרֵי מִשְׁנָה, חֲמִשָּׁה חוּמְשֵׁי תוֹרָה, אַרְבַּע אִמָּהוֹת, שְׁלֹשָׁה אָבוֹת, שְׁנֵי לֻחוֹת הַבְּרִית, אֶחָד אֱלֹהֵינוּ שֶׁבַּשָּׁמַיִם וּבָאָרֶץ.

---

5. The three male rabbis stand outside the closed door and listen for the splash of the water as the woman immerses, as well as the voice of the convert and the female mikveh attendant who ensures the complete submersion of the woman.

It is my strong opinion that the first two options – when the men are in the room – are simply not appropriate. According to the laws of conversion there is no reason for the men to be inside. Many women have described this as a feeling of being abused by the *beit din*.

Male rabbis standing outside the door while the woman is naked (option no. 3) is also unacceptable. There is no reason for the woman to feel as though her body is being inspected by a group of men. A loose fitting robe or sheet can be used in a way that ensures that there are no interpositions. In addition, there should always be a woman present in order to assist and support the potential convert.

There are three practices that I think are appropriate:

WHO KNOWS TEN? I know ten! Ten are the commandments of Sinai; Nine are the months to childbirth; Eight are the days to circumcision; Seven are the days of the week; Six are the orders of the Mishnah; Five are the books of the Torah; Four are the matriarchs; Three are the patriarchs; Two are the Tablets of the Covenant; One is our God in heaven and on earth.

WHO KNOWS ELEVEN? I know eleven! Eleven are the stars in Joseph's dream; Ten are the commandments of Sinai; Nine are the months to childbirth; Eight are the days to circumcision; Seven are the days of the week; Six are the orders of the Mishnah; Five are the books of the Torah; Four are the matriarchs; Three are the patriarchs; Two are the Tablets of the Covenant; One is our God in heaven and on earth.

WHO KNOWS TWELVE? I know twelve! Twelve are the tribes of Israel; Eleven are the stars in Joseph's dream; Ten are the commandments of Sinai; Nine are the months to childbirth; Eight are the days to circumcision; Seven are the days of the week; Six are the orders of the Mishnah; Five are the books of the Torah; Four are the matriarchs; Three are the patriarchs; Two are the Tablets of the Covenant; One is our God in heaven and on earth.

WHO KNOWS THIRTEEN? I know thirteen! Thirteen are God's attributes; Twelve are the tribes of Israel; Eleven are the stars in Joseph's dream; Ten are the commandments of Sinai; Nine are the months to childbirth; Eight are the days to circumcision; Seven are the days of the week; Six are the orders of the Mishnah; Five are the books of the Torah; Four are the matriarchs; Three are the patriarchs; Two are the Tablets of the Covenant; One is our God in heaven and on earth.

---

closer to the Torah of Hashem and the Jewish people. It is my sincere hope and prayer that we might be able to help wipe some of the tears of those who feel most vulnerable.

בברכות התורה וידידות
Rabbi Jeffrey S. Fox
Rosh Yeshiva, Yeshivat Maharat
16 November, 2014

עֲשָׂרָה מִי יוֹדֵעַ? עֲשָׂרָה אֲנִי יוֹדֵעַ: עֲשָׂרָה דִבְּרַיָּא, תִּשְׁעָה יַרְחֵי לֵדָה, שְׁמוֹנָה יְמֵי מִילָה, שִׁבְעָה יְמֵי שַׁבַּתָּא, שִׁשָּׁה סִדְרֵי מִשְׁנָה, חֲמִשָּׁה חוּמְשֵׁי תוֹרָה, אַרְבַּע אִמָּהוֹת, שְׁלֹשָׁה אָבוֹת, שְׁנֵי לֻחוֹת הַבְּרִית, אֶחָד אֱלֹהֵינוּ שֶׁבַּשָּׁמַיִם וּבָאָרֶץ.

אַחַד עָשָׂר מִי יוֹדֵעַ? אַחַד עָשָׂר אֲנִי יוֹדֵעַ: אַחַד עָשָׂר כּוֹכְבַיָּא, עֲשָׂרָה דִבְּרַיָּא, תִּשְׁעָה יַרְחֵי לֵדָה, שְׁמוֹנָה יְמֵי מִילָה, שִׁבְעָה יְמֵי שַׁבַּתָּא, שִׁשָּׁה סִדְרֵי מִשְׁנָה, חֲמִשָּׁה חוּמְשֵׁי תוֹרָה, אַרְבַּע אִמָּהוֹת, שְׁלֹשָׁה אָבוֹת, שְׁנֵי לֻחוֹת הַבְּרִית, אֶחָד אֱלֹהֵינוּ שֶׁבַּשָּׁמַיִם וּבָאָרֶץ.

שְׁנֵים עָשָׂר מִי יוֹדֵעַ? שְׁנֵים עָשָׂר אֲנִי יוֹדֵעַ: שְׁנֵים עָשָׂר שִׁבְטַיָּא, אַחַד עָשָׂר כּוֹכְבַיָּא, עֲשָׂרָה דִבְּרַיָּא, תִּשְׁעָה יַרְחֵי לֵדָה, שְׁמוֹנָה יְמֵי מִילָה, שִׁבְעָה יְמֵי שַׁבַּתָּא, שִׁשָּׁה סִדְרֵי מִשְׁנָה, חֲמִשָּׁה חוּמְשֵׁי תוֹרָה, אַרְבַּע אִמָּהוֹת, שְׁלֹשָׁה אָבוֹת, שְׁנֵי לֻחוֹת הַבְּרִית, אֶחָד אֱלֹהֵינוּ שֶׁבַּשָּׁמַיִם וּבָאָרֶץ.

שְׁלֹשָׁה עָשָׂר מִי יוֹדֵעַ? שְׁלֹשָׁה עָשָׂר אֲנִי יוֹדֵעַ: שְׁלֹשָׁה עָשָׂר מִדַּיָּא, שְׁנֵים עָשָׂר שִׁבְטַיָּא, אַחַד עָשָׂר כּוֹכְבַיָּא, עֲשָׂרָה דִבְּרַיָּא, תִּשְׁעָה יַרְחֵי לֵדָה, שְׁמוֹנָה יְמֵי מִילָה, שִׁבְעָה יְמֵי שַׁבַּתָּא, שִׁשָּׁה סִדְרֵי מִשְׁנָה, חֲמִשָּׁה חוּמְשֵׁי תוֹרָה, אַרְבַּע אִמָּהוֹת, שְׁלֹשָׁה אָבוֹת, שְׁנֵי לֻחוֹת הַבְּרִית, אֶחָד אֱלֹהֵינוּ שֶׁבַּשָּׁמַיִם וּבָאָרֶץ.

---

have taken place "under their direction," as Rav Moshe Klein explains. Once they can hear, they have knowledge that the immersion was accomplished and can be considered to have witnessed the event. Even for those who are not prepared to accept Rav Moshe's *psak* in this way, if a woman expresses discomfort it is certainly acceptable to rely on the first opinion in the *Shulchan Arukh* and not require the *beit din* to actually witness the immersion.

There is no doubt that the situation in Washington, D.C., is currently a *she'at hadechak*. I hope that this *teshuvah* can help bring women and men

CHAD GADYA

ONE KID, one kid,
That father bought for two *zuzim*;
One kid, one kid.

Came a cat and ate the kid
That father bought for two *zuzim*;
One kid, one kid.

Came a dog and bit the cat
That ate the kid
That father bought for two *zuzim*;
One kid, one kid.

---

and gold of Egypt." Our redemption of the firstborn donkey is thus a way of remembering the miraculous exodus from Egypt (see Seforno, ad loc.).

Aside from the two reasons provided by the Talmud, there is deep symbolism behind redeeming donkeys. The mitzvah of *peter chamor* is both a literal commandment as well as a symbolic one. The symbolism of the mitzvah is intended to remind us of the importance of redemption. When we perform the mitzvah of redeeming a donkey, it is supposed to inspire us to dream of redeeming. What other things are we supposed to be redeeming? The answer is everyone and everything.

Parashat Behar is filled with the mitzvah of redemption. The parashah tells us to redeem the land for our relatives. "If your brother becomes impoverished and sells some of his hereditary lands, a close relative should come and redeem what his kinsman has sold" (Vayikra 25:25). Additionally, all hereditary land is redeemed automatically at the Yovel (the jubilee year).

If a fellow Jew is sold to a foreigner we have a responsibility to redeem him from his slavery (25:47). So, too, if someone sells a home within a walled city, he is allowed to redeem it within one year of having sold it (25:29). On the other hand, if someone sells hereditary property then a relative should come and redeem the property even against the buyer's will. (Rashi, 25:25).

There are also more subtle appearances of redemption, such as the commandment not to lend money at interest. The verse doesn't mention

חַד גַּדְיָא

חַד גַּדְיָא, חַד גַּדְיָא

דְּזַבִּין אַבָּא בִּתְרֵי זוּזֵי, חַד גַּדְיָא, חַד גַּדְיָא.

וְאָתָא שׁוּנְרָא, וְאָכְלָה לְגַדְיָא,
דְּזַבִּין אַבָּא בִּתְרֵי זוּזֵי, חַד גַּדְיָא, חַד גַּדְיָא.

וְאָתָא כַלְבָּא, וְנָשַׁךְ לְשׁוּנְרָא, דְּאָכְלָה לְגַדְיָא,
דְּזַבִּין אַבָּא בִּתְרֵי זוּזֵי, חַד גַּדְיָא, חַד גַּדְיָא.

REDEEMING A DONKEY... AND OUR SOULS

Our synagogue invested some funds ($200) toward the purchase of two donkeys. Why would a shul want to be in the donkey business? The reason is that we are not in the donkey business, but we are in the mitzvah business! There is a mitzvah from the Torah to redeem a first-born male donkey – a *peter chamor.*

The Torah states, "Every firstling donkey must be redeemed with a sheep" (Shemot 13:13). Rambam codifies this law in his *Mishneh Torah.* He writes, "It is a positive commandment for every Jewish man to redeem the first [male] issue of a donkey with a sheep" (Hilkhot Bikkurim 12:1). In other words, just like there is a mitzvah of *pidyon haben,* to redeem a firstborn son, so too there is a mitzvah of redeeming a firstborn male donkey. If someone owns a donkey and its first offspring is a male then there is a commandment to take the baby donkey to a *kohen* and give the *kohen* a lamb in exchange for the donkey.

Says the Talmud (*Bekhorot* 5b): "Why is a firstborn donkey different than horses and camels [about whom there is no biblical commandment to redeem]?" The Talmud offers two possibilities as to why the donkey is singled out for redemption. The first explanation is that there is no explanation. It is a decree of Hashem, *gezeirat hakatuv,* which we do because God asked us to. Second, the Talmud suggests that perhaps a donkey is more deserving of our gratitude, because donkeys helped our ancestors when they left Egypt. Our ancestors had no wagons to carry all of their stuff and so they placed their possessions on donkeys instead. According to the Talmud, "There was not an Israelite who did not possess ninety Libyan donkeys laden with the silver

Came a stick and beat the dog
That bit the cat
That ate the kid
That father bought for two *zuzim*;
One kid, one kid.

Came a fire and burned the stick
That beat the dog
That bit the cat
That ate the kid
That father bought for two *zuzim*;
One kid, one kid.

---

purchasing the land. Yirmiyahu gives Chanamel seven *shekalim* (in prison) and ten pieces of silver. He writes down the deed on a document. He demands that the other prisoners serve as witnesses and he weighs out the money on a scale. He then takes the deed of sale and places it in an earthenware vessel so that it will last a long time.

In this story Yirmiyahu is no longer a prophet of doom but a prophet of redemption. As everyone else is preparing for the destruction of the land and selling off their property, Yirmiyahu invests his savings in the redemption of the land. While everyone else is fleeing, he alone believes that redemption will arrive. While everyone else is selling their ancestral lands to the first bidder, Yirmiyahu alone stands up in his prison cell and thunders, "Thus says God: this land will once again see the purchase of fields and vineyards and houses."

The message of Yirmiyahu and the message of our parashah is that we have a responsibility to act as redeemers. We need to redeem our friends and our neighbors. We need to be there for them in their times of need.

Yirmiyahu takes his message of redemption a step further in two crucial ways. Firstly, he tells us that that we should dream of redemption precisely when it seems least plausible. When everyone else is running from the situation and giving up hope, that is when we need to step in and act as redeemers. When everyone else has abandoned hope that is when Yirmiyahu declares his belief that the land of Israel will once again be filled with a thriving population.

And secondly, Yirmiyahu teaches us that our responsibility to redeem does not only refer to the living but also to those who have passed on. Our ancestors planted their trees so we could enjoy their fruits today, and thus we

וְאָתָא חוּטְרָא, וְהִכָּה לְכַלְבָּא,
דְּנָשַׁךְ לְשׁוּנְרָא, דְּאָכְלָה לְגַדְיָא,
דְּזַבִּין אַבָּא בִּתְרֵי זוּזֵי, חַד גַּדְיָא, חַד גַּדְיָא.

וְאָתָא נוּרָא, וְשָׂרַף לְחוּטְרָא,
דְּהִכָּה לְכַלְבָּא, דְּנָשַׁךְ לְשׁוּנְרָא, דְּאָכְלָה לְגַדְיָא,
דְּזַבִּין אַבָּא בִּתְרֵי זוּזֵי, חַד גַּדְיָא, חַד גַּדְיָא.

---

the word *redemption* but the commandment is all about redemption – it is an opportunity to offer someone financial redemption and allow them to get back on their feet. As the verse states, "You must come to his aid. Help him survive" (25:35).

The list goes on and on. So much so that some maintain that all of the commandments of Parashat Behar have as their theme the concept of redemption. All the laws of Shemittah and Yovel, as outlined in this parashah, are really opportunities for redemption – whether it be the redemption of land, of a person's financial status, or of one's personal freedom. (See, for example, Yehudah Shaviv to Parashat Behar, http://www.vbm-torah.org/haftora.html.)

This is why our tradition chooses a beautiful story from Yirmiyahu (chapter 32) as the haftarah for parashat Behar. Yirmiyahu is often referred to as a prophet of doom, but in chapter 32 he is a prophet of inspiration and hope. The story of the haftarah begins with Yirmiyahu sitting in the prison of King Tzidkiyahu. Yirmiyahu has prophesied the destruction of the land by the invading Babylonian army and by this point everyone understands that the land will soon be conquered. The word of Hashem comes to Yirmiyahu and tells him that his relative Chanamel will soon approach him in prison and ask him to redeem his own land from the city of Anatot. Chanamel says to Yirmiyahu, "It is your responsibility to redeem the land" (32:8).

On the face of it this story is absurd. Yirmiyahu was predicting the destruction of the land. This is why he was in prison. And now as he sits in prison, Chanamel comes to him and asks him to pay good money and redeem land that will soon be captured by the Babylonians. And Yirmiyahu says, "Then I knew that it was indeed the word of God. So I bought the land in Anatot from my cousin Chanamel" (32:9).

Not only does Yirmiyahu buy the land, he also makes a show out of

Came the water and quenched the fire
That burned the stick
That beat the dog
That bit the cat
That ate the kid
That father bought for two *zuzim*;
One kid, one kid.

Came an ox and drank the water
That quenched the fire
That burned the stick
That beat the dog
That bit the cat
That ate the kid
That father bought for two *zuzim*;
One kid, one kid.

Came the butcher and killed the ox
That drank the water
That quenched the fire
That burned the stick
That beat the dog
That bit the cat
That ate the kid
That father bought for two *zuzim*;
One kid, one kid.

---

keep the dedications in place, but the synagogues no longer serve the mission for which they were built. Sometimes they are hardware stores, churches, or schools. One synagogue in D.C. even became the site of a morgue!

These synagogues were built with the blood, sweat, and tears of our ancestors. They were built to be shuls. It's tragic that the Jewish community allowed our hereditary property to be sold. Furthermore, it is very possibly a violation of Jewish law to sell a synagogue.

So what did Leon Toubin do? Leon started calling the major Jewish communities in Texas to see if anyone had any interest in his synagogue.

וְאָתָא מַיָּא, וְכָבָה לְנוּרָא,
דְּשָׂרַף לְחוּטְרָא, דְּהִכָּה לְכַלְבָּא,
דְּנָשַׁךְ לְשׁוּנְרָא, דְּאָכְלָה לְגַדְיָא,
דְּזַבִּין אַבָּא בִּתְרֵי זוּזֵי, חַד גַּדְיָא, חַד גַּדְיָא.

וְאָתָא תוֹרָא, וְשָׁתָא לְמַיָּא,
דְּכָבָה לְנוּרָא, דְּשָׂרַף לְחוּטְרָא,
דְּהִכָּה לְכַלְבָּא, דְּנָשַׁךְ לְשׁוּנְרָא, דְּאָכְלָה לְגַדְיָא,
דְּזַבִּין אַבָּא בִּתְרֵי זוּזֵי, חַד גַּדְיָא, חַד גַּדְיָא.

וְאָתָא הַשּׁוֹחֵט, וְשָׁחַט לְתוֹרָא,
דְּשָׁתָא לְמַיָּא, דְּכָבָה לְנוּרָא,
דְּשָׂרַף לְחוּטְרָא, דְּהִכָּה לְכַלְבָּא,
דְּנָשַׁךְ לְשׁוּנְרָא, דְּאָכְלָה לְגַדְיָא,
דְּזַבִּין אַבָּא בִּתְרֵי זוּזֵי,
חַד גַּדְיָא, חַד גַּדְיָא.

---

have a biblical obligation to redeem the lands – the mission and works – of our ancestors.

Today, when the biblical concept of redeeming hereditary land no longer applies to us, we must understand the concept symbolically. Our ancestors' efforts cannot be allowed to disintegrate. We must act as their redeemers.

In Brenham, Texas, the Orthodox community was recently confronted with just such a challenge. In 1893 the community built a synagogue, called B'nai Abraham. The synagogue still stands to this day, but its members no longer fill its pews. Sadly, there are only two members left in the synagogue: Leon Toubin, the grandson of the man who built the synagogue, and his wife Mimi. Since Leon is in his upper eighties he was naturally very worried about the fate of the synagogue.

He had good reason to be worried. If one drives around America, one sees beautiful buildings that were once synagogues but have now been sold. Sometimes the people who purchased the synagogues were kind enough to

Came the Angel of Death
And slew the butcher
Who killed the ox
That drank the water
That quenched the fire
That burned the stick
That beat the dog
That bit the cat
That ate the kid
That father bought for two *zuzim*;
One kid, one kid.

Came the Blessed Holy One
And slew the Angel of Death
Who slew the butcher
Who killed the ox
That drank the water
That quenched the fire
That burned the stick
That beat the dog
That bit the cat
That ate the kid
That father bought for two *zuzim*;
One kid, one kid.

---

require a redeemer. The hero of the story, Boaz, turns to the closest relative, whom the book refers to as the "*goel*" (redeemer), and he asks him, "Will you be the redeemer?" The *goel* declines to redeem the lands and in doing so he forfeits his title as the redeemer. Instead, Boaz becomes the *goel*, the redeemer of Elimelekh's land. Boaz also marries Rut and becomes the father to the ultimate *Mashiach*. Boaz is the redeemer and thus he is the father of the Messiah.

Our faith teaches us that we must all be redeemers. We must all be individual messiahs to another person. Each of us must realize that our number-one responsibility as Jews is to redeem our relatives, friends, and the strangers among us.

וְאָתָא מַלְאַךְ הַמָּוֶת,
וְשָׁחַט לְשׁוֹחֵט, דְּשָׁחַט לְתוֹרָא,
דְּשָׁתָא לְמַיָּא, דְּכָבָה לְנוּרָא,
דְּשָׂרַף לְחוּטְרָא, דְּהִכָּה לְכַלְבָּא,
דְּנָשַׁךְ לְשׁוּנְרָא, דְּאָכְלָה לְגַדְיָא,
דְּזַבִּין אַבָּא בִּתְרֵי זוּזֵי,
חַד גַּדְיָא, חַד גַּדְיָא.

וְאָתָא הַקָּדוֹשׁ בָּרוּךְ הוּא, וְשָׁחַט לְמַלְאַךְ הַמָּוֶת,
דְּשָׁחַט לְתוֹרָא, דְּשָׁתָא לְמַיָּא,
דְּכָבָה לְנוּרָא, דְּשָׂרַף לְחוּטְרָא,
דְּהִכָּה לְכַלְבָּא, דְּנָשַׁךְ לְשׁוּנְרָא, דְּאָכְלָה לְגַדְיָא,
דְּזַבִּין אַבָּא בִּתְרֵי זוּזֵי,
חַד גַּדְיָא, חַד גַּדְיָא.

Fortunately, he connected with Jay Rubin, the head of the Jewish Federation in Austin. Jay and Leon worked together and came up with a plan. They decided to transport the synagogue building by truck over 90 miles to Austin so that another Orthodox synagogue, an up-and-coming congregation located in Austin, can move into the old synagogue and hold its prayer services there!

It would have been cheaper to build a new synagogue from scratch, but sometimes it is not about cost. Sometimes it is about redemption! Leon and Jay acted as redeemers of the B'nai Abraham synagogue, and all those who from now on will daven inside those walls will be fulfilling the spirit of the commandment to redeem the lands of our relatives.

Our job as Jews is to be redeemers, not just of our hereditary lands but of souls. When we see the downtrodden and the weary, the embittered and the lost, the poor and the desperate – be it spiritually, financially, or emotionally – we must be the redeemers. We must be the Yirmiyahus, not of doom, but of inspiration.

This is what we read about on Shavuot. The book of Rut tells us about the hereditary lands of Elimelekh. Elimelekh dies and so do his sons, and his lands

2. The hands of the oldest are washed first by the children to show respect. Often they continue to wash the hands of those at the table until their own hands are washed.
3. The hands are washed before *karpas*, a vegetable, is eaten, but no blessing is said. Only a very small amount is eaten and it is dipped in saltwater or vinegar.
4. Everyone is treated like royalty at the Seder.

KARPAS

1. They are dipping the *karpas* into saltwater.
2. *Karpas* is a Greek word which means vegetable. *Karpas* is often parsley, potatoes, or celery. In our home we sometimes use potato chips or French fries to keep the children interested.
3. It reminds us of the bitter tears of our ancestors when they were enslaved in Egypt.
4. *Borei pri ha'adamah.*

YACHATZ

1. It is a matzah holder. The first picture shows the matzot completely covered up. The second shows the doors opened. The third shows the middle matzah being taken out.
2. It is not always round. It is often square. The important thing about matzah is that it be made only with flour and water and the time spent kneading the dough and placing the matzah in the oven should not exceed eighteen minutes.
3. The middle matzah is broken into two parts. One half is returned to the matzah holder and the matzah holder's doors are shut. The other half of the middle matzah is hidden, to be eaten at the end of the meal.
4. The leader of the Seder hides the *afikoman*. The children find it and hide it in a different place. The *afikoman* must be eaten at the end of the meal. If the children stay awake, they can get a present when the matzah is needed.

MAGGID

1. They have a very important role to play. They are singing the Mah Nishtanah, the Four Questions.
2. We can see a bone; romaine lettuce and horseradish for maror; *karpas*;

ANSWERS TO THE QUESTIONS ABOUT THE ILLUSTRATIONS

THE MNEMONIC

The four events shown in the illustration are:

1. Kadesh: The blessing over wine. Each person has his or her own cup.
2. U'rechatz (and Rachtzah): Children prepare to wash people's hands at their seats using a washing cup.
3. Yachatz: The middle one of the three matzot in the matzah holder is removed, broken in two, and put aside for the *afikoman* to be eaten at the end of the meal.
4. Motzi Matzah: The eating of the matzah.

KADESH

1. Our ancestors were slaves in Egypt. We are free. Free people can enjoy the luxury of having their own cups filled with wine. Thus, each person has his or her own wine cup and drinks four cups of wine at the Seder to remember that we were led out of Egypt, saved, redeemed, and taken by God to be His nation.
2. In ancient Greece, free men leaned to the side as they dined, discussing politics and philosophy. Slaves ate hurriedly so that they could quickly return to work.
3. We lean to the left whether we are right-handed or left-handed because of the danger of choking.
4. People stand when they say or hear the blessing on the wine, the Kiddush. It is a sign of respect. People sit when they drink the wine.

U'RECHATZ

1. Hands are washed at the Seder table itself, and a large pitcher is used to bring water to the table. Water is poured from the pitcher into a round utensil like a cup, often with two handles. The cup is used to pour the water on the hands. The pail catches the water when the hands are washed and the hands are dried.

3. Maror is used as a symbol at the Seder table to represent the bitter lives of the Jews when they were enslaved in Egypt.
4. According to Josephus, the Jews were used as slaves to build the pyramids.

KOREKH

1. Korekh refers to a sandwich made up of two pieces of matzah with maror and charoset in the middle.
2. We want to remember all the aspects of enslavement in Egypt.
3. Everyone, because we are all obligated to reenact the experience of enslavement and the Exodus.
4. Right before the meal is served.

SHULCHAN OREKH

1. The meal.
2. Eggs are a symbol. They are used to show that life is cyclical. Sometimes we are downtrodden and sometimes we are victorious.
3. We dip the eggs in the saltwater to remind us of the bitter tears our ancestors shed in Egypt. We are contrasting the hardships with the cyclical nature of life.
4. Yes, because our doors must be open to the needy on this night. We are obligated to invite all who are hungry to join us.

TZAFUN

1. We eat the *afikoman,* which was hidden.
2. Those children who found the *afikoman,* then rehid it and remained awake until the end of the meal have the *afikoman.*
3. The leader of the Seder gives in to the requests of the children and promises them a present.
4. Nothing is eaten after the *afikoman.*

BAREKH

1. It means *bless,* and is referring to the Birkat Hamazon (Grace after Meals). In this part of the Seder we are thanking God for providing mankind and animals with what they need in order to exist.
2. The entire Birkat Hamazon is both words of prayer and words of thanks.

charoset, which looks like bricks but is made from fruit, nuts, and wine; an egg; and saltwater.

3. To make room on the table. The wine cups were refilled right after Kadesh.
4. Hearing the children say the Mah Nishtanah brings back happy memories of family and fun. Everyone is proud that these children can continue the tradition.

Extra credit: Any language that you understand.

RACHTZAH

1. Their students are coming around to the rabbis with washing cups as in U'rechatz.
2. That was the custom of the time. Individual trays were set up for eating.
3. They are each at their own table and they each perform all parts of the ceremony to show that they are no longer slaves.
4. They were celebrating the Seder, but they were in hiding from the Romans who did not permit the practice of Judaism.

Extra credit: Rabbi Eliezer, Rabbi Yehoshua, Rabbi Elazar ben Azaryah, Rabbi Akiva, Rabbi Tarfon.

MOTZI MATZAH

1. The hands were washed and dried a second time and a blessing was said on the washing of the hands.
2. Two whole matzot and a half matzah, called the middle matzah.
3. Two.
4. *Hamotzi* and *al akhilat matzah.*

Extra credit: *Hamotzi* is the blessing said before you eat a food made from any of the five grains grown in Israel, i.e., wheat, barley, rye, oats, and spelt. *Al akhilat matzah* is the blessing that commemorates the Exodus from Egypt on the night of Passover. It is an obligation to eat the matzah at the Seder so that we can reenact our history.

MAROR

1. Bitter herbs such as horseradish and the core of romaine lettuce.
2. We want to identify with the bitterness of the lives of our ancestors in Egypt.

These last words at the end of Birkat Hamazon express our hope for the future.

3. It is a prayer for a special day, a holiday, that allows us to rejoice in the happiness of the day without any worries.
4. A woman often embodies the power of prayer in Judaism, as shown by the story of Channah, the mother of the prophet Shmuel. This woman is surrounded by flowers, fruit-bearing trees, and all kinds of life because the words of Birkat Hamazon recognize God's rule over the entire world.

HALLEL

1. *Hallel* means thanks. In this part of the Seder we praise and thank God for the miracle of the Exodus from Egypt.
2. The main event in the Exodus from Egypt was the splitting of the Sea of Reeds so that the Jews could escape from the pursuing Egyptians.
3. God created a miracle.
4. They had no choice.

NIRTZAH

1. It means that we have fulfilled our requirements for our Passover Seder and God has accepted our prayers.
2. They are dancing as though they are on the mountain where the Temple once stood in Jerusalem, to which people came three times a year.
3. They are dancing in the hope that Jerusalem and its Temple will be rebuilt to their former glory.
4. They represent Jews from the four corners of the earth.